The Strategic Dynamics of Latin American Trade

The Strategic Dynamics of
Latin American Trade

Edited by

Vinod K. Aggarwal, Ralph Espach, and Joseph S. Tulchin

Woodrow Wilson Center Press
Washington, D.C.

Stanford University Press
Stanford, California

EDITORIAL OFFICES

Woodrow Wilson Center Press
One Woodrow Wilson Plaza
1300 Pennsylvania Avenue, N.W.
Washington, D.C. 20004-3027
Telephone 202-691-4029
www.wilsoncenter.org

ORDER FROM

Stanford University Press
Chicago Distribution Center
11030 South Langley Avenue
Chicago, Ill. 60628
Telephone 1-800-621-2736; 773-568-1550
www.sup.org

2 4 6 8 9 7 5 3 1

Library of Congress Cataloging-in-Publication Data

The strategic dynamics of Latin American trade / edited by Vinod K.
Aggarwal, Ralph Espach, and Joseph S. Tulchin.
p. cm.
Includes bibliographical references and index.
ISBN 0-8047-4900-0 (pbk. : alk. paper) — ISBN 0-8047-4899-3 (cloth :
alk. paper)
1. Latin America—Commercial policy.   2. Latin America—Commercial
policy—Case studies.   I. Aggarwal, Vinod K.   II. Espach, Ralph H.   III.
Tulchin, Joseph S., 1939–
HF1480.5 .S77 2004
382′.3′098—dc22   2003024441

ABOUT THE CENTER

The Center is the living memorial of the United States of America to the nation's twenty-eighth president, Woodrow Wilson. Congress established the Woodrow Wilson Center in 1968 as an international institute for advanced study, "symbolizing and strengthening the fruitful relationship between the world of learning and the world of public affairs." The Center opened in 1970 under its own board of trustees.

In all its activities the Woodrow Wilson Center is a nonprofit, nonpartisan organization, supported financially by annual appropriations from the Congress, and by the contributions of foundations, corporations, and individuals. Conclusions or opinions expressed in Center publications and programs are those of the authors and speakers and do not necessarily reflect the views of the Center staff, fellows, trustees, advisory groups, or any individuals or organizations that provide financial support to the Center.

Contents

Tables and Figures

Tables

Figures

Abbreviations

ALADI	Latin American Integration Association
APEC	Asia-Pacific Economic Cooperation forum
CET	common external tariff
EFTA	European Free Trade Association
FTA	free trade agreement
FTAA	Free Trade Area of the Americas
GATT	General Agreement on Tariffs and Trade
IDB	Inter-American Development Bank
IMF	International Monetary Fund
MERCOSUR	Southern Common Market
NAFTA	North American Free Trade Agreement
OAS	Organization of American States
OECD	Organisation for Economic Cooperation and Development
RTA	regional trade agreement
UNCTAD	U.N. Conference on Trade and Development
WTO	World Trade Organization

Part I

Institutional and Political Elements of Trade Policy

1

Diverging Trade Strategies in Latin America: A Framework for Analysis

Vinod K. Aggarwal and Ralph Espach

Economic relations among the nations of Latin America have entered a new stage. The last twenty years have seen a dramatic shift in Latin American economic policies away from protectionism and import substitution industrialization policies and toward liberalization and the promotion of exports. During the early and mid-1990s in particular, improved economic stability and growth at home and in international markets generated enthusiasm for free trade in various forms. Latin American nations were active at the Uruguay Round of the General Agreement on Tariffs and Trade (GATT), hailed the interest of the United States in creating the Free Trade Area of the Americas (FTAA), and established several important trade accords at the regional level. International investors gushed at this regionwide trend of deregulating trade and investment, and the privatization of state-owned enterprises. Even then, however, when the international climate was favorable to these reforms and foreign investment levels rose across the region, the governments of the region were demonstrating distinctly different paths and styles of liberalization. This divergence was more manifest in the late 1990s, when it began to have significant effects on international relations across the region.

This is especially true regarding trade relations. The diversity of trade agreements established since the mid-1980s, both within Latin America and between Latin American nations and those of other regions, reflects a broadening range of strategic perceptions and orientations. In this volume, we argue that this increasing divergence among the trade arrangements of various Latin American nations reflects fundamental and growing differences among their broader strategic perceptions and political and economic objectives. These, in turn, are grounded in each country's economic profile, the institutional configuration of its trade policy process, and the constraints and opportunities policymakers perceive at the domestic and international levels. This chapter provides a theoretical framework that highlights the political-economic trade-offs entailed in these different trade strategies. This framework provides conceptual background for the more detailed, empirically grounded studies that make up the rest of the volume, including country analyses of Argentina, Brazil, Chile, Mexico, and of the Southern Common Market (MERCOSUR) bloc as a whole.

Both Mexico and Chile have actively pursued transregional opportunities, such as Mexico's free trade pact with the European Union, Chile's accord with Australia, and both countries' active negotiations with Japan. Among Latin American countries, Chile presents the region's best example of successful unilateral liberalization. Its relatively early start at implementing free trade and export promotion programs and maintenance of political support for liberalization have allowed it to pursue trade at the transregional level (through the Asia-Pacific Economic Cooperation [APEC] forum, for example, or with the United States) and global levels simultaneously, while not sacrificing regional trade relations. During the 1990s, Mexico became one of the world's most active bilateral free traders, and its position as a less developed country within the North American Free Trade Agreement (NAFTA) makes its free trade profile unique—while also posing unique challenges. By contrast, Argentina and Brazil have given priority to expanding trade first at the regional level through MERCOSUR. This allows their economies to adapt more gradually to international competition, and gives their governments the strategic option over the long term of using the trade bloc as leverage to negotiate free trade with the European Union or with NAFTA, or through the FTAA on more favorable terms. However, the complicated relations of interdependence that have deepened through MERCOSUR pose different challenges to these countries, which have been exacerbated by Argentina's enduring financial crisis.

To explain the rationales that lie behind this increasing divergence among the trade strategies of our four case study countries, we focus primarily on what we term their *trade preferences*. We can distinguish among four different analytical approaches to trade policies and relations. First, abstract models based on broad economic concepts such as comparative advantage can generate "ideal" trade preferences. An example is classic liberal trade theory, which assumes away political or security concerns and predicts that rational states with perfect information will prefer free trade to any other option. For obvious reasons, ideal trade preferences seldom describe the formulation of trade policies in the real world.

The second approach is the one we undertake, in which we consider the combination of economic, political, and strategic objectives that policy-makers have in mind, as well as the macro-level international constraints they face, when they consider various trade policy alternatives. This complex set of considerations, which naturally differ from country to country based on their resources and perceived options, generates a specific set of political and economic trade-offs between various strategic objectives. For example, Brazil may rationally accept slower growth in the short term, and more limited liberalization, for the ability to nurture the development, over the long term, of more diverse and competitive industries. It can be said that Mexico, for instance, has accepted the internal stress that comes from rapid reforms and deeper dependence on the U.S. market to obtain improved prospects for economic growth and stability. We refer to these sets of political-economic trade-offs, reflected in each country's trade arrangements since the early 1990s, as *trade preferences.*

A third approach to trade relations would focus on the ensuing negotiations and strategic bargaining that take place between trade partners, once their interests or preferences have been assumed.

Lastly, a fourth type of approach would include the outcomes of these negotiations, as well as a variety of domestic and international constraints over time on a government's formulation of its trade preferences and the effective execution of its strategy. The case studies that comprise the second half of this volume are excellent examples of this type of in-depth, comprehensive study.

This introduction presents a simplified theoretical framework by which we can assess each country's trade preferences, defined as the combination of strategic objectives and macro-level constraints that underlie its trade policies. Other chapters in this volume focus either on specific types of constraints or dynamics involved in the formulation of trade policy, or on how existing strategies across the region were formulated, pursued, and either achieved or underachieved.

How might one go about analyzing the origins of countries' trade preferences? Purely economic explanations, which would generally predict increased liberalization as governments, businesses, and consumers enjoy the fruits of free trade, fail to capture both the inconsistency of liberalization and the variation among these countries' political and strategic interests.

Economic demands are certainly important to policymakers in countries with severe debt burdens which depend largely on foreign investment for growth. Yet the aims of economic liberalization coexist—and often conflict—with other important interests. Economic analysis alone, based on estimates of improved efficiency resulting from various trade arrangements, is a poor instrument for explaining or predicting trade preferences.

Our analysis combines economic and political objectives within a liberalized and dynamic trading system, but does not include traditional security objectives, such as military defense or preparations for war. This is a result of our conviction that since the end of the Cold War, and with the spread of democracy throughout Latin America, concerns over inter-state violence play a far less prominent role in regional relations than those of economics and politics. Security concerns today are expressed mostly within an expanded agenda that includes drug trafficking, crime, poverty, and economic instability, in a list of issues so broad that they defy traditional security definitions (see Tulchin and Espach 2001). Those that have clear economic dimensions, and are linked to trade policy formulation, are included in our analysis and in the case studies.

It is worth noting that the analysis in this introduction uses the simplifying assumptions of unitary states as rational actors. The terms states, countries, and governments are used interchangeably—not because we believe that these entities are undifferentiated, but because our analysis lies at the second level of international analysis, that of national interest. For example, we do not question the extent to which national trade policies are shaped by an administration's goal of winning elections. Also, we do not differentiate among government branches, such as the executive and congress, except sometimes in our discussion of individual national behaviors. Domestic dynamics are extremely important; however, using a simple model with assumptions of instrumental rationality allows for generalization and prediction, the results of which can be compared against the more complex empirical analysis of the case study chapters.

We begin the discussion in this chapter by presenting an analytical characterization of different modes of trade liberalization. We show that conventional categorizations of trade arrangements miss important aspects of trade policy choices. We present an overview of existing transregional, regional, and bilateral trade agreements of which our case study countries are signatories in order to demonstrate the significant and increasing divergence we assert. Using this framework, we classify the trade profiles of our case study countries. Next, we examine various types of trade arrangements in detail—unilateralism, bilateralism, minilateralism (i.e., limited multi-lateralism, as in regional trade accords), and broader multilateralism—and the degree to which each is reflected in the trade profiles of our case study countries. This deeper discussion of the trade-offs entailed in each type of trade arrangement leads us to an assessment of the trade preferences that lie behind these nations' trade profiles. These trade preferences are derived from consideration of each country's medium- and long-term economic and po-litical strategic options. In the next section, we revisit the trade profiles of the case study countries and their preferences, and discuss the policy im-plications and predictions suggested by our analytical framework. Finally, we summarize our framework and suggest areas for future research.

Categorizing Trade Arrangements

Over the last fifty years, states have used various measures to promote or control trade flows. In terms of bargaining approaches, these include uni-lateral, bilateral, minilateral (those which have three or more members but limit their membership, as with regional trade blocs), and broader multi-lateral strategies (which have virtually unlimited membership, such as the World Trade Organization [WTO]). In terms of product coverage, measures have ranged in scope from very narrow to broad multiproduct agreements. In addition, some arrangements are geographically concentrated, or "re-gional," while others include distant nations.[1] Finally, these measures have varied in terms of whether the outcome of each is predominantly market closing or market opening. For the sake of simplicity, Table 1.1 and our dis-cussion focus on three dimensions of bargaining approaches—the number of nations involved, product scope, and geographical range—leaving aside other characteristics such as timing, degree of openness, governing party or regime, and so on.

In brief, the top row (cells 1 to 6) refers to different forms of *sectoral-ism,* that is, trade agreements that cover only one or a handful of specially defined products or industrial sectors. Cell 1 includes unilateral measures for sector- or product-specific market opening or restriction, such as the repeal of England's Corn Laws that allowed agricultural imports without reciprocity. In cell 2, we have bilateral agreements among neighbors in specific products, which are relatively rare because they are discouraged by the GATT/WTO. Cell 3 refers to bilateral agreements between countries that are geographically dispersed, which include measures like voluntary export

Table 1.1 Categorizing Modes of Governance in Trade

		Actor Scope				
	Unilateral	Bilateral		Minilateral		Multilateral
		Geographically concentrated	Geographically dispersed	Geographically concentrated	Geographically dispersed	
Product Scope Few products (sectoralism)	Quotas or tariffs on specific products. Repeal of Corn Laws (1)	US–Canada auto agreement (2)	US–Japan Voluntary export restraints (3)	European Coal and Steel Community (4)	Early voluntary sectoral liberalization. The Cairns Group (5)	Information Technology Agreement (6)
Many products	Tariffs such as Smoot–Hawley, or APEC IAPs (7)	US–Canada free trade agreement (8)	Mexico–Chile free trade agreement (9)	NAFTA, EU (10)	FTAA, APEC, EU–MERCOSUR (transregionalism) (11)	GATT or WTO (globalism) (12)

Source: Adapted from Aggarwal (2001: 238).

restraints (VERs). In cells 4 and 5, we have product-specific sectoral agreements. These are also divided according to their degree of geographic concentration. Cell 5 provides an example of dispersed sectoral minilateralism: the case of the early voluntary sectoral liberalization effort that did not pan out among APEC members. Finally, cell 6 provides an example of multilateral accords that are sectorally based but liberalizing, such as the Information Technology Agreement (ITA).[2]

The next row focuses on multiproduct efforts. Cell 7 refers to unilateral, broad-based trade reform. These include Chile's liberalization program in the 1980s, or the infamous protectionist 1930 Smoot-Hawley tariff in the United States. Cell 8 represents the category of geographically concentrated bilateral accords, and cell 9 those of geographically dispersed bilateralism. There are several examples of the latter in Latin America, including Mexico's free trade agreements with Chile and with the European Union. Cell 10 includes geographically focused minilateral agreements, accords traditionally referred to as "regionalism."[3] Cell 11 represents the category of "transregional" trade blocs, including such accords as the Free Trade Agreement of the Americas (FTAA) and APEC that span regions.[4] These "transregional agreements" can also be more formalized and link two regions. Thus, we can refer to cases such as the proposed European Union–MERCOSUR accord as transregional (or interregional) agreements (Aggarwal and Fogarty, forthcoming). Finally, cell 12 refers to the case of global trading arrangements, namely multilateral, multiproduct arrangements such as the GATT and its successor organization, the WTO.

We can use this framework to assess the trade policies of Argentina, Brazil, Chile, and Mexico in the 1990s. While this conceptual framework applies to agreements that are both liberal and protectionist, our focus regarding Latin America is on these countries' liberalization programs. Table 1.2 provides a summary of all existing free trade agreements in Latin America.

Two observations are immediately apparent. First, these nations have only very infrequently pursued liberalization at the sectoral level. Sector-specific exemptions are, in fact, common as components of larger trade agreements, but they are used to protect less efficient and sensitive industries from foreign competition. Part of the reason, as Sylvia Maxfield discusses in Chapter 3, is that sector-specific business associations in Latin America are not as organized or powerful as those within member countries of the Organisation for Economic Cooperation and Development (OECD). For Maxfield, the strength or weakness of state–business collaboration, and the openness of trade policy formulation to organized business groups,

Table 1.2 Overview of Free Trade Agreements in Latin America Effective in 1990s

	Bilateral		Minilateral		Multilateral
Product Scope	Geographically concentrated	Geographically dispersed	Geographically concentrated	Geographically dispersed/transregionalism	Multilateral
Few products (sectoralism)		US–Chile Consultative Committee on Agriculture, 1997; Mexico–Brazil arrangement on trade in autos and auto parts, 2002			
Many products	Costa Rica–Canada, 2001; Mexico–Bolivia, 1994; Mexico–Costa Rica, 1994; Mexico–Nicaragua, 1998	Mexico–European Union, 1995; Mexico–EFTA, 2000; Mexico–Israel, 2000; Chile–Mexico, 1998; Chile–Canada, 1996; Chile–US 2002; Chile–Korea 2002	Central American Common Market, 1960; Latin America Integration Association, 1980; Andean Community, 1996; Caribbean Community and Common Market, 1973; Group of 11, 1984; MERCOSUR, 1991; NAFTA, 1992; Latin American Economic System (SELA), 1975; Chile–Central America, 1999; Dominican Republic–Central America, 1998; CARICOM–Dominican Republic, 1998; Group of 3, 1994; Mexico–Northern Triangle (El Salvador, Honduras, and Guatemala), 2000	Free Trade Area of the Americas, negotiations began in 1994, aimed at completion in 2005; Asia-Pacific Economic Cooperation (Chile, Mexico, and Peru), members, signed 1989, aimed at completion in 2020	World Trade Organization, negotiated 1986–1994, established 1995

Notes: Dates refer to the signing of the agreement. Table does not include partial scope economic arrangements nor economic complementarity agreements.

significantly influence the success of liberalization programs and account, in part, for the differences among our case studies.

In eschewing sectoral agreements, the governments of Latin America are also adhering to the GATT and its successor WTO regime, which prohibits such agreements under Article 24. While this article allows free trade areas or customs unions, it mandates that they cover substantially all trade. By contrast, going back to the 1950s and the textiles and apparel regime, developed countries have been significantly more willing to violate the spirit of GATT Article 19 by convincing developing country partners and Japan to restrict their exports voluntarily, thus avoiding the mandated compensation called for in this article if imports are blocked as well as the provision that restraints be used against all member countries of the GATT. The United States and European Union have used such VERs in steel, consumer electronics, footwear, and other industries as a means of circumventing Article 19. More recently, as broad cross-sector multilateralism has faced difficulty, developed nations have effectively promoted numerous multilateral, sector-specific liberalizing accords, including the ITA and the Financial Services Agreement. These industries benefit from support of the industrialized nations in which they are concentrated, which can cooperate to form a powerful trade lobby for multilateral programs like these. A similar example among less developed countries is the Cairns Group of eighteen agricultural exporting countries, which has labored to little effect to promote lowered tariffs on agricultural goods in developed countries.

The second immediate observation from Table 1.2 is that our case study countries have engaged in a wide variety of trade liberalization practices and agreements. Each country has significantly liberalized its trade policies, both unilaterally and to some degree through international trade agreements. However, each has pushed liberalization to a different degree and in a distinct manner, reflecting the differences in these countries' political-economic profiles and strategies.

With these existing trade arrangements in mind, we can characterize the policy profiles of our case study countries as follows:

- Argentina: *regional partner,* focused at the minilateral (concentrated) level, with transregionalism pursued through collective regional activity
- Brazil: *regional leader,* focused at the minilateral (concentrated) level, with transregionalism pursued through collective regional activity; also extremely active at the multilateral level

- Chile: *multilateral trader,* including unilateral liberalization and agreements at the bilateral (geographically dispersed) and multilateral level
- Mexico: *hub market,* including bilateral, minilateral (concentrated), and transregional trade agreements

Why is it that these four countries, which share similar levels of economic and social development, export a relatively similar range of products (although Brazil and Mexico are significantly more industrialized than Argentina, or especially Chile), and have engaged in economic and trade liberalization, show such distinct trade policy profiles? Economic rationales alone cannot account for the diversity, since all four governments have officially embraced similar policy programs since the early 1990s. To understand these different trade profiles, we must combine these economic orientations with analysis of the political and security aims of each country. As discussed below, each country's choice among economic and political trade-offs—that is, its strategic approach to trade policy—is influenced by its assumptions about the international system and its perceptions of the strategic options available to it. These combinations of political and economic objectives and the trade-offs among them (longer-term strategies and fundamental assumptions) we term *trade preferences.* It is worth reiterating that the case studies in the book trace in depth the process that leads from these preferences to actual policy outcomes; our objective in this chapter is to provide a basic analysis of the various factors and ideologies that drive the development of countries' trade policies.

A Strategic Approach to Trade Arrangements

In this section we examine in more detail the trade-offs entailed in the various arrangements presented in Tables 1.1 and 1.2, and the factors that influence the choices policymakers make between different trade policy options. This discussion is organized around the categorization of trade arrangements already presented. This analysis of the costs and benefits of each arrangement, however, leads us into consideration of individual countries' trade strategies.

Unilateralism

Since the early 1980s each of our case study countries, and virtually all Latin American nations, to one degree or another, have made efforts toward unilateral liberalization. In addition to trade reform, governments have liberalized through reducing the size of state agencies, privatizing state-owned enterprises, enacting regulatory reforms, and other policies. This overarching trend of internal economic reforms is extremely important in that it has provided the domestic political-economic context for the trade policies of this period. Indeed, the successes of MERCOSUR and other regional economic projects in the early and mid-1990s should not be considered in isolation. These achievements came within a period of regionwide liberalization, overall global economic growth and relative stability, and burgeoning extra-regional foreign investment.

Classic economic theory argues that unilateral liberalization, as the most direct route to free trade, maximizes gains from trade by avoiding the messiness of political negotiations and forcing shifts in production across the entire economy to reach optimal efficiency. Unilateral liberalization also frees up state resources that formerly went to protecting or subsidizing weak economic sectors, allowing them to be invested toward long-term productivity gains through improving education, worker training, and national infrastructure. Thus, whether or not trade partners reciprocate, over time these gains in economic efficiency, not to mention the gains to consumers that come from cheaper imports, make unilateral opening a wise policy. These benefits are realized, however, in the long term, since dramatic shifts in resource allocation and productivity take time.

Yet unilateral liberalization has several drawbacks. First, if other countries do not reciprocate, lower trade barriers can place domestic industries at a disadvantage, since they have less opportunity to achieve economies of scale. Without some institutionalized enforcement of reciprocity, unilateral liberalization can open up a country to exploitation by trade partners who subsidize their industries. Second, on the domestic front, unilateral liberalization lacks clear short-term gains except for the diffused effect of lower overall prices, and often entails severe costs for domestic producers and the workers they employ. Resistance by these industries, the workers they employ, and other economic interest groups can make unilateral liberalization politically unfeasible. In contrast, politicians who engage in bilateral or multilateral liberalization can point to reciprocal reforms in partner countries that compensate for domestic costs.

The principal political cost of unilateralism is that, by removing lowered tariffs as a bargaining chit, it reduces a country's leverage to secure trade reciprocity from its trading partners. If a country's main trading partners already have low trade barriers, then all that is gained is increased domestic efficiency and lower costs for imports. However, within a region of uneven progress in liberalization, and when important trade partners (such as Brazil, the European Union, and the United States) engage frequently in protectionist policies, the loss of this bargaining tool can pose a significant opportunity cost. Obviously, this opportunity cost is higher for large countries, whose markets can be extremely attractive to foreign investors, than for small countries. In this regard, a second political drawback of unilateralism is the opportunity cost of foregoing trade liberalization on a collective basis within the rubric of a regional trade accord. Countries with small markets have much to gain from collective bargaining, since alone they have little leverage in pushing their terms of trade against larger countries.

The most prominent Latin American example of unilateral trade liberalization has been the case of Chile, which led the region in embracing the free market model beginning in the mid-1970s. By the 1990s, Chile's tariffs, on the whole, were the lowest in South America, and it has developed a variety of highly competitive export industries, in particular in agro-industry and fisheries, in addition to its traditional strength in mineral exports. Although small, Chile's economy is institutionally stable, which makes it an attractive site for regional investment. This accomplishment is highlighted by the fact that recent financial crises in Mexico, Argentina, and Brazil have had relatively little effect in Chile.

The Chilean model, however, is difficult for other nations to follow. Chile's early efforts had high social costs and were largely unsuccessful. Even in the 1980s, as reforms began to improve economic growth and stability, the Pinochet regime actively repressed social and political resistance through violence. Today it would seem that several factors work against the possibility of aggressive national liberalization programs, such as that of the Fujimori government in Peru. First, there is the popularity of democracy across the region, as well as the increased willingness of regional partners to protest coups and other antidemocratic measures, as was the case with several Latin American nations' responses to the attempted coups in Paraguay in 1996 and Venezuela in 2002 (although in the latter case, the U.S. government showed an unsettling enthusiasm for extra-constitutional regime change). Democratic practice is better understood, more widely embraced by the public, and more deeply institutionalized in most countries than it has been for decades. Also, despite the Bush administration's gaffe in Venezuela, the United States and other economic powers are less openly favorable and generous to authoritarian regimes, reducing the gains such governments may expect from rapid liberalization.

Current efforts to promote unilateral liberalization face economic as well as political challenges. Chile's reform program predated and outpaced those of its neighbors by several years, making it a darling of international investors, development banks, and the governments of OECD countries, which sought to promote its example as the Latin American "tiger." A decade or two later, third-generation export growth programs face increasingly competitive international markets and a less generous attitude from the OECD countries, which now feel the heat from developing country competition. In Chapter 4, Carol Wise argues that Chile should still be considered the most successful liberalization program in the continent, largely due to the state's sophistication and commitment to supporting entrepreneurship, enhanced human capital, and improved dynamism in its export sectors. In Chapter 8, Osvaldo Rosales clearly illustrates Chile's position that through its regional trade, "the country is interested in exporting, on a regional level, the conditions of competition and openness that it has attained on a domestic level."

For the foreseeable future, however, dramatic unilateral liberalization appears to be an unlikely strategy for other countries to pursue. The increasingly dynamic and pluralist qualities of their democratic systems suggest that they will act under domestic political constraints similar to those of other democracies. Also, compared to Chile in the 1980s, Argentina, Brazil, and Mexico have much larger and more diverse economies with powerful industrial and agricultural industries, as well as labor organizations capable of resisting most reforms that bring short-term costs with few politically salient reciprocal benefits.

Multilateralism

Over the last twenty years the project of global multilateral trade liberalization, institutionalized principally in the GATT and WTO negotiations, has run up against hard times. The inability of members to reach consensus on various issues, including levels of agricultural protection, intellectual property, and environmental and labor regulations, coupled with increasingly vociferous and organized public resistance, has stymied progress toward broad, multiproduct liberalization. Most governments profess to be ardent supporters of the WTO and multilateral free trade, at least in its ideal form. However, uncertainty about partners' level of commitment and the feasibility of implementation against strong domestic resistance has led many states to pursue free trade through regional or sectoral trade agreements, in which problems of collective action are easier to overcome.

A multilateralist trade strategy has several advantages.[5] In collective terms, the inclusion of a broad range of goods and a variety of states enables the mobilization of broad domestic and transnational coalitions. Under truly comprehensive, global free trade, there would be very few groups with nothing to gain. Multilateralism also benefits from the high-level fanfare generated by its multinational meetings, which helps governments to mobilize political support at home. However, multilateralist trade strategies are also inherently problematic. With so many countries involved, negotiations are difficult to carry out and fraught with complexity. Without effective leadership by powerful countries, and legitimate, institutionalized enforcement of norms—which is extremely difficult among nearly 150 countries—collective action problems such as free ridership abound. Additionally, the high public profile of these negotiations stimulates social awareness of the potential consequences of free trade and bolsters domestic and transnational opposition.

Each of our case study countries has participated actively in GATT and WTO negotiations. All of them (Brazil most aggressively) have opposed measures to expand the WTO agenda to include extra-trade measures such as labor rights and environmental standards and have pushed for greater attention to the needs of developing countries. In Chapter 2, Joseph Tulchin highlights the role that Chile played as a legitimate voice and proactive negotiator for the less developed world. Despite the activity regarding these contentious issues, the four countries have consistently emphasized their support for the expansion and strengthening of the WTO. Members of regional initiatives such as NAFTA and the MERCOSUR describe these as intermediate steps toward the broader goal of multilateralism. In their design and operations, these regional (or minilateral) initiatives are intentionally nested within the standards and norms of the WTO, so as to minimize conflict with the global free trade project.

An institutionalist approach suggests that the case study nations, as lesser powers in the international system, benefit disproportionately from multilateral institutions. Institutions such as the WTO not only reduce transaction costs, but also provide a more balanced and objective forum for negotiations, constrain the unilateral actions of large powers, and facilitate the organization of coalitions. Less powerful nations can also influence more effectively the norms and values embodied in the international system through institutions than through pressuring powerful states individually. In recent decades, multilateral institutions like the International Monetary Fund (IMF) and the WTO have supported the internationalization of finance and commerce that has helped lead to further development in poor countries. Foreign investment, however, does not come easily. Our case study countries have had to make political and economic sacrifices in the form of privatizations, severe fiscal cuts, the creation of administrative and regulatory institutions, and the acceptance of politically difficult standards and regulations in a variety of areas. Argentina's protracted negotiations with the IMF are just the latest example of the stringency of the demands of the international financial community. On the other hand, as the policy agenda of "globalization" expands to include environmental protection, developing countries around the world have become increasingly sophisticated at demanding reciprocal measures or compensations to offset the costs of these reforms. Multilateral institutions have proven to be valuable instruments for the negotiation of these compensations, as was evident most recently in the concessions won by developing states—in which Brazil and Chile were deeply involved—at the 2001 Doha Round of the WTO.

A country's trade preferences reflect its strategy for embracing or accommodating the various pressures for liberalization and the trade-offs it believes it can obtain for opening its market. The differences among the trade profiles of our case study countries indicate that their strategies for opening to international markets have been affected by political, as much as economic, considerations. It is important to keep in mind, however, that all unilateral, bilateral, and minilateral initiatives of the last two decades have taken place within the context of an increasingly institutionalized GATT/WTO. This global project provides an ideological model, a forum for negotiations, policy and practice standards for fair trade (even if they are not always followed), and most recently a functioning dispute settlement institution. Even the United States and Mexico have begun to bypass NAFTA's arbitration process when they are frustrated by its institutional weakness, as occurred most recently over Mexican telecommunications laws. Progress toward global, multiproduct free trade may recently have fallen behind regional or sector-specific trade accords, but the multilateral regime embodied in the WTO still provides the normative and operational framework for international trade discussions.

In recent years, Chile and Mexico endeavored to meet the standards and practices of more developed countries. In Chile's case in particular, its good standing as a member of the WTO is seen to be an important asset. As Tulchin points out in Chapter 2, Chile's trade regulations and practices meet or exceed the international norm, which along with its institutional stability generates a type of "soft power" that has proved useful in multilateral negotiations. Rosales likewise states in Chapter 8 that Chile's success at the multilateral level, and its aggressive, forward-thinking approach to expanding trade on all fronts without regard for regional protectionism, improves both its political position and economic competitiveness. Mexico has pushed similarly to achieve broader, more rapid liberalization and at the same time—with much less success, thus far—to strengthen the institutional bases of its free market economy. Mexico's efforts, however, are driven more by its attempts to capitalize on its NAFTA membership and to attract investment from non–U.S. sources than they are by WTO standards.

Brazil has been extremely active both in the WTO court as a defendant and plaintiff, and in WTO negotiations as an avid defender of developing countries' interests. Like China and India, at times Brazil has been painted in the United States and European media as a protectionist opponent of free trade, or at least an unfair competitor. Brazil has met these criticisms with some indifference, since its actions at the WTO have been quite effective. Also, Brazil's inclusion with China and India emphasizes its global importance and its self-acclaimed role as regional leader, rightly deserving of a permanent seat on the United Nations Security Council. In Chapter 7, Pedro da Motta Veiga describes how Brazil's distinctive global vision, which is centered on elevating its political power on the global stage, has for decades shaped its approach to trade and economic relations.

Brazil is one of few developing countries with an economy sufficiently diverse and competitive to be involved simultaneously in trade disputes that range from sugar, soybeans, and footwear, to automobiles and steel. Recently it has played a key role in defying the pricing policies on AIDS medications of pharmaceutical multinational corporations that are supported by their home governments. The fact that it (like India) has an established pharmaceutical industry of its own that is capable of producing these products cheaply and efficiently, gives it the ability to be aggressive. Its market size and diversity lend it more political leverage than the other case study countries, and provide Brazil myriad options for sector and issue linkage. Whereas a strategy of aggressive, sometimes protectionist posturing might bring severe costs for a smaller, more trade-dependent economy like Chile's, Brazil perceives it as effective. As President Fernando Henrique Cardoso declared regarding Brazil's actions in the WTO, "Never in Brazil's history have we fought more or gained as much."[6] Moreover, Brazil's diplomatic corps, renowned for its institutional training and professionalism, remains extremely active and influential in the formulation of all international policies, including those concerned with trade. Due to its size, its sense of destiny, and its institutional legacies, the Brazilian government, dominated by its executive branch, tends toward strategic—rather than economic—thinking. Of our case studies, while Chile benefits from quiet compliance with multilateral programs and subtle diplomatic maneuvering, Brazil's trade profile exhibits the most pronounced and contentious multilateral agenda. This is a more risky strategy, perhaps, but one that Brazil's resources and regional importance allow it to believe that it can take.

For the countries of Latin America, the foremost economic prize in the medium term is unhindered access to the U.S. and European consumer markets. A multilateral free trade program, once implemented, would provide this (in exchange for the costs of reduced protection for domestic producers). All the case study countries declare support for a comprehensive WTO, especially one that reduces agricultural protections and nontariff barriers in the developed world. Yet the costs to many local industries of rapid, complete internationalization would be severe. Resistance from domestic industrial, agricultural, labor, and other special interests, which has increased naturally under democratization, has further complicated trade liberalization in these Latin American countries, just as it has in the United States and Europe. Wise emphasizes that the degree to which these governments are successful at translating export-led growth and economic transformation into broad-based economic benefits, especially for the lower-income masses desperate for jobs and cheaper goods will determine the durability of their liberalization programs. For all of our case studies except Chile, these governments have found that by following bilateral or minilateral liberalization strategies they can better mitigate, postpone, or direct the costs and benefits, domestic and international, of free trade.

Bilateralism Geographically Concentrated

Theoretically speaking, bilateralism between neighbors has many political-economic advantages. Geographic, cultural, and historical similarities provide a favorable atmosphere for dialogue and partnership, especially considering that Latin America is a relatively peaceful community of nations. Also, free trade between neighbors encourages mutual confidence and trust in political and security terms, and creates diverse opportunities for the spill-over of cooperation in several issue areas. Bilateral trade is also simpler for policymakers to consider and for diplomats and economists to negotiate. Whether concentrated or dispersed geographically, bilateral trade agreements allow policymakers the most clear and predictable situations of industrial complementarity and economies of scale. Bilateral negotiations are easier to start, less costly, and usually less complicated politically than are mini- or multi-lateral negotiations.

The disadvantages of bilateralism include the possibility of significant trade diversion, since efficiency gains are generally lower than they would be under minilateral or multilateral free trade. Also, when a country signs several different bilateral agreements with various partners, the different tariff levels, exceptions, deadlines, standards, and so on can lead to confusion and overall inefficiency. As José Salazar-Xirinachs discusses in Chapter 5, the potential for developing a "spaghetti bowl" of multiple, overlapping trade accords is a common criticism of current trends in hemispheric trade. Moreover, the specific terms and conditions of each bilateral agreement compromise to some degree the member countries' participation in broader free trade projects, where they are unlikely to be able to secure such detailed, sensitive treatment. Finally, bilateralism can be a poor option for smaller nations because it forces them to negotiate one-on-one with larger nations from a disadvantaged position, since smaller-country producers stand to gain more from access to large markets than do large-country consumers or producers from access to the smaller market. For example, Chile pursued a free trade agreement with the United States without success for almost a decade. This delay was due not to any concern with Chile's credentials or lack of effort, but because free trade with Chile was such a minor issue in the United States that it was easily lost or set aside. Also, because the effects of U.S.–Chilean free trade are so concentrated on tiny agricultural industries, these small lobbies were able to prevail against lukewarm general support for the measure until 2002.

As Table 1.2 indicates, bilateral trade accords between neighboring nations are uncommon in Latin America. When they have occurred, as between Chile and its neighbors or between Argentina and Brazil in the mid-1980s, they were typically part of a larger program of political and security cooperation. These broad political and military gains in the form of improved mutual confidence and security far outweighed their economic benefits, at least in the short term.

In Chile's case, its bilateral economic complementation agreements with the various member countries of the Andean Group, and its associate membership in MERCOSUR, reflect its preference for flexibility instead of full membership in subregional pacts that would tie it to relatively protectionist policies. Following its unilateral liberalization efforts in the 1980s, bilateral trade agreements have been advantageous for Chile since they entail either access to larger markets or the pressuring of regional neighbors to match Chile's lower tariff levels. Chile's stable and fast-growing economy and its increasing consumer market give it leverage over its poorer Andean neighbors, while the competitiveness of its exports and international corporations serves it well in the much larger Argentine and Brazilian markets. Chile's bilateral agreements with Mexico and Canada, and now with the United States, are means of access to the NAFTA market, and represent in our framework an overlap between regional dispersed bilateralism and transregionalism.

Our other case study nations are full members of regional trade blocs. In the case of MERCOSUR, Argentina and Brazil have emphasized the need for the group to negotiate free trade with non-member countries or other trade blocs in a collective fashion. As long as this commitment holds, it precludes broad bilateral agreements between MERCOSUR members and nonmembers. Collective negotiations have proved difficult, especially in the case of MERCOSUR's negotiations with the Andean Group. Nevertheless, negotiating from a single consolidated position is likely to yield a more advantageous outcome than could be obtained by any one member negotiating alone. This is particularly important as MERCOSUR continues its transregional free trade negotiations with the European Union and NAFTA members, as well as within the Free Trade Area of the Americas project.

The value of geographically concentrated trade in Latin America, whether bilateral or minilateral in form, is fundamentally limited. Compared to the complementarity seen in trade between the United States and Mexico (the sort of free trade envisioned in classic economic trade models, that is, between two nations with abundance in two different factors of production), trade among less developed economies offers limited opportunities for mutual gains. Trade among similar Latin American economies often heightens competition in primary goods, driving down profits. It does little to increase technological innovation and application or productivity, since competition among manufacturing or technology-based firms remains meager; in fact in many cases it simply invites expanded monopolies. With low complementarity, free trade among similar economies brings few efficiency gains for the region as a whole. Trade within the Andean Pact, for instance, or the Caribbean Community, has never generated significant economic growth.

Bilateralism Geographically Dispersed

Two of the case studies—Chile and Mexico—have engaged widely in geographically diffuse bilateralism. Similar to geographically concentrated bilateralism, negotiating on their own allows these governments tactical flex-ibility in setting the terms, conditions, and scheduling of tariff reductions. Both countries are in advanced stages of economic liberalization: Chile as a result of its unilateral reforms and development, and Mexico from its unilateral efforts and its NAFTA-driven transition process. Many of these agreements have been with larger and more successful exporting countries, or even with giants like the European Union (Mexico), Canada (both), Japan (both in process), or the United States (Chile). These bilateral agree-ments provide improved access to the world's most lucrative markets and they open these economies to the world's fiercest competition. However, Chile and Mexico engage in these agreements with somewhat different strategic motivations.

Since the establishment of NAFTA, Mexico has strategically positioned itself as the hub in a "hub-and-spokes" strategy of multilateral trade (see Smith 1996; Aggarwal 1994; and Ravenhill 2002).[7] Membership in the world's second-largest free trade market makes it an extremely attractive partner to countries around the world, and bilateral negotiations present less of the tricky social and nontariff issues required in direct negotiations with Canada or the United States. Mexico has signed or is negotiating a host of free trade agreements with countries in South America, the European Union, and Asia. In addition to increased trade, Mexico's position as a gate-way to NAFTA has attracted billions in foreign direct investment. However, as Antonio Ortiz Mena L.N. explains in Chapter 9, Mexico's aggressive transregional bilateralist program reflects both a strategic advantage—its NAFTA membership—and a defensive maneuver. Since joining NAFTA, Mexico's trade profile has become increasingly dominated by trade with the United States, and much of its growth in trade has been by way of di-version from countries in Asia or other regions, due largely to NAFTA's hefty and complicated set of rules of origin. While Mexico is more pro-active in accepting and responding to these circumstances than many crit-ics suggest, such overwhelming dependence on trade with and investment from the United States causes serious concern. Free trade with Europe, Japan, and Latin American countries is intended to mitigate this trade diversion and other effects of increased interdependence with the United States.

Chile, already deeply committed to a high degree of economic liberal-ization and export-led growth, has little to lose and much to gain from free trade with as many and as varied a set of partners as possible. Rosales em-phasizes that by increasing its trade with Asia, the European Union, and sub-regional neighbors (especially the MERCOSUR countries), as well as with the United States, Chile has avoided dependence on any one or two foreign markets. As in the Mexican case, however, there are certain political costs to negotiating or signing on to free trade agreements at the terms of larger, more developed countries. For Chile, however, having already suffered through the severe short- and medium-term effects of economic dislocation, and with a range of competitive export industries, these political costs are borne more easily. In fact, as Wise argues, Chile's success at maintaining relatively stable growth during the 1990s has allowed it to make progress in social investment, including its education, health, and pension systems.

Minilateralism Geographically Concentrated

Regional trade agreements have proliferated worldwide since the 1960s, a reflection of the tactical and political advantages of these groupings. Similar to bilateralism, cultural, historical, or institutional similarities can promote feelings of regional community and facilitate the compromises required in reaching agreements. Likewise, regional free trade is often concomitant with collaboration in security or political issues as well, and takes place within a broader regime of interdependence that enhances the incentives for success. In negotiations, it is relatively easy for like-minded countries to agree on norms and rules, and the potential industrial complementarities and economies of scale are more clear and predictable at the regional—rather than the transregional or global—level. Also, it is often easier to resolve collective action problems at the minilateral level, since the grouping is small and governments are more familiar with one another and because the power balance is more clearly understood. On the other hand, minilateral trade, like bilateral trade, can lead to trade diversion and regionally specific norms, rules, or procedures that complicate progress toward free trade on a larger scale.

In recent decades the rise of minilateralism, in the form of subregional trade agreements, has been the most pronounced trend in Western Hemispheric trade relations. Although defined as projects for economic liberalization and integration, many of these agreements—including NAFTA and MERCOSUR—were established largely with improved regional security and political relations in mind. Several early subregional projects were influenced by dependency theory. The work of Raúl Prebisch and others promoted the creation of protected regional markets in order to nurture local industrialization through economies of scale and reduce dependency on imports from the United States and Europe. With the severe debt crises of the 1980s and the failure of import-substitution-industrialization policies, dependency theories and their radically protectionist prescriptions were widely discredited (if not virtually banned by international creditors, the IMF, and the U.S. Treasury). With the rise of the "Washington consensus" in the 1980s, the rationale for these subregional groups shifted to emphasize their utility as frameworks for gradual free market reform. The question of whether such regionalism is a help or hindrance to the broader goal of nondiscriminatory multilateral free trade is still up for debate.

At its creation in 1994, NAFTA institutionalized and formalized free trade measures among countries that already shared porous borders and massive trade flows. To some extent, Mexico's membership was an acceptance of the inevitable deepening of its ties—particularly in economic and security affairs—with the United States, which had always been dense but were rapidly increasing. Costs to Mexico include a degree of trade diversion, the constraints on its foreign and domestic political autonomy that come with deeper interdependence with the United States, and the distance this special relationship with the United States created between Mexico and its traditional Latin American partners. To some degree these costs can be mitigated through Mexico's aggressive pursuit of bilateral and transregional trade relations, although the long-term prospects for this attempt at "balancing" are uncertain at best.

These economic and political costs for Mexico of NAFTA membership are balanced by the gains accrued from the growing importance of its partnership with the global superpower. In terms of both its economic welfare and its national security, the United States now has a clear stake in the improvement and stability of Mexico's economy and political system. This new significance was evident almost immediately, in 1995, in the $40-billion rescue package patched together by the Clinton administration following the devaluation of the peso. Since taking office, the Fox administration has proactively engaged the United States on several key issues, including border control and a more reasonable migration policy, and economic development. Just as importantly, the rise of cross-border transactions among individuals, firms, and local state agencies has improved the institutionalization of negotiations and dispute settlements, generating dense networks of cooperation at several levels.

MERCOSUR is the world's largest and most successful example of a regional free trade bloc among countries of the South. MERCOSUR grew out of a set of bilateral agreements signed in the second half of the 1980s that were intended to alleviate political and security tensions between Brazil and Argentina and to bolster support for these countries' fledgling democratic governments. This bilateralism, once in place, expanded into subregional cooperation in several areas, including the dramatic improvement of security relations. The explosion of intra-MERCOSUR trade in the early 1990s largely reflected the extraordinary lack of subregional trade up until that point. Throughout the 1990s, MERCOSUR was an important international complement to, and instrument of, the liberalization programs of its member countries. However, apart from MERCOSUR's economic benefits, it always held political and strategic importance, especially for Brazil.

Despite its title as a common market initiative, the MERCOSUR project has been as effective at reducing security tensions, bolstering democracy, and enhancing the international political and economic profile of the Southern Cone as it has been at increasing regional trade and growth.[8] As noted before, the massive regional increase in foreign investment and economic growth over the 1990s had more to do with these countries' domestic reform programs, and the overall health of the global economy, than with effects directly accountable to MERCOSUR. As international conditions have worsened since the East Asian financial crisis in 1997–1998, and with the collapse of Argentina's economy at the end of 2001, MERCOSUR is under severe strain. However, considering its various economic, political, and social benefits over the period of its existence, MERCOSUR has had an overwhelmingly positive impact on its members.

MERCOSUR's economic pattern is principally that smaller members gain access to Brazil's enormous consumer market, especially for their agricultural and low-level manufacturing exports, while opening their markets to Brazil's manufactures and capital goods. Several regional industries have gained in efficiency by establishing cross-border production and distribution networks. In terms of exports, the smaller members have generally gained disproportionately, at least until the devaluation of the Brazilian real in 1999. It is important to point out, however, that with the exceptions of Paraguay and Uruguay, intraregional trade remains a relatively insignificant portion of these countries' portfolios, which continue to be dominated by trade with the United States and Europe. A South American Free Trade Area, if it were to exist, would not alter this pattern.

As Motta Veiga emphasizes, the value of MERCOSUR for Brazil is political and strategic as much as economic. If MERCOSUR can organize itself to negotiate collectively in trade negotiations vis-à-vis the European Union and within the FTAA process, its members stand a better chance of achieving more favorable terms, such as flexible scheduling for tariff reduction, regulatory leniency, and support for social and economic programs that assist less competitive industries and groups affected by economic transition. Leadership in MERCOSUR and in various South American political and economic initiatives is also an important card in Brazil's bid to enhance its power and legitimacy in global affairs, including its campaign for a permanent seat on the U.N. Security Council. According to Motta Veiga, Brazil's behavior within MERCOSUR and its leadership of the bloc in negotiations with the European Union and other transregional partners cannot be understood without considering its larger national political agenda.

Argentina originally valued MERCOSUR for the subregional security and democratic and peaceful norms that it represented, as well as for the access it gave to the Brazilian market. During the 1990s, Argentina gradually came to terms with its growing dependence on the massive Brazilian economy and the added political leverage this gave Brazil in regional affairs. However, this asymmetry grew more difficult to accept—especially for the irascible former economy minister Domingo Cavallo—as the country slogged through a prolonged recession. With Brazil's currency devaluation in 1999 and its reluctance to abandon protectionist sectoral policies, its regional partners began to complain openly about its shortcomings as a regional power, which should voluntarily bear a greater share of the burden of a regional partnership that serves its interests. Calls for deeper institutionalization of MERCOSUR, including for multinational autonomous decision making and a supranational dispute settlement mechanism, achieved little. Brazil was reluctant to agree to any collaborative measures that may impinge on its sovereignty, and the creation of a supranational bureaucracy faced domestic opposition in all member states. Brazil's image and capacity as a regional leader will be sorely tested by the challenges of assisting Argentina through its current troubles. Certainly the stabilization of the peso at a lower value will improve macroeconomic conditions for cooperation. However, a review of events in 1995–1997, a previous period of stability and growth when MERCOSUR failed to broaden state collaboration and to institutionalize, does not inspire confidence. A stronger, more effective MERCOSUR demands political commitment and leadership from Brazil more than it has thus far been willing to give.

Transregionalism—Minilateralism Geographically Dispersed

The FTAA project, which would combine the various subregions of the Americas, is the most important example of transregionalism. All 34 participants stand to gain, either by increasing their exports to the enormous North American market or, for NAFTA members, by gaining access and fair treatment in the growing Latin American markets. However, the project has encountered problems of collective action. Collective action problems abound within a group that ranges from Caribbean microstates, to impoverished states like Haiti, Honduras, and Bolivia, to OPEC (Organization of Petroleum Exporting Countries) members Venezuela and Mexico, to mammoth Brazil and the United States. Governments find it difficult to commit to painful reforms with uncertain outcomes, while trusting that most of the other nations of the hemisphere will do roughly the same. Even if most governments showed the political will to agree to the wide-ranging objectives of the project, mobilizing the resources and institutional capacity needed to implement lower tariffs (which reduce state income) and a host of new regulations and standard practices would be a tremendous challenge. Most importantly, there is a prevailing attitude of skepticism about the U.S. commitment to further trade liberalization, based on its long-standing protectionism in certain sectors and its appetite for antidumping cases. An implementable FTAA, one with reduced sectoral protectionism across the board and with realistic, reasonable measures to reduce nontariff barriers based on health, labor, or environmental standards, would be the optimal framework for hemispheric economic growth. Yet the hemisphere's array of dynamic democracies—which allowed the FTAA its initial impetus—may prove too complex an environment for the wide-ranging consensus demanded by the project in its current form.

Transregionalism has emerged over the last decade as a popular strategy, one that complements more concentrated, regional minilateralism. As a half step between minilateralism and global multilateralism, transregionalism has the advantages of more focused negotiations, while significantly increasing and diversifying the aggregate market. For all of our case study countries, transregional free trade has the principal value of adding balance and diversity to a nation's or economic group's trade profile. Rosales suggests that Chile's free trade ties across the Pacific Ocean and with Europe offer much broader returns than focusing on hemispheric relations. For Mexico, membership in the Asia-Pacific Economic Cooperation (APEC) and a free trade agreement with the European Union invite extraregional investment and reduce Mexico's dependence on the United States. MERCOSUR's ongoing negotiations with the European Union follow the same logic. Why should the establishment of hemispheric trade dominated by the United States receive so much attention at the expense of consolidating historical trade and cultural partnerships in Europe? Although a free trade agreement with Europe does nothing to preclude the subsequent creation of free trade with the United States or within the FTAA, it would certainly be of advantage to European firms and investors. It would also increase the political and economic leverage of Latin American countries in FTAA negotiations.

It is far from certain, however, that achieving a trade agreement that meets the goals of MERCOSUR negotiators will be any easier in Europe than within the FTAA. To satisfy Southern Cone exporters, European leaders would have to overcome opposition from powerful domestic opponents of open markets, most specifically the French-supported protectionist agricultural regime. Despite the apparent progress made at the Doha Round of WTO talks in 2001, protectionism by developed countries in key industries such as agriculture and textiles is not likely to disappear.

Chile and Mexico (along with Peru) are members of APEC. However, with the lack of institutionalization and the decreased demand in Asia for Latin American exports since the 1997 crisis, membership in APEC has not produced important benefits other than encouraging trade and investment with Asian countries. The example of APEC, with its dramatically large and diverse membership, has failed to institutionalize coordination on various issues and policies. This example may prove instructive for negotiators and observers of the FTAA initiative (see Aggarwal 1994 and Pastor 2001).

The fact that none of the authors of our case studies devotes much space to outlining prospects or arguing the importance of expanded transregionalism (although Rosales mentions these negotiations as important) can be interpreted to mean that thus far, formal transregional agreements have proved either of too little benefit, or too difficult to establish, for our case study countries to engage in them more fully. Certainly the former is not the case. Every Latin American economy depends on trade and investment relations with developed countries in North America, Europe, and/or Asia. The difficulty of negotiating these agreements, however, lies largely beyond the power of these countries. Unless the developed countries reduce their protectionism toward agriculture and other key industries, more formalized free trade would come largely at the expense of Latin American workers and producers. As is the case with global multilateralism embodied in the struggling WTO, it is these failures on the part of developed countries to live up to their commitments of free trade that drives the continued interest in Latin America for various regional projects. Regionalism may be an inferior alternative to the ideal of free trade with the United States or Europe, but it may be the best option currently available.

Trade Preferences and National Strategies

Table 1.3 summarizes the economic and political trade-offs entailed in various trade strategies. With these in mind, we can consider the individual trade preferences of Argentina, Brazil, Chile, and Mexico over the last decade.

We have characterized the trade profiles of our case study countries as follows:

- Argentina: *regional partner,* focused at the minilateral (concentrated) level, with transregionalism pursued through collective regional activity
- Brazil: *regional leader,* focused at the minilateral (concentrated) level, with transregionalism pursued through collective regional activity; also extremely active at the multilateral level
- Chile: *multilateral trader,* including unilateral liberalization and agreements at the bilateral (geographically dispersed) and multilateral level
- Mexico: *hub market,* including bilateral, minilateral (concentrated, dominated by U.S. hegemony), and transregional trade agreements

Table 1.3 Advantages and Disadvantages Associated with Various Trade Strategies

	Unilateralism	Bilateralism	Minilateralism	Multilateralism
Economic	Maximum individual efficiency, but can disadvantage local industries without reciprocity	Risk of trade diversion; relatively clear assessment of costs and gains; flexible terms	Wider economies of scale; risk of trade diversion; less flexibility	Maximum global efficiency
Political	Flexibility, but minimum political leverage	Improves security and cooperation among neighbors; most easily established; strongly favors larger member	Improves regional security and cooperation; small group can overcome collective action problems; favors larger members	Collective action problems, and complexity of achieving success among diverse members; coalition-building dominant strategy

A comparison of these trade profiles to the political-economic trade-offs presented in Table 1.3 helps us piece together these nations' trade preferences, and patterns among their preferences. At least for the time being, Argentina and Brazil have centered their foreign economic policies around the enterprise of regional integration and political solidarity. The economic benefits of MERCOSUR have been significant, but alone they are insufficient to justify these commitments if MERCOSUR comes to be viewed as an obstacle to broader free trade, or to more far-reaching political goals. As Alcides Costa Vaz in Chapter 10 makes clear, enhanced economic interdependence paid off handsomely when Argentina's and Brazil's macroeconomic cycles were in sync (in particular between 1994 and 1997), but differences in monetary regimes and lack of economic policy coordination have proven costly. Politically, Argentina gains significant bargaining power as a member of MERCOSUR, which is especially important considering that President Carlos Menem's several overtures of strategic partnership with the United States fell on deaf ears in Washington. However, the costs and benefits of its economic partnership are unclear, as many of its more developed industries have suffered at the hands of Brazilian competition, especially since the Brazilian devaluation in 1999.

MERCOSUR has fallen far short of establishing a common regional market, and trade among members even declined in the late 1990s. Since then, with Argentina's financial collapse and the resulting contagion affecting Uruguay and Brazil, prospects for MERCOSUR appear even bleaker, at least in the short term. In Chapter 6, Eduardo Ablin and Roberto Bouzas assess in detail Argentina's continued minilateral regional strategy, which reflects a combination of strategic ambivalence toward liberalization and an incapacity for coherent policymaking due to the complicated domestic political situation under Presidents Menem and Fernando de la Rua. Fixing the peso to the U.S. dollar was a powerful gesture of commitment to stability; however, the government was unable to implement domestic fiscal and institutional reforms required to fulfill that commitment. Bouzas emphasizes the complexity of Argentina's external relations, with Brazil, which faces similar domestic uncertainties, in a region undergoing rapid change, and in a global environment radically different from that of 1990. Less than a strategy, perhaps, Argentine leaders negotiated the establishment of MERCOSUR, its evolution, and other trade matters in a somewhat ad hoc fashion, pushed by short-term economic and domestic political demands. For Argentina, MERCOSUR seemed to offer a more hospitable climate for liberalization than entering highly competitive global markets.

Also, from a strategic viewpoint, regional integration and cooperation still offer the country its best platform for the expansion of free trade within the Americas or with Europe. Since Brazil has often acted as a largely unpredictable and slow-moving partner, however, Argentina may yet reconsider its bilateral options. At present, because of financial collapse, the Argentine government is unable to think beyond its short-term needs. Nevertheless, if MERCOSUR membership comes to appear more as a hindrance than a source of assistance as it emerges from these difficult times, Argentine trade preferences could be dramatically revised. Argentina is unlikely to abandon MERCOSUR, considering the success of the project in several areas, but it may resist its more restrictive aspects. On the other hand, Brazil could come to play a significant role in helping Argentina's recovery, and the devalued peso (along with a devalued Uruguayan peso) will reduce significantly the gap in competitiveness that had plagued the regional community. As Ablin and Bouzas suggest, Argentina's future trade preferences, and therefore its strategy, will likely depend on what leader or coalition emerges to pull it out of its current woes and reestablish its economic footing.

Brazil has gained prestige by adding regional political leadership to its position as the economic engine of South America. Increased political coordination—manifested most importantly in MERCOSUR's free trade negotiations as a bloc with the European Union and the FTAA—yields the benefit of enhanced international legitimacy and bargaining power. Also, Brazil thus far has managed to expand its trade and to strengthen and diversify its economy while protecting some of its key sectors, including the sugar and automotive industries, from the effects of rapid liberalization. Brazil's trade has been dramatically liberalized. However, using the advantages of being a regional hegemon in a minilateral strategy, and as Argentina's financial troubles and institutional impediments weakened its competitiveness, Brazil has maintained control over the pace and form of its liberalization.

Regionally, Brazil's use of its hegemonic position and its gradual, state-controlled dance with liberalization reflect neo-mercantilist considerations, especially within its largely insulated foreign ministry. The country's political agenda is particularly pronounced at the multilateral level, where Brazil has exerted significant effort in several international organizations. Brazil's global political pretensions, including its campaign for a permanent seat on the U.N. Security Council, its activism as a leader of the developing world, and its proactive use of WTO dispute procedures set it apart from the other case study countries. MERCOSUR's future may hinge on Brazil's ability and willingness to assist Argentina and its other neighbors through the current crisis. If MERCOSUR weakens further, Brazil's strategy of leading a South American bloc in FTAA negotiations will be dealt a severe blow. Until now, however, Brazil's hedging strategy has served its interests relatively well. It remains uncommitted to deeper institutionalization of MERCOSUR, has successfully resisted an FTAA based on the NAFTA model or on piecemeal negotiations with the United States, and it maintains significant political autonomy, all while still claiming several efficiency benefits from gradual liberalization. The generosity to Brazil shown by the IMF in August 2001, while loans for Argentina were curtailed, reinforces the view that Brazil is perceived to be different from its neighbors. Like Mexico, which has embraced interdependence with the United States, Brazil appears to have attained the privileged status of a country that the international financial system cannot afford to allow to fail. Moreover, this has occurred with far less of the political and economic constraints imposed by a formalized regional agreement such as NAFTA.

With its unilateral liberalization and broad bilateralism, Chile pursues a high level of export growth and competitiveness without committing itself to the rules and standards of minilateral regionalism. Chile's successful liberalization program, active state-led development, and the stability of its political institutions have earned it the reputation as South America's most stable and well-governed economy, making it an attractive trading partner. The cost of its unilateralist strategy is that, as a small country negotiating trade pacts on its own, Chile has little market leverage vis-à-vis the United States, Japan, or Brazil, and can do little to resist their terms of agreement. Since today most Chilean industries are relatively competitive, this cost is more manageable for Chile than it would be for Brazil, for example. However, Chile's experience regarding accession to NAFTA membership, for which it had to wait for almost a decade, despite its competitiveness and willingness to meet the conditions of the pact, illustrates these costs.

During the last decade, Chile's trade preferences have centered on economic more than political objectives. Its strategic outlook and its agenda of export-led growth and legitimization as a rule follower rather than as a challenger of the system, reflect the ideological dominance of the free market model, as well as a keen awareness of its options as a small country. From 1990 to 1997, when a strong U.S. economy and relative stability in regional markets boosted economic growth and investment throughout South America, Chile fared well. Also, as Tulchin highlights in Chapter 2, Chile recently played a central role in negotiations at the Doha Round of the WTO, and appears to have attained a position of importance far beyond that which would be expected, considering its limited economic and strategic resources. However, if the global economy enters a period of slowdown, heightened competition, and protectionist entrenchment, and if trade agreements must be negotiated one by one in painstaking fashion, Chile's go-it-alone strategy may leave it vulnerable to marginalization and various forms of discrimination, both in the large markets of the North and its regional neighbors.

The trade-offs of Mexico's hub-market strategy—based on its NAFTA membership—are rapid, more stable economic growth for reduced political autonomy. Deeper interdependence with the United States does not completely eliminate instability, especially in the case of a slowdown or shocks in the U.S. economy. However, these tighter relations guarantee U.S. assistance and support in times of crisis, because trouble in Mexico will generate significant costs for the United States. If NAFTA is deepened to include some redistributive and economic development policies, according to the model of the European Union, the advantages of membership could be much improved, arguably for the United States and Canada as well. On the other hand, any additional involvement of U.S. funds or expertise in Mexican development also increases U.S. leverage in Mexican internal affairs through a wider variety of economic and social policies (although military action is virtually unthinkable). As Ortiz Mena argues, Mexico's entry into NAFTA can be viewed as a pragmatic, but quite visionary, proactive decision to manage the inevitable tightening of its relations with the United States. The ever-increasing numbers of Mexican immigrants and American citizens of Mexican background, and the boost this gives to cross-border business, tourism, and social and cultural exchanges—with NAFTA just a tool for formalizing and managing this inevitable trend—means that Mexico is likely to continue to have markedly different trade and strategic preferences from our other case studies. Within this context of Mexico's special relations with the United States, its transregional, bilateral hub-market trade profile reflects its optimal strategy for capitalizing on NAFTA membership.

Mexico's trade preferences underwent a radical transformation during the 1980s and 1990s, driven both by ideological shifts among the ruling elite and changes in the international system. In a strategic sense, this change can be regarded as radical in its softening of a long-held conservative concept of state sovereignty necessary to pursue the tangible benefits of economic growth, development, and the pressures that NAFTA brings for modernized governance. The country's—or at least, the government's—

dramatic transition from avid anti-Americanism to President Fox's innovative, proactive enthusiasm for cooperation requires explanation on several
levels. Regarding trade relations specifically, Mexico's revised preferences
and strategy are related to the rise of commitment to liberal trade theory
(mostly through the ascension to office of a generation of technocratic
leadership), ambivalence regarding multilateral institutionalism (as highlighted by Ortiz Mena), and a competitive strategy of capitalizing on its
unique position vis-à-vis other developing nations.[9] Over the long term, the
evolving political nature of its NAFTA partnership and the effects of its
deepening interdependence with the United States will be as important as
its economic gains in shaping Mexico's future.

Conclusion

This chapter argues that analysis along any single axis—be it economic or
political interests—cannot explain the growing diversity among recent trade
strategies of these four Latin American countries. An assessment of long-
term political calculations, including trade-offs inherent in pursuing multilateral, minilateral, or unilateral arrangements, and the recognition that these
states do not share a common vision regarding their potential roles within
the international system, reveal the various preferences that underlie these
strategies. Our focus on trade preferences, derived from an analysis of economic and political bargaining, is useful in categorizing these strategies and
suggesting the objectives and risks that they entail.

This analysis gives rise to two questions to which the concept of trade
preferences and the strategic framework that we have presented could be
usefully applied. First, what factors and processes influence a country's
trade preferences? How much are they—and the diversity among them—
the result of distinct strategic perceptions among top-level policymakers, or
how much are they driven by subnational interests and institutions? The
authors in this volume take up several of these questions in their chapters.
The influence of domestic constraints, actors, and shifting coalitions is the
focus of the analysis by Sylvia Maxfield, who assesses the role of business
groups, and Carol Wise, who analyzes various countries' state-led export
programs. These chapters point to several fruitful avenues for further in-
vestigation. A related question is to what extent can we generalize from
these four cases to test, for instance, a hypothesis that a specific institutional
trait or traits within a government or its foreign or trade ministry shape its

liberalization in a specific way? What role do regional relations and integration play in this process? Each of these questions calls out for further exploration.

A second interesting area of further inquiry is how much the examination of these four cases reveals patterns of preference or behavior that can be generalizable to other developing countries in other parts of the world. Do transition economies or young democracies tend to act differently from more developed countries, for whom the domestic costs of trade liberalization are less severe (although certainly severe enough for certain groups, such as farmers)? Are foreign policymaking dynamics and decision making best analyzed along geographical lines—based on the idea that geographically proximate countries share common cultural, historical, and/or institutional characteristics that shape their behavior—or along other lines of distinction such as size or degree of economic development? These four countries were selected partly to control for the effects of dramatic differences in economic development levels, or trade industries. To compare Brazil, or even Chile, against a much smaller and less developed economy such as Ecuador would be problematic. However, smaller countries likewise face a range of alternatives in their trade relations, and have political and strategic goals in addition to economic growth. Therefore, the application of this type of analysis to those cases could be useful as well.

These important questions are beyond the purview of this introductory chapter. We hope, however, that this analysis and the others in this volume represent a step toward an improved understanding not only of current trends in Western Hemispheric trade and trade policy formulation, but of the trade-offs and preferences that lie behind international trade strategies in general.

Notes

This research has been supported by grants from the Center for Latin American Studies and the Clausen Center for International Business of the University of California–Berkeley, and the Latin American Program of the Woodrow Wilson International Center. We are grateful to Roberto Bouzas, Antonio Ortiz, Joseph Tulchin, Diana Tussie, and João Paulo Cândia Veiga for their extremely useful comments and suggestions. Special thanks go to Priyanka Anand and Sonia Khan for their research assistance.

1. It is worth noting that this category is quite subjective, since simple distance is hardly the only relevant factor in defining a "geographic region." But despite conceptual difficulties, we find this to be a useful category.

2. Other examples include the Basic Telecom Agreement, or the recent Financial Services Agreement. For a discussion of these agreements, see Aggarwal (2001) and

Aggarwal and Ravenhill (2001). Examples of multilateral protectionist sectoral agreements include the Multifiber Arrangement in textiles and apparel.

3. As should be clear from the table, however, cells 2, 4, and 8 are also forms of "regionalism," although theoretically they may have quite different political-economic implications.

4. Note that the definition of what constitutes a "region" is to a large extent subjective.

5. See Aggarwal and Lin (2002) for a general discussion of the costs and benefits of various approaches to trade liberalization.

6. *Estado de São Paulo,* February 7, 2002.

7. See Smith (1996), and Chapter 9 in this volume for the unfolding implications of this position.

8. Although intraregional trade and investment multiplied under MERCOSUR, it never accounted for more than around 20 percent of its members' total trade. For a variety of viewpoints on the importance of MERCOSUR and its future development, see Tulchin (2002).

9. Regarding the rise of technocratic leadership, see Centeno (1997).

References

Aggarwal, Vinod K. 1994. "Comparing Regional Cooperation Efforts in the Asia-Pacific and North America." In *Regimes in the Asia-Pacific Region,* edited by Andrew Mack and John Ravenhill. Sydney: Allen & Unwin.

———. 2001. "Economics: International Trade." In *Managing a Globalizing World: Lessons Learned Across Sectors,* edited by P.J. Simmons and Chantal de Jonge Oudraat. Washington, DC: Carnegie Endowment for International Peace.

Aggarwal, Vinod K., and Kun Chin Lin. 2002. "Strategy Without Vision: The U.S. and Asia-Pacific Economic Cooperation." In *APEC: The First Decade,* edited by Jürgen Rüland, Eva Manske, and Werner Draguhn, 91–122. London: Curzon Press.

Aggarwal, Vinod K., and Edward Fogarty, eds. Forthcoming. *EU Trade Strategies: Between Regionalism and Globalisation.* Basingstoke, UK: Macmillan.

Aggarwal, Vinod K., and John Ravenhill. 2001. "How Open Sectoral Agreements Undermine the WTO." *Asia Pacific Issues* 50 (February).

Centeno, Miguel Ángel. 1997. *Democracy within Reason: Technocratic Revolution in Mexico,* 2d ed. University Park: Pennsylvania State University Press.

Pastor, Robert A. 2001. *Toward a North American Community: Lessons from the Old World for the New.* Washington, DC: Institute for International Economics.

Ravenhill, John. 2002. *APEC and the Construction of Pacific Rim Regionalism.* New York: Cambridge University Press.

Smith, Peter H. 1996. *Talons of the Eagle: Dynamics of U.S.–Latin American Relations.* New York: Oxford University Press.

Tulchin, Joseph S., ed. 2002. *MERCOSUR at a Crossroads.* Washington, DC: Woodrow Wilson Center Press.

Tulchin, Joseph S., and Ralph Espach. 2001. *Latin America in the New International System.* Boulder, CO: Lynne Rienner Publishers.

2

Using Soft Power to Enhance Trade Strategies

Joseph S. Tulchin

In Chapter 1, Vinod Aggarwal and Ralph Espach discuss various trade strategies and their implications. They make a significant contribution to our understanding of foreign policy and international relations by organizing this variety of experiences into a typology that allows us to understand the relationships among differing strategies. They deliberately and explicitly leave for others to consider a number of variables normally associated with the study of international relations and foreign policy, especially at the intrastate level of analysis. In this chapter, I want to refer to some, but by no means all, of those variables and set trade strategies into the broader context of international relations. In so doing, I suggest an approach that may be taken as a complement to the Aggarwal and Espach approach.

Where Aggarwal and Espach deal with a comprehensive set of strategies in trade policy or trade preferences, they quite properly restrict themselves to policies and behaviors that refer to international trade. Their goal is to encompass as complete a set as possible of trade strategies that nations might adopt and to explain how each might be used to achieve specific goals in a range of situations over time. They admit that each of these strategies might be the result of a set of contesting or disparate interests within the nation-state—interests that might well determine a particular trade strategy at a specific moment in time. They also recognize that domestic division and debate among interest groups may well produce an outcome or a policy that is less than optimal. Nevertheless, they prefer to leave those domestic political issues aside,[1] and focus instead on outcomes.

My purpose is to insert trade and trade strategies into the wider context of geopolitics, in which trade is but one factor, although an important one, in the determination of a nation's foreign policy. In the formal academic study of geopolitics, trade has had an important place as an element of national power since the beginning of the nineteenth century. Four centuries earlier, in the era of sea-going empire, trade was monopolized by the state and considered an attribute of state power, even when private agents were used to conduct the activity. With the rise of capitalism, as the private and public sectors became autonomous from one another, trade continued to be taken as part of a nation's power, and trade policy was an integral part of a nation's foreign policy and development model. Alexander Hamilton and George Washington understood this relationship in the early years of the republic.[2] But while it is relatively easy to document that trade was an integral part of a nation's sense of its place in the world and has long been considered a central facet of a nation's power and particularly its capacity to project its power beyond national boundaries, it was difficult to isolate trade strategies as distinct elements of broader national policy until an institutional framework for multilateral trade negotiations had been created in the aftermath of World War II. Once institutions such as the General Agreement on Tariffs and Trade (GATT) were in place, it was possible to speak of multiple trade strategies and to evaluate trade strategies against one another.[3]

Since the end of the Cold War, however, the subject has become more complex. Thanks to the work of Joseph S. Nye, Jr., and Robert O. Keohane, among others, we now understand that a nation's influence beyond its borders has to do with a whole range of attributes and behaviors that are not considered part of traditional or "hard" power. Following their lead, we can understand trade strategies as part of traditional national power (e.g., the size of GDP) and "soft power" (e.g., respect for human rights). I argue that the success of a nation's trade policy has as much to do with its management of the diverse instruments of soft power (Nye and Keohane 1988; Nye 2001) as it does with the size of its gross national product, military might, or perspicacity of its trade policy (Nye and Keohane 1988; Nye 2001).

Trade and trade strategies, therefore, must be considered within a broad framework of geopolitics that today includes global governance, the roles of nonstate actors, global regimes, and international institutions, and even institutions that are not directly concerned with trade. And, in the case of Latin American nations, the role of domestic actors must be taken into account as they would be in studies of the most industrialized nations, since Latin American nations are now all functioning democracies in which contestation is normal and healthy and such public discussion of domestic differences over policy is new. Indeed, the heart of the argument presented by Eduardo Ablin and Roberto Bouzas is that domestic, sectoral interest groups virtually prevent the formulation of rational trade strategies in Argentina, at least in the sense of that term as used by Aggarwal and Espach. As I shall indicate below, the Ablin and Bouzas approach is correct as far as it goes, but it does not give full weight to the geostrategic debate within the Argentine government over the nation's proper role in world affairs. It is true that Argentina's trade strategy was less than optimal because of the gridlock among private medium- and small-scale actors. It is not true that the trade strategy was inconsistent with the government's broader policy, at least during the administration of President Carlos Menem.

Trade policy strategies emerge out of a matrix of domestic and international pressures that shape a nation's strategic vision and determine the trade and nontrade elements of a nation's participation in the international community. Furthermore, trade strategies can be strengthened or weakened by developments in areas that have little or nothing to do with trade.[4] For example, in Latin America in the past decade, both the shape of trade strategies and their success were influenced by policies related to arms control or proliferation in the case of Argentina; or related to the environment, in the case of Brazil; or related to leadership in the struggle for international recognition of human rights, as in the case of Chile.[5]

The framework I shall construct is a state-centered model to understand how nations in Latin America deliberately use a panoply of instruments to insert themselves into the post–Cold War international system. I am intent on showing the breadth of instruments available and the fluid and complex environment in which they might be selected for use.[6] In addition, I take for granted the broad consensus among students of international relations that state-to-state bargaining can be understood in terms of game models or game strategies.[7] And, finally, the nature of policymaking has been discussed at length in the literature and need not be reviewed here.[8]

In the examples I use, there is evidence of conscious, deliberate, and strategic mixing of soft and hard power to enhance, influence, and optimize outcomes. The effectiveness of trade strategies is a function of the conscious insertion of trade policy by decision makers into the broader matrix of geopolitical strategic considerations. In other words, the relative success of trade strategies is determined, at least in part, by effective application of soft power. This is demonstrated in the trade strategy adopted under President Carlos Menem in Argentina and the trade strategy adopted under President Ricardo Lagos in Chile. In both cases, the same trade strategy was less effective when it was not coordinated carefully with other elements of soft power under Menem's successor, Fernando de la Rua, or Lagos's predecessor,

Eduardo Frei.[9] In the case of Mexico under Vicente Fox, we can see how trade strategy, already fixed within the North American Free Trade Agreement (NAFTA), is used as the foundation for a broad shift in geopolitical policies and the more deliberate use of soft power to enhance trade advantages. Brazil is a case treated in detail by Aggarwal and Espach, so I shall not deal with it at length. Suffice it to say that Brazil's trade policy is driven by a long-standing geopolitical vision, a vision that many observers consider outmoded, and that in my view, Brazil is a case of not taking advantage of a nation's potential soft power.[10]

In constructing my argument, I make four assumptions based on a broad consensus in the recent literature about the post–Cold War period:

- All nations in the hemisphere understand that the bipolar competition has ended and that, insofar as the Western Hemisphere is concerned, the United States is the only superpower.
- All nations of the hemisphere are making an effort to become more democratic in their domestic governance than they were before and during the Cold War, and all are seriously considering a transition to a more open economy than they had before the end of the Cold War. Democracy and free markets are part of these nations' strategy of insertion into the international system.
- All nations of the hemisphere are disposed to participate to some degree in multilateral agencies, such as the United Nations and the World Trade Organization (WTO).
- All nations of the hemisphere are more or less affected by globalization, especially in terms of access to information technology and communications and the increased role of non-governmental actors in the formulation of rules of the international game.[11]

The last three assumptions, taken together, indicate that the nations of Latin America are more profoundly inserted into the international system than they have been at any time in their history, and that they will be more affected by the international system than ever before. Obviously, this can be a severe constraint on national policy, as it was for Argentina throughout its fiscal crisis from 2000 to 2002. On the other hand, as I have argued elsewhere, these assumptions suggest that if they were so disposed, the nations of the hemisphere could play more protagonistic roles in the international community than they ever have before, and that this protagonism should form part of their trade strategies in order to optimize the expected results. While there is a clear sense that the United States is the hegemonic power in the region, there is considerable ambiguity as to how the United States might use its power. This ambiguity is both an opportunity and a constraint for the nations of the region. In the response to the terrorist attacks of September 11, 2001, the United States became even more preoccupied than ever with events outside the hemisphere. In previous episodes of U.S. distraction, the nations of Latin America complained of being ignored. In the post–Cold War world, this distraction is an opportunity for greater influence by Latin American nations.[12]

As the international trading system becomes more global and as the volume of trade increases, along with the share of foreign trade in national economies, trading strategies become more significant.[13] By the same token, since the region's insertion into the international system has to do with so many more issues than trade, the exogenous factors that influence foreign policy become more numerous and weightier, while at the same time the transition to democracy increases the pressures of endogenous factors on foreign policy.[14]

Trade Strategies as Strategic Instruments

The earliest evidence of anything resembling a conscious trade strategy comes with the drive for the accumulation of wealth at the heart of maritime imperial adventures from the fifteenth century onward. Without exception, the states of Europe were directly involved in promoting trade. The state—monarchs and their allies among the nobility—invested in private ventures, created charter companies with monopoly privileges in trade, and generally used all instruments available to them to increase the value of their trade and to retain the state's control over that trade. In a mercantile world, trade had to be controlled within very strict institutional bounds. As the middle class expanded through the nineteenth century, the role of the state diminished in relative terms. Trade increasingly became an activity of private individuals and corporations.

As the distance between public and private spheres increased, it became possible to talk for the first time of a government trade strategy, in the sense of an autonomous public policy designed to influence efforts by private members of the national community, although until the middle of the twentieth century, it seemed essentially a question of more is better. There were two major schools of thought on trade strategy in the nineteenth and early twentieth centuries. One was the free trade school, led by the United Kingdom, which held that the best way to expand trade is by lowering tariffs and other barriers to international exchange. The other school, led by Germany, took a more interventionist posture, considering trade as a complement to industrialization. Trade was part of industrial policy.

From its inception, the United States has been torn between the two schools and the national debate over trade, mainly over the level of tariffs, has moved back and forth between free trade and protection for industry and agriculture. Beginning with Alexander Hamilton, the debate included a clear, strategic vision for national development that included protection for infant industries and state promotion of key exports. At no time since the presidency of George Washington has the state withdrawn from strategic intervention in the economy as a whole. Even when free traders dominated the debate over tariffs in the United States, the federal government was deeply involved in strategic investments in areas such as infrastructure and consistently formulated competition policy and banking regulation, which enhanced the competitiveness of U.S. exports. There was also a fairly broad consensus among the governing elite that trade was an essential element of national power. Trade took the flag to the far corners of the world. That flag had to be defended. Military power and economic power were inseparable elements of a nation's capacity and influence.[15] The linkages between power and economic activity became more articulated in World War I, when access to or control over communication, finance capital, and fuel became part of strategic planning, with trade often taking a back seat to other forms of international economic activity.[16]

In Latin America, there were very few, isolated voices that were in concert with this realist understanding of the relationship between private economic activity, public policy, and national power. The vast majority held fast to a traditional concept of the international division of labor and comparative advantage where trade was considered a "natural" attribute of a nation's resources and that the international market would maximize trade without state intervention on either side of the exchange.[17] Under this simple strategy, a nation should produce for the international market the products in which it had a natural price advantage. The ruling elites of the major trading nations in the hemisphere believed that there always would be markets for their products and that the industrialized nations of Europe always would be willing to sell them the manufactured products they might need at rates of exchange that would be advantageous. This was the first conscious strategy by the nations of Latin America to be inserted into the international system: to prepare the infrastructure and organize the nation's institutions to maximize the use of their natural resources, including labor, that would maximize exports to markets in the industrialized countries that were expected to grow indefinitely.[18]

The United States never followed this approach to its insertion into the international system. It always had a strategic sense of how trade fit into a broader view of influence and autonomy. It is noteworthy that the discussion of trade policy in the executive and legislative branches in the United States remained fairly simple right up until World War II, at least compared to the multifaceted debate over industrial policy and regulatory policy.[19] Economists and policymakers were concerned to know, as Charles P. Kindleberger (1962: 4) put it, "What determines the nature and amounts of the goods a country buys and sells in international trade?" and "What is the impact of foreign trade on national economic life?" Such studies started from the assumption that the best economy is one in which private enterprise generates economic activity with as little interference from the state as possible. This bias, as we might put it today, led to discussions of trade policy without making strategy a central concern. Dumping and other constraints on trade were considered "problems" (Viner 1923).[20]

The cases of Nazi Germany or the Soviet Union in the 1930s were considered to be extreme examples of state interference, where trade was not just part of industrial policy but part of an overt strategic posture and a search for power and influence. These examples provided opportunities to comment on state trade strategies, but always with the implication of criticism. Nazi Germany and the Soviet Union were perverse cases. The protectionist policies of the United States and the nations of Western Europe in the same period were considered to be inevitable, understandable, and unfortunate responses to the aggressive bloc trading of the Germans and the Soviets— "second-best policies" (Kindleberger 1962, chapters 9 and 10).

But if the trade policies of the Soviet Union and Nazi Germany were counter to economic orthodoxy, even perverse, they certainly were clear examples of how trade was manipulated strategically for broader objectives. Trade was a critical element in the struggle for international influence and power. Trade was clearly a weapon in an international struggle with an adversary. The instruments used to control trade for strategic purposes were the same as those used during wartime. The same zero-sum calculations were made to determine what trade would be encouraged, with whom, and under what conditions. In wartime, the tendency toward mercantile, zero-sum calculations is carried to its most extreme form. In the Great Depression of the 1930s, we can see experiments conducted to control trade for strategic purposes and have trade used as a weapon short of war. Indeed, the Japanese alleged that unfair trade practices by the United States in Asia were the principal cause of the attack on Pearl Harbor.[21]

It is worth noting that during this period between the world wars, we can see the first strategic approach to trade in Latin America in Getúlio Vargas's government in Brazil. Vargas was able to set the United States and Germany against one another to Brazil's advantage in negotiating trade preferences and credits for strategic investments in the steel industry. For Vargas, trade was one of the many instruments he used to achieve his vision of a corporatist, industrialized nation. Brazil's ability to deal with the United States and Germany during the war is in marked contrast to Argentina's reliance on an older strategy of comparative advantage that no longer worked.[22] Just prior to the onset of the Great Depression, there were some Argentine economists, who, as a reaction to the dislocations created by the World War I, argued that Argentina's national security required a trade strategy that served the long-term goals of establishing the nation's autonomy from the national goals of other states. The two most influential of this group, Alejandro Bunge and Raúl Prebisch, argued that trade should be used deliberately to build the nation's industrial base, precisely to reduce its international dependence.[23] Their arguments were drowned out by those who insisted that the industrialized nations, especially Great Britain, had to return to an international division of labor that would maximize Argentina's benefits.

During the Cold War, we can see a shift away from mercantile thinking about trade and a resurgence of classic free trade doctrine. At the same time, the Soviet Union represented a constant reminder of trade as strategic instrument. And yet, both the United States and the Soviet Union used trade with the Third World—the developing countries that were either marginal to or unaligned in the bipolar struggle—as an instrument to win influence against the adversary. As international trade accelerated after 1960 and as institutions were created to deal with the trading community of nations, it became possible for the first time to speak of trade strategies in the sense used in this volume.

Latin America and the New International System

In the aftermath of the Cold War, the nations of Latin America began to seek new ways to achieve their national goals. For the first time in fifty years, they were free from the pressure of being caught between the two great powers, the United States and the Soviet Union, and locked in a struggle for dominance. In that struggle, the United States, long the dominant external power in the region, had taken the position that neutrality was a hostile position. In response, foreign policies in Latin America were conceived in terms of how they would play in Washington and Moscow. In the first moments that they felt free of this straitjacket, two curious things happened. The governments in the region, without exception, expressed diffidence in assuming autonomous positions on global issues. Instead, they focused attention on long-dormant territorial disputes with their neighbors, disputes that the United States had encouraged them to ignore so that they could focus their energy on the Cold War and the global adversary outside the hemisphere or on subversion within their own borders.

In some cases, as between Peru and Ecuador, this produced armed hostilities or a number of "hot" borders. In others, fortunately, historical hypotheses of conflict were addressed and either eliminated, as between Argentina and Brazil, or set firmly on the path toward resolution, as between Argentina and Chile. In both cases in which Argentina moved to reduce friction with a neighbor, national leaders, first Raúl Alfonsín (with Brazil) and then Carlos Menem (with Chile), sought to maximize attributes of soft power in the global community. Alfonsín wanted to maximize the advantage of the transition to democracy to achieve Argentina's international goals and to protect his government against hostile groups within his own armed forces. Menem wanted to demonstrate to the international community that Argentina had left behind the period of irresponsible behavior and had become a worthy site for investment and trade.

In the 1990s, the nations of the region did experiment with different ways of achieving their national goals. They participated in multilateral agencies, but generally as rule takers, not rule makers. High-profile examples by Brazil included hosting the U.N. environment summit and participating as a member of the GATT and U.N. Conference on Trade and Development (UNCTAD) to block rules being made. The same was true of Mexico's participation in multilateral agencies. The only exception to this was Argentina's participation in peacekeeping efforts all around the world. More significant were rare efforts to join forces with other nations in the region to project Latin American influence, individually or collectively, on a global or even a regional stage.

Perhaps the most dramatic shift in the role of Latin American nations in the international system was their insertion into the community of nations as democracies. Virtually all of the nations in the hemisphere began a transition to democratic government in the final years of the Cold War. Several enjoyed honeymoon periods of influence in the international system as a result. For example, Argentine President Alfonsín, a strong opponent of the military regime in his country, was lionized in international forums and multilateral agencies for most of his term because of his history of strong support for democratic values. Alfonsín used the transition to democracy in Argentina to move boldly to eliminate potential nuclear competition with Brazil. He never used his country's new democratic status to enhance Argentine trade. Instead, he tried to use his personal influence to recreate the nonaligned movement just as that group was rendered anachronistic by the collapse of the Soviet Union. While defenders of Alfonsín's policy claimed that it was an example of idealism (*principismo*), it was counterproductive because the idealism of the period was moving rapidly from a bipolar view of the world to a world that might be governed by international, egalitarian institutions such as the United Nations.

Taking a very different approach, the new democratic government of Patricio Aylwin, in Chile, used support for human rights and democratic institutions as an instrument in his government's foreign policy, including Chile's relations with Europe, the United States, and multilateral agencies. There is little doubt that Chile enjoyed greater influence in world affairs during the decade of the 1990s than its size or the size of its economy—its hard power—might indicate.[24] Chile, thanks to its record as a democratic country and defender of human rights, had earned the right to become a rule maker in the international community and graduate from the mass of ruler takers.[25] Chile immediately tried to convert its soft power into a trade advantage by gaining privileged access to NAFTA in 1995. It failed. It succeeded, however, in winning special status in the Southern Common Market (MERCOSUR) and in securing a bilateral free trade agreement with Mexico. It also succeeded in becoming the first nation in Latin America with which the new Bush administration would negotiate a bilateral free trade treaty in 2001. While the bilateral negotiations dragged on into 2002, irritating the government of Ricardo Lagos, the fact remains that only Chile was admitted into the club of bilateral negotiations, only Chile could lobby the U.S. Congress with a clear conscience, and only Chile, despite its modest size, could adopt such a flexible trade policy with success. The trade treaty was signed in 2003. Compare the response of the Bush administration to Chile's request for trade negotiations to the response to Argentina's request for help in its financial crisis.

With the end of the Cold War and the emergence of multilateral institutions as forums for setting rules for the international community, Latin American nations found themselves with multiple venues in which they could express their interests and in which they might attempt to achieve influence. At the same time, it became clear that the international community in its noninstitutional, almost inchoate state, was in the process of establishing rules of the game in a variety of areas—crimes against humanity, trade, intellectual property, the environment, immigration, coping with international crime, whether it was trafficking in illegal drugs or money laundering, arms trafficking, and many others—in which many nations, large and small, could make their influence felt, although asymmetries of power remain important. In this situation, small nations as well as large nations could exert influence. In many cases, the larger nations, even the largest and most powerful, including the United States, could not find the means to exert their superior power and were forced to work with smaller nations whose interests coincided with theirs. In this fashion, soft power in the post–Cold War era became a significant feature of the international community. In this brave new world, trade strategies were another instrument of soft power and another way in which nations could achieve their broader goals and objectives.

Trade Strategies as Access to Rule Making

Historically, as relatively weak states, the nations of Latin America have attempted to use multilateral institutions as modes of access to international rule making and as havens of protection from the more powerful Darwinian states. Caught in the straitjacket of the bipolar conflict, a number of nations in the region adopted idealist postures toward international institutions (principismo) and attempted to forge roles for themselves under the banner of international law within the United Nations, and through a number of international conventions on arms regimes, human rights, and the law of the sea. On occasion, even nations such as Argentina, which claimed to be idealistic members of an international system governed by consensual institutions, were cynical users of the system when it suited their purposes. In one of the more curious uses of international institutions, Argentina voted against the United States in the U.N. from 1960 to 1990, more than any nation in the world except Cuba, Libya, and Yemen (Escudé 1997). Apparently, the Argentine foreign ministry considered the U.N. so insignificant that it could use it as a forum to express its residual jealousy of and disdain for the United States. On other occasions, Latin American nations felt them-selves used and abused as part of international institutions, such as when the Organization of American States (OAS) served as a fig leaf to cover the U.S. intervention in the Dominican Republic in 1965. To this day, the na-tions of the hemisphere are ambivalent about the OAS, seeing it as a po-tential forum to defend their interests, even against the United States, and as a weapon used against them by the United States. This ambivalence, the result of the historical legacy of hegemonic behavior by the United States, is seen again in the 1990s, in the participation of the OAS in the efforts to restore and consolidate democracy in Haiti. There is still no example of Latin American nations using the OAS to promote their interests in situa-tions where such promotion might run counter to strongly held views of the United States.

Latin American nations more recently have attempted to use their membership in other multilateral agencies as instruments of leverage in bar-gaining. An example of successful multiple strategies is Argentina's mem-bership in the Cairns Group, which represents the interests of nations that export agricultural products. Because it is one of the very few areas in which Argentine interests coincide almost perfectly with those of the United States, Canada, and other democratic nations with active roles in the inter-national system, it gives the Argentine government access to the bargaining table alongside some of the most powerful trading nations in the world. Argentine membership in the Cairns Group has served to increase Argen-tine influence in the negotiations between MERCOSUR and the European Union, since agricultural protection is one of the most sensitive issues to be negotiated. Looking at domestic political factors, we find that exporting firms in Argentina that are cool to MERCOSUR, or even those that are hos-tile to it, have supported talks between the European Union and MERCOSUR because they already have had experience in relying on international groups or institutions to defend their interests by either complementing national institutions or replacing them. Agricultural exporters probably have more to gain from the Cairns Group than they do from their own governments. This domestic interest group support strengthens the Argentine position within MERCOSUR.

In Chapter 1, it is clear that both Brazil and Argentina have attempted to use MERCOSUR as an instrument in their individual bargaining with other nations. As the leader of the trade group, Brazil has given the group more value as a negotiating unit. Argentina, while giving lip service to MERCO-SUR as a negotiating instrument, also has pursued bilateral strategies. The result for Argentina has been to weaken the credibility of both its strategies, a clear case of failing to do what Katzenstein, Keohane, and Krasner (1998) called combining collaboration and cooperation. By appearing consistent and steadfast, Brazil has earned a greater respect that may neutralize the hostility to its pretensions in the region and to its persistent public statements in opposition to U.S. leadership that is felt throughout the U.S. government, including the Congress.

The key to understanding the success of trade preferences, at least for the relatively weak nations of Latin America, in addition to the accuracy of decisions among unilateral, bilateral, and multilateral strategies, is the way in which a nation manages its store of soft power. The only nations in the region with any measurable store of global hard power are Mexico and Brazil.[26] Mexico's hard power derives from its position in NAFTA, its store of petroleum, and its size. Its soft power today depends primarily on the way in which the Fox administration handles the transition to democracy. That is the background for the dramatic shift of Mexican foreign policy toward protagonism in multilateral agencies and toward more collaboration with South American nations.

Brazil is caught in the dilemma of whether to pursue a regional strategy or a global strategy. Its size and certain foreign policy pretensions, such as the desire for a permanent seat on the U.N. Security Council, indicate a nation as a global player. Its dominant geopolitical strategy is that of a regional player. Until that dilemma is resolved, perhaps by some form of mini-maxing, Brazilian trade strategies will be reduced in effectiveness, except within MERCOSUR. The very size of the Brazilian economy makes reliance on MERCOSUR problematic in the long term. Because the other members of the group—Argentina, Paraguay, and Uruguay—do not add enough real power to make the common market an effective unit in bargaining aside from the effectiveness of Brazil by itself, the ambivalence of Brazilian strategic posture actually reduces the country's international influence. The foreign ministry of Brazil, Itamaraty, insists in mantra-like fashion that Brazil is a poor nation, a nation made weak by inequality and underdevelopment. And yet, it is a nation that successfully blocks U.S. strategies in the region, because it is inconceivable to establish hemispheric rules or a hemispheric community without Brazil. Brazil is a case of a nation with significant hard power and great potential soft power, a potential that it refuses to use. Its hard power is of less value in hemispheric affairs, where the United States is unquestionably the hegemon. Does this mean that Brazil should lead? Or does it suggest that Brazil's greatest influence would come eventually, if not immediately, on a global stage, not just a regional one, where its combination of soft and hard power could be put to greatest advantage?

The fact that trade is part of a larger context can work to the detriment of a nation's trade strategies. For example, the financial crisis that affected Argentina in the second half of 2001 virtually brought the nation to its knees. Its trade preferences were undermined. Its ability to use multilateral and bilateral strategies were all but wiped out as the government was forced to demonstrate fiscal discipline as the starting point for negotiations on all other matters.[27] As B. J. Cohen (1996) has argued, the global financial system can be taken as an opportunity, but it also can become a constraint on national policies. The interim government of Eduardo Duhalde attempted to sell a multiple trade strategy as part of its argument for financial aid with the International Monetary Fund and to move away from tightly focused support of the United States in all matters that had been the cornerstone of the Menem administration's policy (WWICS 2002).

Perhaps the most flexible trade strategy in the hemisphere is Chile's.[28] The Chilean trade strategy is also the most closely tied to the nation's broader geopolitical plan. Not only does the Chilean government have a sense of what it wants to accomplish, its representatives are well prepared. The efficiency of Chilean diplomats in negotiation actually improves their strategy. In the current negotiations between Chile and the United States for a bilateral free trade treaty, the Chilean delegation achieved more of its objectives than either government anticipated simply because they were better prepared than their U.S. counterparts. Given the endogenous pressure on the U.S. side to get something done, and quickly, the lack of preparation by the U.S. negotiators cannot be used as an excuse, so the talks plowed ahead, much to the benefit of the Chilean negotiators. Ending the talks without a treaty would have been a mortal blow to the Bush administration's much-trumpeted goal of a free trade treaty for the hemisphere.

That the bilateral talks even started is a tribute to the Chilean understanding of soft power and its potential. Given its modest attributes of hard power, Chile has been the most successful nation in the region in adapting to the post–Cold War rules of the game.[29] Once the military regime had been replaced by an elected, democratic government, the fact that Chile had been the first nation in the region to privatize and to open its economy immediately became significant assets. Chile was the favorite son of the international community for most of the decade of the 1990s, despite the fact that its democracy was seriously hampered by an autonomous military establishment; by the continued presence of the dictator, Augusto Pinochet, on the political scene; and by the total dominance of its media by the unreformed right wing. It is important in understanding how the elements of soft power are interconnected to note that the arrest of Pinochet in London in 1998 virtually eclipsed Chile's role as a model state for over a year. Finally, when the new government of Ricardo Lagos made it perfectly clear that Pinochet would be judged in Chile under the laws of the land, the nation began to recover some of its international influence. If the cliché is that if you live by the sword and you die by the sword, then there must be some equivalent for the rules of soft power. If you build your influence in the international system by soft power, you must follow all the rules.

The Lagos government, represented by Vice Minister Heraldo Muñoz, was one of the stars at the November 2001 WTO meetings in Doha. Newspapers all around the world, including the *New York Times,* picked up a photo by Agence-France Presse to run on their front pages in which Muñoz is shown gleefully shaking hands with the representatives from Canada, South Africa, and Brazil. Canada is the recognized leader in the Western world in the use of soft power in the international system. But, Chile? The small, developing nations took advantage of the heightened sense of interdependence among the larger, more developed nations after September 11, 2001, to secure major victories at the Doha meeting.[30] Brazil also was a major player at Doha, and the success of foreign minister Celso Lafer in the talks dealing with intellectual property, especially pharmaceutical patents, is one of the few instances in the past decade in which Brazil has consciously manipulated the soft power adhering to poor nations because of their healthcare crisis.[31]

The final lesson is clear: Brilliant trade strategies are better than rigid, mediocre strategies; but brilliant trade strategies are more effective when they take advantage of a nation's soft power as well as its hard power.

Notes

1. For a view of trade strategies at the firm level in Europe and Asia, see Aggarwal (2001).

2. On the role of trade in early U.S. foreign policy, see Gilbert (1958).

3. Of course, there were isolated cases of international trade groups and prehensile institutions in the nineteenth century, and the British Commonwealth served as a framework for trade among members in the period between the two world wars. Nevertheless, a comprehensive, global framework only came into existence after 1945. For a historical view of institutions and the evolution of the concept of power, see Steinmo et al. (1992) and Pierson (1996).

4. On the notion of global governance, see Vayrynen (1999). On the new world order in which trade forms part of a complex web of state and non state actors, see Slaughter (1997).

5. On the impact of arms control policies on international influence, see Diamint (1996). On the impact of environmental policy on Brazil's influence in the world, see Guimarães (1986). Finally, on the Chilean human rights leadership as a role in international affairs, see Rojas Aravena (1998).

6. I have developed these ideas previously in Tulchin (2001a).

7. For an early view of how social science theory could be applied to the study of international relations, see Knorr and Verba (1961), especially the chapters by Richard E. Quandt ("On the Use of Game Models in Theories of International Relations") and Thomas C. Schilling ("Experimental Games and Bargaining Theory").

8. The concern for process in policy decision making, especially in subjects where economics and politics intersect, was first explored in a systematic way by Dahl and Lindblom (1953) and Braybrooke and Lindblom (1963). Both were concerned with domestic decision making and domestic policy questions. The classic study of foreign policymaking as decision-making process is Allison and Zelikow (1999).

9. It is also worth admitting that some portion of the variance in outcomes is attributable to the changes in the external environment, something that I also leave aside, at least in the systematic sense.

10. As examples, see Chapters 7 and 8 in this volume.

11. On the growing role of NGOs in the international community, especially in setting the agenda on such issues as the environment, see Slaughter (1997) and Tuchman Matthews (1997). On nonstate actors in Latin America, see Sikkink (1993a, 1993b). For a recent review of the literature on the role of international institutions in foreign policies, see Martin and Simmons (1998).

12. On the debate over how the Latin American nations should view this ambiguity, see the chapters by Tulchin (2001b), Muñoz (2001), and Van Klaveren (2001).

13. For an evaluation of trade strategies in a globalizing economy, see Krugman (1996).

14. On the rising number of exogenous factors impinging on foreign policy, see Cooley and Ron (2002).

15. The classic work in this school is Mahan (1980). On the consensus among opinion leaders, see May (1991).

16. For a discussion of the linkages among trade, communication, finance, and oil, see Tulchin (1971).

17. Given the trajectory of his later career with the U.N. Economic Commission for Latin America, it is interesting that one of Raúl Prebisch's first professional publications argued for the strategic use of trade and protected domestic industry; see Sociedad Rural (1927).

18. For a general discussion of the nineteenth-century approach to the international system, see Cortés Conde (1974). On the deliberate formulation of strategy based on trade by Argentina, see Tulchin (1990).

19. For a comprehensive history of industrial policy, see Graham (1992).

20. Other examples are Hexner (1945), and Meade (1953), an early study of trade constraints in economic unions.

21. See Hirschman (1971, 1998), which links the Nazi experience to the development experience of Latin American nations.

22. For Brazil's trade strategy under Getúlio Vargas, see Wirth (1973). On the Argentine strategy, see Tulchin (1990).

23. For the arguments of these early advocates of closed economies for strategic purposes, see Tulchin (1990), chapter 1.

24. See Van Klaveren (1996) and Wilhelmy (1996).

25. On the distinction between rule making and rule taking, see Tulchin (2001a).

26. Chile has a very modern air force that serves as effective hard power in a regional setting, keeping Bolivia and Peru at bay and holding on to the territories taken from those two states in the War of the Pacific over a hundred years ago. Venezuela's oil represents hard power, but it is diluted by participation in the collective decision making of the Organization of Petroleum Exporting Countries (OPEC), especially since the terrorist attacks of September 11, 2001, when the United States returned to a zero-sum rhetoric of considering nations "with" us or "against" us.

27. On the Argentine financial crisis and the harsh view taken by elements of the international financial community, see Dunn and Spiegel (2001), and the comments by Secretary of the Treasury Paul O'Neill in the *Wall Street Journal,* October 31, 2001.

28. For a detailed case comparing Chile's success and Argentina's failure (because of a lack of flexibility), see Diehl (2002). See also Heritage Foundation and *Wall Street Journal* (2000).

29. For a small sample of how recognition by the international community of international good behavior, especially in the area of human rights can benefit a nation's influence and how Chile has benefited from this relatively new phenomenon, see Fox (2000/2001), Schulz and Bolton (1999), and Behr (2000).

30. Kahn (2001); Cooper and Winestock (2001b); and BRIDGES (2001).

31. *Wall Street Journal* (2001).

References

Aggarwal, Vinod K., ed. 2001. *Winning in Asia, European Style.* New York: Palgrave.

Allison, Graham T., and Philip Zelikow. 1999. *Essence of Decision: Explaining the Cuban Missile Crisis.* 2d ed. Reading, MA: Longman.

Behr, Peter. 2000. "Companies Sign Pact on Human Rights: Conduct in Developing Nations Targeted." *The Washington Post,* December 21, p. E10.

Braybrooke, David, and Charles E. Lindblom. 1963. *A Strategy of Decision: Policy Evaluation as a Social Process.* New York: Free Press of Glencoe.

BRIDGES. 2001. "Regional Trade Developments in the Wake of Doha." *BRIDGES Weekly Trade News Digest* 5, no. 40 (November 8). Available at: http://www.ictsd.org.

Cohen, Benjamin J. 1996. "Phoenix Risen: The Resurrection of Global Finance." *World Politics* 48: 268–96.

Cooley, Alexander, and James Ron. 2002. "The NGO Scramble: Organizational Insecurity and the Political Economy of Transnational Action," *International Organization* 27, no. 1 (Summer): 5–39.

Cooper, Helen, and Geoff Winestock. 2001. "Tough Talkers: Poor Nations Win Gains in Global Trade Deal, as U.S. Compromises," *Wall Street Journal,* November 15, p. A1.

Cortés Conde, Roberto. 1974. *The First Stages of Modernization in Spanish America.* New York: Harper and Row.

Dahl, Robert A., and Charles E. Lindblom. 1953. *Politics, Economics and Welfare*. New York: Harper.

Diamint, Rut. 1996. "El Gobierno Norteamericano ante El Caso del Condor II: Sistema Burocrático y Toma de Decisiones." Working Paper 224. Washington, DC: Latin American Program/Woodrow Wilson International Center for Scholars.

Diehl, Jackson. 2002. "Escapees from a Vicious Cycle." *The Washington Post*, July 8, p. A17.

Dunne, Nancy, and Peter Spiegel. 2001. "Argentina in Crisis." *Financial Times*, December 22, p. 8.

Escudé, Carlos. 1997. *Foreign Policy Theory in Menem's Argentina*. Gainesville: University Press of Florida.

Fox, Robin. 2000/2001. "Human Nature and Human Rights." *The National Interest*, no. 62 (Winter): 77–86.

Gilbert, Felix. 1958. *To the Farewell Address: Ideas of Early American Foreign Policy*. Princeton, NJ: Princeton University Press, 1958.

Graham, Otis L. 1992. *Losing Time: The Industrial Policy Debate*. Cambridge, MA: Harvard University Press.

Guimarães, Roberto. 1986. *Environmental Politics*. Boulder, CO: Lynne Rienner Publishers.

Heritage Foundation and Wall Street Journal. 2000. *Index of Economic Freedom*. Washington, DC: Heritage Foundation and Wall Street Journal.

Hexner, Ervin. 1945. *International Cartels*. Chapel Hill: University of North Carolina Press.

Hirschman, Albert. 1971. *A Bias for Hope*. New Haven, CT: Yale University Press.

―――. 1998. *Crossing Boundaries*. Cambridge, MA: MIT Press.

Kahn, Joseph. 2001. "Nations Back Freer Trade, Hoping to Aid Global Growth." *New York Times*, November 15, p. A12.

Katzenstein, Peter J., Robert O. Keohane, and Stephen D. Krasner. 1998. "*International Organization* and the Study of World Politics." *International Organization* 52, no. 4: 645–86.

Kindleberger, Charles P. 1962. *Foreign Trade and the National Economy*. New Haven, CT: Yale University Press.

Knorr, Klaus, and Sidney Verba, eds. *The International System: Theoretical Essays*. Princeton, NJ: Princeton University Press, 1961.

Krugman, Paul, ed. 1996. *Strategic Trade Policy and the New International Economy*. Cambridge, MA: MIT Press.

Mahan, Alfred Thayer. 1980. *The Influence of Sea Power Upon History 1660–1805*. Englewood Cliffs, NJ: Prentice-Hall.

Martin, Lisa L., and Beth Simmons. 1998. "Theories and Empirical Studies of International Relations." *International Organization* 52, no. 4: 729–58.

May, Ernest R. 1991. *American Imperialism: A Speculative Essay*. Chicago: Imprint Publications.

Meade, James E. 1953. *Problems of Economic Union*. Chicago: University of Chicago Press.

Muñoz, Heraldo. 2001. "Goodbye U.S.A.?" In *Latin America in the New International System*, edited by Joseph S. Tulchin and Ralph Espach, 73–90. Boulder, CO: Lynne Rienner Publishers.

Nye, Joseph S., Jr. 2001. *Soft Power: The Illusion of American Empire*. New York: Oxford University Press.

Nye, Joseph S., Jr., and Robert Keohane. 1988. *Soft Power.* New York: Knopf.

Pierson, Paul. 1996. "The Path to European Integration: A Historical Institutionalist Analysis." *Comparative Political Studies* 29: 123–63.

Rojas Aravena, Francisco. 1998. "Confidence Building Measures and Strategic Balance: A Step Toward Expansion and Stability." In *Strategic Balance and Confidence Building Measures,* edited by Joseph S. Tulchin and Rojas Aravena, 121–38. Stanford, CA: Stanford University Press.

Schulz, William F., and John Bolton. 1999. "What Price Human Rights? An Exchange." *The National Interest,* no. 56 (Summer): 112–20.

Sikkink, Kathryn. 1993a. "Human Rights, Principled Issue-Networks, and Sovereignty in Latin America." *International Organization* 47: 411–51.

———. 1993b. "The Power of Principled Ideas: Human Rights Policies in the United States and Western Europe." In *Ideas and Foreign Policy: Beliefs, Institutions and Political Change,* edited by Judith Goldstein and Robert O. Keohane, 139–72. Ithaca, NY: Cornell University Press.

Slaughter, Anne-Marie. 1997. "The Real New World Order." *Foreign Affairs* 76, no. 5 (September/October): 183–97.

Sociedad Rural [La]. 1927. *Informe Anual.* Buenos Aires: La Sociedad Rural.

Steinmo, Sven, Kathleen Thelen, and Frank Longsteth. 1992. *Structuring Politics: Historical Institutionalism in Comparative Analysis.* New York: Cambridge University Press, 1992.

Tuchman Matthews, Jessica. 1997. "Power Shift." *Foreign Affairs* 76, no. 1 (January/February): 50–66.

Tulchin, Joseph S. 1971. *Aftermath of War.* New York: New York University Press.

———. 1990. *Argentina and the United States: A Conflicted Relationship.* Boston: Twayne.

———. 2001a. "Introduction: A Call for Strategic Thinking." In *Latin America in the New International System,* edited by Joseph S. Tulchin and Ralph Espach, 1–33. Boulder, CO: Lynne Rienner Publishers.

———. 2001b. "Toward Innovative Strategic Policies: A Conclusion." In *Latin America in the New International System,* edited by Joseph S. Tulchin and Ralph Espach, 219–22. Boulder, CO: Lynne Rienner Publishers.

Van Klaveren, Alberto. 1996. "Understanding Latin American Foreign Policies." In *Latin American Nations in World Politics,* 2d ed., edited by Joseph S. Tulchin and Heraldo Muñoz, 35–60. Boulder, CO: Westview.

Vayrynen, Raimo, ed., 1999. *Globalization and Global Governance.* New York: Rowman & Littlefield.

Viner, Jacob. 1923. *Dumping: A Problem in International Trade.* Chicago: University of Chicago Press.

Wall Street Journal. 2001. "O'Neill Suggests U.S. Won't Back More IMF Aid," *Wall Street Journal,* October 31, p. A16.

Wilhelmy, Manfred. 1996. "Politics, Bureaucracy, and Foreign Policy in Chile." In *Latin American Nations in World Politics,* 2d ed., edited by Joseph S. Tulchin and Heraldo Muñoz, 61–80. Boulder, CO: Westview.

Wirth, John D. 1973. *Vargas and Brazil.* Stanford, CA: Stanford University Press, 1973.

Woodrow Wilson International Center for Scholars. 2002. *Getting Out of the Economic Crisis.* Argentina Policy Bulletin 3. Washington, DC: Latin American Program, Woodrow Wilson International Center for Scholars, June.

Part II

The Political Economy of
International Trade in the Americas

3

The Dynamics of State–Business Relations in the Formulation of Latin American Trade

Sylvia Maxfield

This book focuses on the differences in Latin American countries' trade policy preferences and performance. Aggarwal and Espach's introduction asks about the relative roles of government and non–government actors and of international/regional relations in shaping trade. It explores the importance of both economic and political concerns in trade relations and bargaining. In this chapter, I take the strategic bargaining framework Aggarwal and Espach espouse at an international level of analysis to the domestic level. In an effort to explore variation in Argentine, Brazilian, Chilean, and Mexican trade processes, I evaluate whether there is an elective affinity between modes of business government collaboration and types of trade strategies. The chapter outlines the possible causal links underlying a correlation between encompassing business organizations' rational-technical interaction with government and successful pursuit of open regionalism in trade relations. But case studies of the role of business in each country's recent trade policy suggest a complex, somewhat path-dependent, reciprocal interaction between the history of business organization, business–government collaboration, and the trade process. The theoretical contribution of this chapter is to highlight how information and organization shape the translation of interests into economic policy, especially in the dynamics of government and business collaboration around trade policy and performance.

More research is clearly needed to explore some of the causal connections identified in the case studies. These include the simple idea that close government–business collaboration stimulates investment in export-oriented business, without which trade liberalization fails. "Policy partnerships" provide information to businesspeople with which to understand the potential of new, export-oriented business models. Through collaboration, businesspeople gain confidence that the government will be responsive and flexible in the policy process, resulting in greater trust—the social glue of capitalism. Collaboration may also help make trade negotiations more successful by providing the government with information and expertise, improving the quality of policy, and bolstering the government's negotiating strength.

But close government–business interaction can just as easily descend into a vicious spiral of greed and corruption. Maxfield and Schneider (1997) explore how and when collaboration is constructive or destructive for economic policy processes and performance. The histories of business organization summarized here suggest that two factors provide part of the answer: the stance of government, that is, whether it is responsive to particularistic pressures; and the history of business organization, specifically whether it succeeds in aggregating interests.

Causal Connections in Business–Government Relations and Trade Policy

Close government–business relations improve the possibility for successful trade liberalization, whether pursued unilaterally or regionally, simply because collaboration helps encourage business investment. In Chapter 4, Carol Wise argues that Latin American growth rates respond best to trade liberalization where governments pursue active export promotion policies. Classic interpretations of Japan's "miracle," an extreme case of government-designed export-led growth, highlight the importance of close government–business collaboration. In fact, Japan is the model for Johnson's (1982) description of the capitalist "developmental state," in which he attributes Japan's economic success to the features of state organization and government–business interaction. The state guides the market but does so through "numerous institutions for consultation and coordination with the private sector" (Wade 1990: 26). These consultations are an "essential part of the process of policy formulation and implementation" (Wade 1990: 26). The developmental state model is also routinely applied to other East Asian countries including South Korea and Taiwan. Wade refers to this as the "governed market" theory of East Asian success.

The comparison between Chilean and East Asian success with export-led growth focuses attention on the institutional and political requisites for structural adjustment and growth in Latin America. Chile is frequently viewed as the "Asian tiger" of Latin America. Although copper still dominates Chilean exports, the number of export products grew from 200 in 1975 to 3,800 in 1998 and copper has fallen from roughly 80 percent of export revenue to under 40 percent (Agosin 1999: 82). Gross investment averaged 23.5 percent between 1971 and 1995, and Chile grew more than 6 percent annually for most of the 1980s and 1990s.

Although Chile did not mimic the government-controlled banking system or the extreme form of capital controls behind Japan's export push, the Chilean government did explicitly promote exports and collaborated closely with business. Chile's Trade Promotion Commission, termed ProChile, dates to 1974. By the 1990s, ProChile's main functions were sustaining an international network of thirty-two trade attaché offices and coordinating hundreds of product-specific Export Committees. These committees are comprised of businesspeople and supported by the government; ProChile covers the costs of administration and foreign activity for up to six years.

Government–business collaboration played an important supporting role in Chile's successful export promotion. Silva's (1998: 313) definitive study describes the interaction between government and business:

> Top policymakers set the agenda for incremental changes. After their technical commissions drew up draft legislation, it was circulated to the appropriate peak [business] association. For each initiative the business organization formed a technical commission to study the proposal and make observations. Policymakers and business leaders then negotiated on the basis of these reports.

Imagine a continuum running from successful trade liberalization and export-led growth on one end to trade liberalization without growth on the other. Among Latin American countries, Chile would be on one end of the continuum and Argentina close to the other. As a member of the Southern Common Market (MERCOSUR), a customs union with a common external tariff well above those of countries pursuing open regionalism, Argentina had to selectively reduce tariffs on imports in order to promote exports. Argentina's export promotion program, the Regimen de Especialización Industrial (REI), allowed companies to earn import tariff breaks by documenting improved export performance. However, though sectoral business associations were supposed to mediate the approval process, the government did not respect the associations' role. Individual businesses were known to have appealed directly to the government for special exemptions. In one case, a representative of the textile association notes specific instances where the associations' rejection of a company's request for import tariff reductions undermined the government's efforts to lower tariffs (Sirlin 1999: 109). This example points to a pattern of particularistic interaction between business and government that undermined business organizations' collective action.

Cursory depiction of Japan, Chile, and Argentina suggests that there is an association between characteristics of government–business collaboration and trade liberalization, which when properly managed can lead to a successful growth strategy. Government–business collaboration in Japan and Chile helps explain the success of export promotion strategies. But particularistic patterns in government–business collaboration can undermine programs for economic growth, as has been partly the case in Argentina's dismal experience with trade liberalization.

While government–business collaboration is a theme in Latin American political economy, this essay explores connections between the nature of government–business collaboration and trade negotiation strategies. Although the choice of strategy belongs undoubtedly to government, the success of strategies involving sectoral negotiations arguably hinges on information flowing both ways between government and business. Collaboration may also help build trust between government and business, which helps create social capital, particularly in developing countries. This is part of the mystery of successful capitalism. Fukuyama (1995) sees social capital as the glue that holds otherwise centrifugal market forces at bay (see also Putnam 1993).

Business–government collaboration is a component of the trade policy process to varying degrees in advanced industrial countries. For example, business–government consultation on trade negotiations is institutionalized in the United States under the 1974 Trade Act, requiring, among other things, that the Office of the Special Trade Representative consult regularly with sectoral business groups. These advisory committees provide information and advice on U.S. negotiating objectives and bargaining positions *before* the United States negotiates agreements on aspects of implementation and operation of trade agreements and on U.S. trade policy generally. The trade policy advisory committee system includes thirty-three advisory committees with up to a thousand members. Recommendations for membership come from Congress, business associations, and other sources. Members pay for their own travel and related expenses and are chosen based on qualifications in the trade area, geographical considerations, and committee needs. As former Clinton administration trade representative Charlene Barshevsky's negotiations with China evidence, this collaboration helps trade negotiations succeed (Sebenius and Hulse 2001).

Case studies and deductive logic help spell out the causal logic linking government–business collaboration to trade policy and performance. Close government–business collaboration stimulates investment in export-oriented business, without which trade liberalization fails. Without private investment, government spending and consumption must drive growth. Scholars ranging from Schumpeter (1964) to Hirschman (1971) and Lindblom (1977) have tried to understand the "animal spirits" impelling private individuals and enterprises to invest. Business–government collaboration stimulates investment in at least two ways, which are described below.

First, the close government–business collaboration helps governments successfully promote export-led growth because it induces business investment in export-oriented activities. Being part of a policy partnership provides business with information that can reduce the uncertainty surrounding new business models. A similar logic underlies an analysis of delayed policy reform in developing countries during the 1980s and 1990s. In the so-called "war of attrition" models of delayed reform, one source of delay was actors' uncertainty over how reforms would impact them from an economic standpoint. However, close collaboration with government can reduce this uncertainty as trade policy changes. Cason (2001: 18) highlights this uncertainty in his analysis of MERCOSUR: "Many [businesspeople] will be reticent about integration," he notes, "because they do not know what its consequences will be."

Second, collaboration may induce business investment by giving business confidence that government will be responsive and flexible in the policy process. This formula may sound like "regulatory capture," the notion that businesses "capture" government policy and adjust it to serve their own ends, but the idea is that collaboration actually serves to build trust. Describing how this process worked in Chile, Silva (1998: 314) wrote that business "began to trust in the Concertación's readiness to compromise, perhaps not on all issues, but on enough to keep business from rebelling and engaging in investment strikes. . . . No one's fundamental interests would be gored."

Discussing Mexican government–business collaboration in the North American Free Trade Agreement (NAFTA) negotiations, Kleinberg makes a similar point. "Because the whole structure of the negotiations created

what [COECE leader] Gallardo termed "a quality of dialogue" unprecedented in the private sector's relationship with the state," she argues that a
majority of private entrepreneurs "started to view the state as . . . more
'transparent,' consistent, credible and trustworthy. . . . [A]fter the negotiations, there was [a] strong sense of confidence that the state would accommodate the needs of . . . business."

Collaboration may help make trade negotiations a success by providing
government with information and expertise that improves the quality of
policy and even bolsters the government's negotiating strength. Collaboration provides government with specific operational information about the
potential effects of particular negotiation outcomes. Government negotiators
can very credibly stonewall negotiations, arguing that the national business
community would not tolerate any further international concessions. Collaboration may also help convey the operational knowledge and expertise
of businesspeople and make government policy design better. Traditional
theories of economic integration posit that institutionalization defines success. Business–government collaboration and the business organization
behind it may help the institutionalization process.

The problem with business–government collaboration is that it can just
as easily promote greed and corruption. Identifying modes of business–
government interaction and their causes is no less important in the trade policy process than in other economic policy arenas (Maxfield and Schneider
1997). Silva and Durand (1998: 12) draw a distinction between government–
business exchange based on rational-technical criteria or particularism. The
behavior of Chilean and Mexican peak business associations mostly falls
into the rational-technical category. Government accessibility can help move
associations in one direction or another. Sectoral organizations had easy
access to government in Brazil and Argentina, which encouraged business
groups and even individual enterprises to interact directly with government
rather than work through business associations. Particularism occurs when
"lobbying" yields partial policy change or special relief for specific sectors
or industries. This creates little incentive for business associations to overcome divisions that hinder their professionalism. Of the cases examined in
this volume, Argentina illustrates how government instability can directly
contribute to organizational weakness among business associations and can
create openings for particularistic business pressure that undermines association cohesion. At the extreme, particular businesses or business groups
are seen as "gaining control" of a government ministry.

Both the stance of a government and the nation's history of business organization help promote or hinder the mode of government–business collaboration that is an important ingredient in the recipe for trade strategies of open regionalism. According to Silva and Durand (1998: 19),

> [I]n countries where encompassing business associations have existed, they have tended to provide more specific, early, broad, consistent private sector demands for free market economic reforms. By contrast, in the absence of encompassing business associations, early, cohesive private sector support for economic liberalization was more ambivalent and fractured, and organized business provided conflicting signals to policymakers.

Among the cases considered in this volume, Mexico, Chile, and Argentina had "encompassing business associations" but they were not all equally cohesive. Encompassing business organizations only facilitate professional business–government collaboration if the organizations are cohesive, and capable of aggregating interests and maintaining a unified front.

Martinelli (1991) argues that organizational structures make the difference between cohesive or fragmented business associations. Governance and membership rules are a tool through which to manage representation. Successfully representing broad interests is the core of business association legitimacy for both governments and members. Rules such as automatically rotating association presidencies among the sectors or requiring a quorum to bring issues to the table can help minimize conflict within encompassing business associations.[1]

Mexican Business–Government Collaboration Reinforces Open Regionalism

The case of Mexico helps illustrate how information flows between government and business can help reduce uncertainties and create virtuous cycles that reinforce collaboration and successful trade negotiation. The Mexican government sought business input for NAFTA negotiations even though business ambivalence only a decade earlier contributed to the scuttling of Mexico's membership to the General Agreement on Tariffs and Trade (GATT). The Mexican government needed expertise that only business could provide. Schneider (2001) observes that when NAFTA negotiations began, government staff knew relatively little about North American business and trade, especially compared to the knowledge of Mexican exporters themselves. Mexican officials sought data to bolster their formulation of negotiating positions and also relied on business associations to poll members about their reservations. However, factors other than the government's needs made this collaboration possible.

Silva and Durand (1998) draw a distinction between business associations with "reactive, defensive, political, and ideologically based" stances on the one hand, and those with "proactive, economically based" modes of action on the other. Of the cases considered in this volume, Chile and Mexico fall into the latter group, while Brazil and Argentina's associations are closer to the former. As for Mexico, making the shift from reactive to proactive associations is an important part of its story that began with a long history of voluntary, encompassing business associations.

State-sponsored, compulsory membership business associations existed in Mexico alongside voluntary business associations that partially defined their mission as providing an independent voice for businessmen. Party politics excluded business to perhaps a greater extent in Mexico than anywhere else in Latin America (Schneider 2002). Exclusion was a strong incentive for independent business organization, and opposition to the government and governing political party was a defining feature of several of these voluntary associations. By the 1970s, for example, many members of the Confederación Patronal de la República Mexicana (COPARMEX) were PAN (National Action Party, historically, Mexico's largest opposition party) sympathizers.

Mexico has a large number of multisector, voluntary business associations, especially compared to other Latin American countries. Mexico's four such associations are COPARMEX, the Consejo Mexicano de Hombres de Negocio (CMHN), the Consejo Coordinador Empresarial (CCE), and most recently the Coordinadora de Organismos Empresariales de Comercio Exterior (COECE). There are diverse explanations for the cohesion of these associations (see Table 3.1). The CMHN is a small body with a membership rule requiring unanimous approval of existing members. The CCE initially suffered from internal dissent stemming from the core manufacturing industries organized in the Cámara Nacional de la Industria de Transformación (Canacintra), although within a year of its founding Canacintra had elected leadership supportive of the CCE (Tirado 1998: 89). The CCE also downplays regional representation to minimize geographically based divisions (three of eight CCE affiliates have a regional organization structure).

Government accessibility clearly helped shape the extent to which the actions of Mexico's encompassing organizations took on a technical-rational

Table 3.1 Mexico's Major Voluntary Business Associations

	Date Founded	Membership	Governance and Functions
Confederación Patronal de la República Mexicana (COPARMEX)	1929	Open to anyone from manufacturing, services, agriculture, and professions; membership currently at 17,000	Regional centers, governed by a council of directors composed of more than 100 members, lobbies for deregulation, sound fiscal/monetary policy, other classic liberal economic causes and for genuine procedural democracy
Consejo Mexicano de Hombres de Negocio (CMHN)	1962	Business owners spanning diverse economic sectors; new members approved unanimously by existing members; currently, over 40 members	Governed by president and ad hoc working groups; meets monthly for lunch with a senior government official
Consejo Coordinador Empresarial (CCE)	1975 (by CMHN)	Association of all major Mexican business associations; nearly 1 million individual businesses represented; controversy over poor representation for small/medium businesses	Schemes for selection of president have varied over time; holds assemblies with government guest speakers; extensive research capacity
Coordinadora de Organismos Empresariales de Comercio Exterior (COECE)	1990 (by CCE)	Composed of hundreds of business subsectors	Analyzes, promotes, and coordinates Mexico's international trade policy through joint government–business advisory committees

or particularistic mode. Damage to government–business relations wrought by the 1982 Mexican bank nationalization encouraged the Mexican authorities to seek more consistent collaboration with business. For example, the Economic Solidarity Pact ("Pacto") negotiations of 1987, brought labor, business, and government together to negotiate key aspects of economic policy. Thacker (1999: 60) writes, "Government negotiators, orchestrated by . . . presidential candidate Salinas de Gortari, clearly led the way, but they were careful to court the participation of key allies in the private sector." A primary purpose of these meetings was to provide a political foundation for inflation control. Through this forum the government achieved labor and business support for wage and price restraint. One unique aspect of Mexican

inflation stabilization was the government's success linking trade liberalization to inflation control. The Salinas government argued that putting an
end to inflation required structural adjustment, particularly trade liberalization, and the Pacto meetings provided an important forum for building private sector support for trade liberalization via the argument that over the
long-term stabilization required trade liberalization.[2]

When the Mexican government began efforts to pursue NAFTA membership, ministry officials and private sector representatives drew on the
experience of government–business collaboration in negotiating the Pacto.
The Salinas administration called on the private sector to help prepare for
free trade. The CCE worked hard to convince small and medium-sized business that benefits of free trade would be greater than the risks. "Clearly the
CCE was concerned about projecting a unified position vis-à-vis the state,"
writes Kleinberg (1999: 76).[3] The CCE president contacted the Consejo
Empresarial Mexicano de Asuntos Internacionales (CEMAI), which formed
an ad hoc working group to consult with the private sector, gather information and bring issues to the negotiating table. The COECE grew out of the
U.S.–Mexico Committee of the CEMAI. COECE's first act was to contact
Canadian trade advisory groups. This interaction revealed how little technical capacity and information the Mexicans possessed.

COECE played a huge role in the NAFTA negotiations. Initially it included seven coordinating groups, of which six were sector specific and
one dealt with cross-sectoral issues. The seven groups were comprised of
140 subgroups, including representatives from each of the subsectoral business chambers. The CCE think-tank, Centro de Estudios Económicos de
Sector Privado (CEESP), created a data collection methodology for these
140 industry-specific subgroups. Within a year COECE had a general profile of each of the 140 subsectors. For "the first time in Mexico's economic
history," Kleinberg (1999: 77) writes, "the private sector had complete data
on its own activities." These subsectoral reports were discussed with the
Secretaría de Comercio y Fomento Industrial (SECOFI) in over 1,400 meetings in the second half of 1991.

As NAFTA talks began, COECE's structure changed to complement the
structure of the negotiations. Thacker (1999: 62) describes these changes as
follows:

COECE created essentially a parallel bargaining unit that mirrored the
organization of the Mexican government negotiating team. Just before a
negotiating round, government and private sector leaders would typically

meet in Mexico, in groups that imitated in number and specialization of the actual negotiating table, to discuss issues and strategies. A team of private sector representatives would then accompany the government negotiators to the various, alternating Canadian, Mexican and U.S. negotiating sites. COECE would typically reserve hotel rooms as close as possible to actual negotiating rooms to facilitate regular contact with the Mexican government negotiating teams.

The close collaboration between government and business, coupled with the organizational strength of business, launched a virtuous cycle during the NAFTA negotiations. The importance of the activity of business associations during the negotiations forced them to become more cohesive. Schneider (2001) interviewed one businessman involved in the negotiations, and reported that "[w]ithin various advisory groups, representatives of upstream and downstream firms realized that they had to work out differences before taking action proposals to government" in order to maintain credibility and influence with the government.

But COECE achieved cohesion partly at the expense of representation. Silva and Durand (1998: 13) suggest that the CCE created COECE because the CCE's heterogeneity was problematic.[4] Whatever their intent, the CCE and COECE leadership went to considerable lengths to promote COECE's representative image. During the NAFTA negotiations, COECE included 200 subsectors of Mexican business and according to its president, consulted systematically with all members to "achieve the universality, unity and true representativeness" of the entire Mexican private sector (Kleinberg 1999: 78). COECE held thousands of meetings during the NAFTA negotiations, but Thacker (2000) argues that small business fell away because it lacked the resources to participate in the process.

While the requisite of maintaining credibility in its partnership with the government reinforced the organization of business associations, another virtuous cycle emerged from the close government–business relationship that developed during the NAFTA negotiations. This dynamic centered on the government's need to maintain credibility with investors. Leading Mexican businessman Fernando Canales Clariond reported that collaboration gave investors important information that helped reduced uncertainty as businesses planned future investment (Schneider 2001: 4). Both private and public sector elites agreed that this was the first time business had been consulted so extensively before economic policy was made (Kleinberg 1999: 78). Seeing Mexican businesses invest in plans that responded to the new trade environment reinforced the government's commitment to their strategy of open regionalism.

This analysis highlights two instances where uncertainty and incomplete information shape the domestic political economy of trade negotiations. Government is unsure of business interests and capabilities as trade policy changes. Close government business collaboration provides government with important information to formulate negotiation positions. Furthermore, understanding business costs can strengthen negotiators' positions by allowing them to credibly claim certain terms as non-negotiable because anything less is unacceptable to national businesses. On the other side of the government–business interaction, collaboration (or concertación) also reduces uncertainty for businesspeople whose investment in new business models is crucial to the long-term viability of government trade strategies.

Organizationally Dysfunctional Business: Causes and Consequences of Brazil's Closed Regionalism

Two conditions facilitated creation of the virtuous cycles that helped reduce both government and business uncertainty in ways that reinforced Mexico's open regional trade strategy. First, the government had clear incentives to bring business into the negotiation process from the start. Second, Mexico benefited from a substantial history of successful business organization and representation. Neither the first nor the second element was present in the Argentine and Brazilian cases. This may help explain why Brazil and Argentina persist, within MERCOSUR, in discriminatory regionalism.

The original initiative and early efforts toward MERCOSUR came from the founding governments of Brazil and Argentina. This was a state-led process that did not initially include business as it had in Mexico. MERCOSUR grew out of the bilateral integration treaty signed by the two countries in 1986.

Cason (2000a: 207) emphasizes that the Argentine-Brazilian Economic Integration Program (ABEIP) was a government-to-government diplomatic effort: "From the beginning the initiative was clearly state-led. The private sector was generally not involved in the early negotiations." Manzetti (1990: 115) notes that "the main drive behind the integration process was not so much pressure from industrial and agricultural groups as the converging political interests of the Sarney and Alfonsín administrations." Both administrations saw the agreement as a way to solidify democracy in their

Table 3.2 Timeline of MERCOSUR Evolution

1986	Argentine Brazilian Economic Integration Program (ABEIP) signed
1988	Argentina and Brazil announce intention to create a free trade agreement within ten years
1990	Buenos Aires Act: Argentina and Brazil agree to establish a free trade area by the end 1994. Paraguay and Uruguay express desire to join, while Chile declines
1991	Asunción Treaty creates MERCOSUR, a customs union with agreements of scheduled tariff reductions to coordinate macroeconomic policy, develop sectoral accords, and set up institutions for trade dispute litigation
1992	Las Leñas Protocol sets timetable for harmonization
1994	Ouro Preto Protocol establishes guiding institutions for MERCOSUR
1995	Limited customs union rules go into effect (some tariffs remain and special rules apply to automotives and sugar)
1996	Bolivia and Chile become associate members
2000	Complete free trade between Argentina and Brazil
2001	Complete free trade within Argentina, Brazil, and Uruguay, and common external tariff
2006	Paraguay to be added to customs union; free trade between associate members and MERCOSUR core

respective countries and to end a tradition of military rivalry. The locus of policymaking was the two countries' foreign ministries, which required important institutional adjustments for each government's foreign ministry. The Brazilian Ministry of Foreign Affairs (Itamaraty) traditionally kept more distance from business than other Brazilian executive branch entities.[5] Business was surprised and shocked when the government announced the ABEIP. Although the approach to negotiating ABEIP was sectoral, the government did not try to involve the private sector when negotiations turned to specific sectors. Birle (1997: 292) writes that business had no involvement in the decision making leading up to the Asunción Treaty of 1991.

In subsequent rounds of trade negotiations, the Brazilian government did encourage formation of business groups that could support the integration process. One was the Foro Consultivo Económico-Social (FCES). The purpose of the Foro was primarily to help educate the business public on MERCOSUR and secondarily to channel information between government and business. FCES brought together business, labor union, and consumer representatives in large meetings that entertained various opinions on integration, although they resulted in few conclusions.

A second business group involved in MERCOSUR's evolution was the Consejo Industrial MERCOSUR (CIM). In 1991, the CNI of Brazil and the Unión Industrialista Argentino (UIA) of Argentina formed a commission to coordinate policy. At the end of the same year their Uruguayan and Paraguayan counterparts joined the commission, resulting in the formation of the CIM. By joining forces, the various business groups hoped to pressure their respective governments regarding MERCOSUR, though they met only sporadically until 1994. Although the CIM supported the integration process, members saw major deficiencies in the Las Leñas (1992) and Ouro Preto (1994) accords (Birle 1997: 291). After 1994, however, the CIM met regularly, more closely resembling their Mexican and U.S. trade advisory counterparts. The CIM included a series of working groups on harmonization and sectoral issues that included government representatives, business-people, and labor leaders from each of the four MERCOSUR countries. These working groups drew in members of a variety of different business associations but had little influence on the integration process, partly because divergent interests prevented them from forwarding of joint strategies. In contrast to the Mexican case, working group meetings were often gripe sessions rather than professional exchanges of information about policy and business activity. Business representatives in Working Group Number Seven of the CIM, charged with harmonizing industrial and technology policies, spent their time at meetings complaining that government tariff reductions threatened their existence (Birle 1997: 291–292).

The mode of business–government interaction around trade strategy in Argentina and Brazil stands in stark contrast to the Mexican case. To the extent that business organized around trade, it was to oppose, instead of to discuss or to formulate, government-proposed policies. As MERCOSUR evolved, negotiations moved quickly on issues such as across-the-board tariff reductions, whereas progress on sectoral issues stalled because business associations opposed collaboration.

Brazil's and Argentina's relatively low trade dependence in the early 1990s and lack of business competitiveness internationally are important explanations for the dysfunctional interaction between business and government and help to explain the persistence of closed regionalism. But these patterns reflect a tradition of poor government accessibility and business organization. Scholars of Brazil contend that Brazilian business is more poorly organized than anywhere else in Latin America (Kingstone 1999; Schneider 1997/1998; Weyland 1998). Brazil is one of few remaining Latin American countries without an encompassing business association such as the CCE or COECE in Mexico. Prominent business associations, such as the

Federação de Industria do Estado de São Paulo (FIESP) and the Confederação Nacional de Industria (CNI), are state-initiated compulsory organizations whose heterogeneity and organizational rules hinder their cohesion and effectiveness. Weyland (1998: 89) writes,

> Where business has an effective encompassing peak organization, it can participate in the design and enactment of neoliberal reform. Given its economic weight, Brazil's private sector would be a prime candidate for such an influential role, but the absence of a peak association poses obstacles that have so far proved insurmountable.

Brazilian business associations are plagued by size, sectoral, and regional differences. The São Paulo business community, for example, remains quite distinct from that of Rio de Janeiro, and has traditionally been more protectionist. The São Paulo business association, FIESP, is significantly bigger and stronger than the CNI, which is based in Rio. However, São Paulo is home to an extremely diverse range of industries, and the FIESP charter defines sectors at a high level of disaggregation, which complicates the formation of coherent political positions. Schneider (1997/1998) gives the example of the Association for Cane and Umbrella Manufacturers, with only twelve members. Not only does this disaggregation enlarge the size of FIESP, but the "one organization, one vote" principle in this case enhances the power of small industries. "It is not surprising," notes Schneider (1997/ 1998: 103), "that the president of FIESP has often been a marginal figure in Paulista industry." This does little to raise the credibility of the organization in the government's eyes.

Patterns of business access to government also hindered cohesion and representation in Brazilian business associations. Brazil's military governments (1964–1985) gave businesspeople particularistic access. Examples include Brazil's unique "bureaucratic rings" that brought individual businesspeople into close contact with government officials, and the habit of the Finance Ministry under President Ernesto Geisel to submit proposals to business associations for comment (Weyland 1998: 78).

The president of the CNI in 1995 argued in a newspaper column that business fragmentation reflected government fragmentation. "Although we have . . . great access to President [Fernando Henrique] Cardoso," he wrote, "we have not managed to institutionalize negotiation with other levels of government. We are constantly taken by surprise by initiatives that go completely against our interests . . . " (cited in Schneider 1997/1998: 111).

Fragmented business interacting in largely particularistic fashion with a fragmented government was not conducive to building the technically oriented state–business dynamic evident in Mexico and Chile. When Brazilian associations tried to act as a unified group, they failed. In 1996, for example, FIESP organized 3,000 industrialists to fly to Brasilia to lobby Congress to pass the constitutional amendment on pension reform, with the support of President Cardoso. Congress voted down the measure, dealing a heavy blow to whatever legitimacy business associations had as effective lobbyists.

Failed efforts at reforming FIESP during the 1980s spawned a variety of voluntary organizations that spanned the typical regional and sectoral divides of Brazilian business associations. But whatever cohesion these associations initially enjoyed eroded quickly. Several frustrated FIESP reformers left to found new associations, including the União Brasileira de Empresarios (UBE), Forum Informal (FI), Instituto de Estudos para o Desenvolvimento Industrial (IEDI), and Pensamento Nacional das Bases Empresariais (PNBE), among others. Most of these organizations had political aims, and in some cases they became vehicles of a single individual or firm. Tensions with other associations hindered their growth and development into encompassing, coherent, representative organizations like their counterparts in Mexico and Chile. "None has gained prominence within the private sector," concludes Weyland, "not to speak of managing to unify it" (Weyland 1998: 81).

The UBE was founded in 1986 to coordinate lobbying for auto parts manufacturers in the upcoming constituent assembly. The organization suffered from internal strife over constitutional issues such as restraints on foreign investors and became dormant in 1988. Several institutional problems led to the collapse, including the creation of incentives for individual presidents to use the UBE platform for their own goals, and short presidential terms of six months and prohibiting reelection, which limited the accumulation of experience and technical expertise.

Although the UBE eventually lost steam, FIESP felt threatened enough by UBE that it established a competing voluntary association, the FI, to prevent UBE's ascendance. FI, based in São Paulo, had frequent conflicts with other business associations. The PNBE, a cross-sectoral association representing mostly small- and medium-sized business, was formed explicitly to oppose FIESP and exhibited regional bias, reflecting the largest fault line in Brazilian business organization. The Brazilian government further aggravated disunity in the private sector by playing business groups off one another. President Fernando Collor de Melo, for instance, favored the PNBE in order to weaken FIESP (Weyland 1998: 83).

IEDI probably had the greatest chance of evolving into an encompassing Brazilian business association. Its membership, limited to thirty representatives, initially consisted of business owners, CEOs, and individual businesspeople involved in a range of sectors and regions. It mimicked the CMHN to some extent, but unlike the CMHN it was set up partly as a think tank on industrial policy. It attempted to use publications to bring business, government, political parties, and even labor together to discuss policy ideas. IEDI's first document, titled "Changing to Compete," defined commercial opening not as a means to stabilization but as an element of long-term growth. However, as IEDI became more partisan and more involved in lobbying, it became less effective, as its members became caught up in the day-to-day task of adjusting to economic reform. Eventually, IEDI also failed in its fight to link trade opening with industrial promotion policies (Kingstone 1998). Schneider (1997/1998: 107) writes,

> [T]he trade liberalization after 1990 had a profoundly disarticulating impact on IEDI. Members responded in highly varied manner. Some of the industrialists among IEDI founders became service sector enterprises. Others did not adjust and continued to push IEDI toward a protectionist stance unacceptable to other members.

Encompassing business associations that might have partnered with the government to push for opening trade, faltered under unstable patterns of government access and organizational dysfunction. Partly for geopolitical reasons, the government clearly set the tone and direction of trade strategy; however, neither government nor business understood the professional planning and organization required to induce uncompetitive industries to adjust and help government successfully negotiate sectoral-based (open) regional trade agreements. According to Kingston (1998: 78), "The system encouraged atomization over collective action, promoted the concerns of the least sophisticated business people over the most sophisticated, and promoted rent seeking rather than real leadership on policy questions."

Patterns of Particularism in Argentine Business–Government Relations

The Argentine government was more interested in business collaboration than the Brazilian government, although organizational history prevented the kind of planning exemplified in the Mexican case. Like Mexico, Argentina has voluntary associations but they have suffered extreme factionalism. The Union Industrialista Argentino (UIA) split in 1981 into two internal currents, the Movimiento Industrial Argentino (MIA) and the Movimiento Industrial Nacional (MIN). Historically, the MIA supported more liberal economic policy while the MIN more closely resembled Peronist party positions, evincing a proclivity for protectionism and government intervention in the economy (Viguera 2001). As different factions rose and fell within the UIA, Argentina's most influential businesses vacillated between more and less direct involvement with the association. Both the UIA and the Sociedad Rural Argentina (SRA) had an affinity with Argentina's military governments, which left the early postdictatorship administrations hesitant to associate too closely with these organizations.

Beyond their association with the military government, the UIA and its factions were at best ambivalent about trade liberalization, whereas the MIN was uniformly opposed. The MIA was divided between one faction—which included the food industry—that supported trade liberalization, and a second—including textiles, metallurgy, and electronics industries—that opposed liberalization. The Cámara Comercial Argentina, consisting of retail and wholesale enterprises such as supermarket chains and import-export companies, was a consistent voice supporting trade liberalization, but was not sufficiently encompassing to credibly represent broad support.

Although factionalism in Argentine business associations followed sectoral divides to a greater extent than in Brazil, where the strongest divisions were regional, the Argentine associations also suffered from geographic jealousies. For example, Argentina's Confederación General de la Industria (CGI) was founded by provincial industrialists who felt that the UIA failed to represent their interests.

There are several Argentine associations that are both voluntary and cross-sectoral. The Consejo Empresarial Argentino, founded in 1967, is similar to the CCE in Mexico. Its membership consists of individual CEOs, and its objective is to advise the government on nonsectoral economic policy issues. Another cross-cutting, peak-type group, known in the press as the "Capitanes de la Industria" or Grupo Marias, garnered considerable media attention in the 1990s. It was never formally organized, however, and so never gained the legitimacy of a broadly representative, interest-aggregating association such as COECE.

More than in Brazil, government instability in Argentina tended to draw business associations into a political stance. Between 1955 and 1973, politicization was the norm rather than the exception for most Argentine business associations. The Confederación General Económica (CGE) was explicitly Peronist. The Acción Coordinadora de las Instituciones Empresarias Libres (ACIEL) and Asemblea Permanente de Entidades Gremiales Empresarias (APEGE) were formed to counter the political influence of the CGE. "The relationship between the CGE, the ACIEL, and the APEGE and their respective associations (for example, the CGI, and the UIA) was conflictual. Each denounced the other's interests as 'illegitimate.' They were trapped in a web of contending political and social alliances" (Acuna 1998: 64).

As in Brazil, the lack of access to collective business information hindered unity and promoted a particularistic mode of business–government interaction. For example, although business associations occasionally gained "control" of government ministries (as was the case with CGE in 1973–1974), a new pattern emerged under the Menem government, which coincided with the apogee of the Grupo Marias. President Menem designated Miguel Roig and Nestor Rapinelli, both from the large Argentine conglomerate Bunge y Born, as successive economy ministers. Reflecting a decades-old pattern in government–business relations, businessmen lined up behind Miguel Roig in order to "stay in the game" and not because they shared a common view of economic policy. Whereas business in Mexico was systematically excluded from party politics and government, businessmen in Argentina would become confidantes of prominent government officials. When Rapinelli succeeded Roig, the complaint was that he would not let other businesspeople participate in the policymaking process. Viguera (2000: 103) writes that leaders of "big business wanted to be close to Menem to insure the possibility, not of criticizing from the outside, but influencing decisions from the inside."

The system of nontariff barriers in place in Argentina prior to 1988 presented a challenge to the Argentine associations and encouraged private lobbying. Viguera argues convincingly that, as MERCOSUR evolved, the predominant model of Argentine business associations followed the historical pattern of reaction and defense. Even when the associations seemed unified around a gradual, compensated export model, they continued to work to slow liberalization, asking for exceptions and limitations. Viguera suggests that even the more ideologically committed economic liberals in the business community begged for protection the minute imports threatened their profitability (Viguera 2001: 202). Each new government measure was followed by individual requests for exemptions, a game in which each instance of government participation only served to reduce the likelihood of collective action. In the early Menem years, power over economic policy was highly concentrated within the government, which meant discretion was easily realized, further encouraging private lobbying. The general attitude of Argentine business was to support liberalization publicly in hopes of negotiating a better particular outcome.

Argentine businesspeople tended to interact with the government primarily to seek exceptions from trade liberalization. Throughout the Menem years, business never achieved a consistent, institutionalized form of collaboration with the government over economic policy. Many business associations found themselves unable to count on consensus around any given policy issues, factions and associations saw their power rise and fall, and individual business people sought special access to pursue their own interests. The virtuous cycles involving important flows of information back and forth between business and government, evident in the Mexican case, never had a chance to take hold.

Turning to Closed Regionalism Weakens Encompassing Business Associations in Chile

Chile's mode of business–government collaboration on trade issues is similar to Mexico's. Chile's encompassing business association, the CPC, enjoyed extraordinarily close collaboration around the technical aspects of export policy in the 1980s. Business in Chile was always very close to the government at the negotiating table, whether over terms of association with MERCOSUR in the 1990s or multiple ongoing bilateral negotiations throughout the world. Depending on government protocol, business might be at the table or in the room next door with cell phones, as occurred during NAFTA negotiations in the Mexican case. (In one extreme situation, a Chilean business association staffer was sent to negotiate for the government.) As Schneider (2001) points out, this gave sectoral associations strong incentives to invest and for members to remain active.

The Chilean case suggests that the relationship between modes of business–government interaction and trade strategy involves complex dynamics. Recent Chilean experience challenges the simple notion of an elective affinity between the type of business–government collaboration (encompassing, rational-technical) and open regionalism substantiated by the contrast between Mexico, on the one hand, and Brazil and Argentina on the other. In the mid-1990s while the Chilean government was inclined toward NAFTA accession, at least until it became clear that Clinton was not going to go forward with fast track negotiations, Chile's benchmark encompassing, rational-technical business association, the CPC, along with two other important Chilean business associations, favored a shift from Chile's open unilateralism to the discriminatory regional strategy implied by joining MERCOSUR. While these associations had varied motives for supporting Chile's entry into MERCOSUR, their behavior belies the simple correlation between modes of business organization/government collaboration and trade strategies. The Chilean case suggests that the type of trade strategy may influence the nature of business organization.

In Mexico, NAFTA negotiations helped reinforce Mexico's encompassing business associations and reinforced the burgeoning rational-technical mode of business–government collaboration. In Chile, negotiations around joining MERCOSUR threatened to shift power to Chile's sectoral associations and weaken the encompassing CPC. Schneider (2001: 14) concludes that conflict between the agricultural and industrial associations

> exceeded the consensus building capacity of the CPC which recused itself from discussion with the government on trade. Sofofa [Federation of Chilean Industry] staffers felt this breakdown of consensus building hurt industry [in the MERCOSUR negotiations] because agriculture was able to get a lot of protection.

In exchange, MERCOSUR industries in Argentina and Brazil got protection from Chilean manufacturers. The Chilean example suggests a complex reciprocal dynamic between the nature of business–government collaboration and trade strategies. The turn toward a more closed regionalism in Chile undermined Chile's encompassing business associations. Fortunately, although closed regionalism induced a shift toward sectoral business associations, the historical rational-technical mode in business–government collaboration continues.

Conclusion

Grounded in rationalist assumptions that interests bear an important connection to economic policy and performance, this essay has explored the nature of government–business collaboration and its consequences for trade negotiation strategies by looking at how information and organization shape the translation of interests into economic policy and performance. In Mexico and, more broadly speaking, in Chile, information flows and organization helped reinforce a constructive pattern of government–business interaction that contributed to Mexico's successful open regionalist trade policy. Collaboration provided information pertinent to evaluating new business models and built trust that changed risk perceptions. Mexican business invested heavily in the government's trade liberalization strategy.

In Argentina, government business collaboration was very different. The currency of collaboration was not technical information or exchange of ideas about trade negotiations, but the give and take of favors for particular businesses and government officials. The history of business organization, lacking encompassing associations capable of aggregating varied interests, hindered successful trade policy formulation and implementation. Government–business collaboration reinforced businesses' perceptions of uncertainty and risk.

There are many reasons for Brazil's partially discriminatory, minilaterally focused trade strategy, which is arguably more politically than economically motivated. Although circumstances may be changing in the early years of the twenty-first century, Brazil's history of particularistic business–government collaboration and weakly organized business associations is not consistent with the requirements for a successful open trade strategy that are suggested by the Mexican and Chilean cases.

Business actions are always conditioned by uncertainty and risk; this is rational. When patterns of government–business interaction facilitate "technical" information exchange and seed funding, investors are more likely to accept a certain degree of uncertainty and risk. Opening formerly closed economies involves great risk. Business is more likely to "buy into" open trade strategies such as those pursued by Mexico and Chile when information flows fluidly along a wide two-way street between business headquarters and government buildings. Joan Robinson (1956) referred to investors as "animals" whose "spirits" guided capital accumulation. Those spirits are crucial in the story of Latin American trade strategies and they respond partially to the way information and organization shape patterns of government–business interaction.

Notes

1. This is a fruitful area for future research because existing case studies point out contradictions about certain governance principles. Silva (1998) argues that the one-

organization–one-vote rule in Chile's encompassing association promotes unity while studies of Brazil and Mexico argue the opposite.

2. This is the standard view pioneered by Heredia and Kaufman (1994). Interestingly, one of Mexico's preeminent scholars of business organization suggests that Pacto negotiations involved government promises *not* to liberalize trade (Tirado 1998).

3. There was some controversy within the CCE initially over whether members were being manipulated or whether the government was acting in good faith.

4. The strongest opposition to COECE came from the Asociación de Industrias de la Transformación (ANIT), a Canacintra splinter group. In a slightly exaggerated claim, ANIT leadership accused COECE of representing only 2 percent of Mexican businesses (Conchiero 1996).

5. Argentina's Regimen de Especialización Industrial did allow for business to push ahead with integration, as occurred in the chemical sector where sectoral associations in Brazil and Argentina signed an agreement in 1987.

References

Acuna, Carlos. 1998. "Political Struggle and Business Peak Associations." In *Organized Business, Economic Change and Democracy in Latin America,* edited by Francisco Durand and Eduardo Silva, 51–72. Coral Gables, FL: North-South Center Press.

Agosin, Manuel. 1999. "Comercio y Crecimiento en Chile." *Revista de la CEPAL* 68 (August): 79–100

Bartell, Ernest, and Leigh A. Payne, eds. 1995. *Business and Democracy in Latin America.* Pittsburgh, PA: University of Pittsburgh Press.

Birle, Peter. 1997. *Los Empresarios y la Democracia en la Argentina.* Buenos Aires: Editorial de Belgrano.

Borquez, Elvira Conchiero. 1996. *El Gran Acuerdo.* Mexico City: Era.

Cason, Jeffrey. 2000. "On the Road to Southern Cone Integration." *Journal of Interamerican Studies and World Affairs* 42, no. 1: 23–35.

———. 2001. "Vulnerable Integration." Middlebury, VT: Department of Political Science, Middlebury College.

Fukuyama, Francis. 1995. *Trust: The Social Virtues and the Creation of Prosperity.* New York: Free Press.

Hirschman, Albert O. 1971. *A Bias for Hope.* New Haven, CT: Yale University Press.

Johnson, Chalmers. 1980. *MITI and the Japanese Miracle.* Stanford, CA: Stanford University Press.

Kingston, Peter R. 1998. "Corporatism, Neoliberalism, and the Failed Revolt of Big Business: Lessons from the Case IEDI," *Journal of Interamerican Studies and World Affairs* 40, no. 4: 73–95.

———. 1999. *Crafting Coalitions for Reform.* University Park: Pennsylvania State University Press.

Kleinberg, Remonda Bensabat. 1999. "Strategic Alliances: State–Business Relations in Mexico." *Bulletin of Latin American Research* 18, no. 1: 71–87.

Lindblom, Charles E. 1977. *Politics and Markets: The World's Political Economic System.* New York: Basic Books.

Manzetti, Luigi. 1993–1994. "The Political Economy of Mercosur." *Journal of Interamerican Studies and World Affairs* 35, no. 4: 101–141.

————. 1990. "Argentine–Brazilian Economic Integration." *Latin American Research Review* 25, no. 3: 109–140.

Martinelli, Alberto, ed. 1991. *International Markets and Global Firms: A Comparative Study of Organized Business.* New York: Sage.

Maxfield, Sylvia, and Ricardo Anzaldua Montoya. 1987. *Government and the Private Sector in Contemporary Mexico.* San Diego, CA: University of California-San Diego, Center for U.S.–Mexican Studies.

Maxfield, Sylvia, and Ben Ross Schneider, eds. 1997. *Business and the State in Developing Countries.* Ithaca, NY: Cornell University Press.

Montero, Cecilia. 1997. *La Revolución Empresarial Chilena.* Santiago: Cieplan and Domen.

Schneider, Ben Ross. 1997/1998. "Organized Business Politics in Democratic Brazil." *Journal of Interamerican Studies and World Affairs* 39 (Winter): 95–127.

————. 2001. "Business Politics and Regional Integration: The Advantages of Organization in NAFTA and MERCOSUR." Evanston, IL: Department of Political Science, Northwestern University.

————. 2002. "Why Is Mexican Business So Organized?" *Latin American Research Review* 37, no. 1: 77–118.

Schumpeter, Joseph A. 1964. *Business Cycles.* New York: McGraw Hill.

Silva, Eduardo, and Francisco Durand. 1996. "From Dictatorship to Democracy." *Comparative Politics* 28, no. 3: 299–317.

————. 1998. "Organized Business and Politics in Latin America." In *Organized Business, Economic Change and Democracy in Latin America,* edited by Francisco Durand and Eduardo Silva, 1–50. Coral Gables, FL: North-South Center Press.

Sirlin, Pablo. 1999. "El Regimen de Especialización." *Revista de la CEPAL* 68 (August): 101–113.

Thacker, Strom. 1999. "Nafta Coalitions and the Political Viability of Neoliberalism in Mexico." *Journal of Interamerican Studies and World Affairs* 41, no. 2: 57–83.

————. 2000. *Big Business, the State and Free Trade.* Cambridge: Cambridge University Press.

Tirado, Ricardo. 1998. "Mexico: From the Political Call for Action to a Proposal for Free Market Economic Reform." In *Organized Business, Economic Change and Democracy in Latin America,* edited by Francisco Durand and Eduardo Silva, 183–216. Coral Gables, FL: North-South Center Press.

Viguera, Anibal. 2000. *La Trama Política de la Apertura Económica en la Argentina.* La Plata, Argentina: Ediciones al Margen.

Wade, Robert. 1990. *Governing the Market.* Princeton, NJ: Princeton University Press.

Weyland, Kurt. 1998. "The Fragmentation of Business in Brazil." In *Organized Business, Economic Change and Democracy in Latin America,* edited by Francisco Durand and Eduardo Silva, 73–98. Coral Gables, FL: North-South Center Press.

4

The FTAA: Trade Preferences and the Art of the Possible

Carol Wise

Since the launching of formal negotiations for a thirty-four-member Free Trade Area of the Americas (FTAA) agreement in April 1998, the FTAA process has been put to considerable testing. External shocks, antiglobalization protests, mounting domestic political instability in Latin America, and a marked antipathy toward the deepening of trade liberalization in the U.S. Congress have all given pause to the realistic prospects for sealing this ambitious deal by the targeted 2005 deadline. Nevertheless, with the election of President George W. Bush in 2000, it appeared as if new leadership in Washington would jump-start the FTAA initiative as Bush himself declared the strengthening of U.S.–Latin American trade ties to be a top priority for the incoming administration (DePalma 2000: C23).

The main issues at stake on the FTAA negotiating agenda—market access, services, investment, agriculture, and trade remedies—were admittedly tough, but with the appointment of the formidable Robert Zoellick as chief U.S. trade negotiator and a renewed White House commitment to advance the hemispheric agenda, the obstacles were still deemed surmountable (Carmichael 2001: 13–14). With a Republican majority in both houses of the U.S. Congress, it appeared that other barriers to the completion of the FTAA on the U.S. side, including the passage of the necessary "fast-track" negotiating authority and the resolution of differences over how to properly address the environmental and labor market effects of trade liberalization, could finally be overcome. As a show of good faith, the Bush administration proceeded immediately with the moribund U.S.–Chile free trade negotiations, languishing since 1995 and initially brought back to life in 2000 by the outgoing Clinton team.

Alas, the year 2001 turned out to be the Western Hemisphere's *annus horribilis,* as a series of economic and political events converged to inject a fresh dose of uncertainty into the FTAA process. On the economic front, the unprecedented growth and dynamic productivity rates that had prevailed in the United States from 1994 to 2000 proved to be too good to last. As always, a slowdown in North America augurs recession for the rest of the hemisphere and this period was no exception. Yet, this particular slowdown came at a point when all but Mexico were still struggling to recapture the 5-to-6 percent regional growth rate that had finally been achieved by 1997. A combination of external shocks (Argentina, Brazil, Chile, and Uruguay); impartial reform implementation (Argentina, Bolivia, Brazil, Colombia, Peru, and most of Central America); or the lack of any serious reform at all (Ecuador, Paraguay, and Venezuela) helped derail the process.

The fact that Latin American exports to the United States and Canada had expanded from 44 percent of all exports in 1990 to nearly 60 percent by 1999 was testimony to the progress that had been made in expanding regional markets[1]; but stronger trade ties also meant an even quicker transmission of the recession southward. In the aftermath of the September 11 terrorist attacks on the World Trade Towers, the deepening recession in the North kicked some parts of Latin America into economic depression, especially the Southern Cone. The Argentine economy, still reeling from the Brazilian devaluation of January 1999, literally imploded as the country was forced to abandon its decade-old currency board and default on some $144 billion in external public debt. Although financial contagion had been largely contained through the discounting of Argentine debt by international banks, the trade shocks from the Argentine devaluation were deeply felt by Brazil, Paraguay, and Uruguay, its partners in the Southern Common Market (MERCOSUR).

On the political front, U.S. foreign policy had understandably succumbed to security concerns, momentarily eclipsing earlier debates in Washington concerning the fate of the FTAA. Against this backdrop, when the Bush administration and the U.S. Congress did return to the question of trade policy, the post–September 11 debate had become ever more protectionist. Whereas previous commercial policy disagreements in the U.S. Congress had been weighted toward trade-related issues, such as the need for labor and environmental standards in future agreements or the private sector's insistence on the right to litigate against dumping and unfair subsidies from abroad (Destler and Balint 1998), Congress had now turned its attention to the provision of tariffs, subsidies, and other barriers to shield U.S. producers from further competition. For instance, in December 2001, the House of

Representatives finally passed a fast-track bill (or "trade promotion authority" package as U.S. Trade Representative Zoellick rephrased it) with just a one-vote margin, but only because of last-minute concessions made to agriculture and textile-producing states in the United States—concessions that actually benefited Mexico due to its exemption as a member of the North American Free Trade Agreement (NAFTA).

Apologist explanations from the Bush team centered on the need to offer selective protection in sensitive sectors (steel and softwood lumber producers subsequently won important tariff concessions) in the short run in order to secure the necessary congressional votes for the trade promotion authority (TPA) bill in the long run. For those Latin American trading partners most affected by rising U.S. barriers, the presumed relationship between short-run protectionism and longer-run trade opening did not add up (Rohter and Rich 2001: W1). This became apparent when the TPA bill was finally passed by the U.S. Senate in July 2002, where it was subjected to a further round of protectionist demands, including an unsuccessful effort to delete any language from a trade agreement that changes U.S. trade-remedy laws.

Given this context of escalating protectionism, deep economic recession in Latin America, and ongoing security concerns on the part of U.S. policymakers, the question of trade preferences and strategic policy choice vis-à-vis the FTAA is perhaps even less clear than when the negotiations started. The pressures from continued international economic volatility and the apparent weakening of political will for deeper liberalization throughout the hemisphere have fueled earlier predictions concerning the futility of the FTAA project. At the same time, those who still champion the FTAA argue that, if anything, the steady stream of external economic and political shocks, combined with the favorable trade gains achieved thus far from liberalization and subregional integration, have strengthened the resolve of hemispheric leaders and policymakers to see the FTAA negotiations through to a successful finish.[2]

In this chapter, I set aside these largely rhetorical debates and instead approach the FTAA, flaws and all, as the most viable venue for further integration of the Western Hemisphere at this particular historical juncture. In light of the difficulties that have surrounded efforts to launch a new "millennium round" at the World Trade Organization (WTO), even the gradualist and piecemeal nature of hemispheric integration under the auspices of the FTAA seems more promising at this point.[3] The countries in the Western Hemisphere have advanced the integration process considerably on the basis of bilateral and subregional accords. However, with the finalization of the U.S.–Chile free trade agreement (FTA) and the formal launching of negotiations for an FTA between the United States and five Central American countries,[4] it appears that bilateral and subregional approaches are also reaching their limits. As Vinod Aggarwal and Ralph Espach point out in Chapter 1, bilateral pacts may be simpler to negotiate and less politically complicated, but they can also lead to significant trade diversion and overall inefficiency. Similarly, while subregional negotiations (NAFTA, MERCOSUR) were a highly rational response to obstacles at the multilateral level in the early 1990s, these too have generated overly specific rules and procedures that detract from trade liberalization on a larger scale such as the FTAA.

On this last point, none of this is to suggest that multilateralism will be superseded by the brand of regionalism embodied in the FTAA. Rather, since the launching of the General Agreement on Tariffs and Trade (GATT) Uruguay Round negotiations in 1986, multilateralism and regionalism have simultaneously moved forward in a complicated pattern (Hart 1999). It was, for example, the prolonged impasse at the Uruguay Round that prompted the United States to pursue the NAFTA negotiations with Canada and Mexico; in turn, NAFTA's ability to advance in areas that had eluded agreement at the Uruguay Round (dispute settlement, intellectual property rights) provided new pressures and incentives for the completion of the GATT negotiations and the creation of the WTO in 1994. Now, this same cycle appears to have swung back in favor of regionalism: in essence, the FTAA represents trade policy as the art of what's politically possible for the Western Hemisphere at this point in time.

Further down the line, it is quite likely that concrete progress with FTAA negotiations will provide similar incentives for negotiating breakthroughs at the multilateral level. For now, however, there remains the question of how such progress can be achieved at the FTAA negotiating table. Apart from Canada and the United States, the four Latin American countries on which successful hemispheric integration will most depend are Argentina, Brazil, Chile, and Mexico (Hinojosa-Ojéda et al. 1997). Other chapters in this volume have analyzed the various policy choices and institutional settings within which these key states have pursued commercial reform since the mid-1980s. In their introductory chapter, Aggarwal and Espach categorize these individual strategies as Chile (unilateral liberalization/multilateral trader); Mexico (bilateral liberalization with Canada and the U.S./hub market in the Latin American context); Argentina (regional partner/minilateral liberalization); and Brazil (regional leader/minilateral liberalization combined with multilateral activism).

In this chapter I dig deeper into the actual trade strategies that have been embraced within these general categories, how they have been manifested in a subregional context, and the kinds of collective action bottlenecks that have worked to slow the deepening of liberalization and integration at the FTAA negotiating table. At the same time, as lingering economic recession in Latin America and the prospects for further liberalization are feeding directly back into domestic politics across the hemisphere, I explore the possibility for a more strategic bundling of the FTAA with a set of credible adjustment policies that offer to strengthen the economic position of weaker players in the market.

The FTAA in Retrospect:
Political, Economic, and Institutional Evolution

One way of understanding the current challenges regarding the FTAA is to look at the initial inspirations and various policy motivations between North and South America. For the United States, proposals to negotiate a bilateral FTA with Canada in the 1980s, and subsequently the NAFTA agreement with Canada and Mexico, stemmed from fears over the country's declining competitiveness, as well as frustration over the Uruguay Round's slow progress in reducing trade barriers in Europe and Asia. Canada, which faced these same troublesome international trends, pragmatically accepted U.S. overtures toward bilateralism in recognition that its earlier foothold in European markets could no longer be taken for granted. While Mexico's request in 1990 to negotiate a bilateral FTA with the United States was badly received in Ottawa, in the end, Canada joined the NAFTA negotiations in order to avoid the diversion of trade and investment that it would have otherwise suffered.

Whereas Canada and the United States turned to bilateral initiatives long after each had liberalized its trade and investment regime, the rapid proliferation of subregional trade schemes in Latin America was part and parcel of the region's efforts at deep structural reform. As trade liberalization became an integral part of macroeconomic stabilization efforts in the late 1980s, an initial round of unilateral tariff and nontariff reductions quickly brought most Latin American countries in line with the mandates of GATT.

Simultaneously, policymakers sought to maximize the potential of trade reform as a powerful tool for microeconomic restructuring. In contrast to the macroeconomic turmoil and inward-looking integration schemes of the 1960s in Latin America, subregional integration in the 1990s became a main means for "locking in" hard-fought macroeconomic stabilization gains, and for institutionalizing new liberal trade and investment initiatives.[5] As the editors pointed out in Chapter 1, the paths toward integration may have been different, but the ultimate goals were basically the same.

For Latin America, it was President George Bush's 1990 announcement of a new Enterprise for the Americas Initiative (EAI) that shaped expectations for the creation of a full hemispheric accord that would amount to more than the sum of its subregional parts. The stated strategy of the former Bush trade policy team in the early 1990s was to proceed simultaneously with the Uruguay Round at the multilateral level and with NAFTA negotiations at the subregional level. It was assumed that the negotiation of a larger hemispheric accord would follow once these more immediate goals were achieved. Although the NAFTA and Uruguay Round agreements were later secured by the Clinton administration, in the aftermath it had become apparent that in pursuing a joint subregional/multilateral strategy, U.S. trade policymakers were now operating under new kinds of opportunities and constraints.

On the side of opportunity, for example, some of NAFTA's achievements clearly went beyond the GATT. This was so with the removal of virtually all border barriers to trade among Canada, Mexico, and the United States over a fifteen-year time period, and in NAFTA's more comprehensive coverage of foreign direct investment (FDI), trade in services, intellectual property rights, and dispute settlement (Lawrence 1996: 67–75). These advances revealed the extent to which NAFTA was as much about investment as it was about free trade. And, despite open disagreements in Washington as to whether the United States had any business launching subregional negotiations in the midst of the Uruguay Round (Bhagwati and Krueger 1995), hindsight does show that the very prospect of NAFTA provided the United States with the leverage it needed to finally wrap up the Uruguay Round agreement in early 1994.

Yet, the NAFTA negotiations also drove home the constraints inherent in a hemispheric approach to integration. Having entered the NAFTA negotiations at a fairly early stage in its own trade opening, Mexico was primarily interested in market access and bargaining over crucial sectoral concerns (automotives, textiles, and agriculture). As advanced liberal capitalist economies,

Canada and the United States were more intent on securing the kinds of legal trade norms mentioned above, goals that continue to prove extremely challenging to accomplish at the multilateral level. Underpinning these different motives for subregionalism, of course, were the huge disparities between North and South. Because of its close preexisting economic ties with the North American bloc, Mexico had a tremendous amount to gain by conceding on legal norms in exchange for guaranteed access to this market—so much so that the Mexican government was willing to forego any special breaks in the NAFTA negotiations for its developing country status.

But neither the U.S. public, nor political leaders along with their constituencies in the southern part of the hemisphere have been able to overlook these asymmetries. In the United States, while there was substantial consensus amongst economists of all theoretical preferences that NAFTA would have a modest net gain of 100,000 to 200,000 jobs over its first ten years, the long-term trend toward corporate downsizing and wage stagnation gave U.S. workers understandable cause for concern. If NAFTA signified a free flow of goods, services, and capital among all three countries, what was to stop the flow northward of environmental pollution and illegal immigrants willing to work for a fraction of the minimum wage? Why risk the lowering of labor and environmental standards that workers and consumers in the United States had fought to achieve since the 1930s?

With the negotiation of special labor and environmental side agreements to address these concerns, the Clinton administration finally won enough congressional votes to pass the controversial NAFTA bill in November 1993. However, by the time of NAFTA's implementation in January 1994, all of the various protagonists that took part in the original debate had dug their heels in even deeper than before. Labor and environmental activists were embittered that the side agreements provided for enforcement of national legislation that already existed, but stopped short of strengthening and harmonizing North American standards in these areas. Indeed, the side agreements actually impinged very little on national sovereignty, yet the North American private sector saw them as going much too far in this direction. These divisions grew with the rise of a conservative Republican congressional majority out of the 1994 mid-term elections in the United States, which uncharacteristically viewed the idea of further market opening with suspicion. Mexico's December 1994 peso crisis, which generated the need for a massive $50 billion multilateral bailout, did little to assuage these fears. Within a year of NAFTA's launching, the question of further accession to the agreement, or congressional reauthorization of fast-track negotiating authority, was basically precluded by these other political and economic forces.

South of the Mexican border, just as NAFTA had elicited contrasting views in North America about what we should expect from government, the role of markets, and strategies for economic development, so too did the prospect of its expansion southward trigger similar debates in these countries. Although the possibility of NAFTA accession became increasingly remote as the 1990s wore on, policymakers in other Latin American countries were still left to grapple with three main challenges: (1) the huge asymmetries summarized in Table 4.1; (2) unanimous opposition to the direct linking of labor and environmental issues to a regional trade agreement; and (3) the very different core concerns that North (international commercial law, trade remedies) and South (market access) brought to the negotiating table. These concerns would continue to shape trade policy preferences, as the key actors turned their attention to the strengthening of subregional and extraregional ties, and to the prospects for negotiating a full hemispheric FTAA accord.

Within this scenario, only Mexico's bilateral integration with the United States, and secondarily with Canada, constituted the realization of a set of trade preferences proper. For others, such as Argentina and Chile, whose hopes for negotiating bilaterally with the United States were thwarted by U.S. congressional intransigence on trade policy post-1994, the eventual paths taken boiled down to trade preferences as the art of what was possible at that particular point in time. For Brazil, with its conflicting aspirations to assume regional integration leadership, maintain its own regime of selective protectionism, and place multilateralism above regionalism, thus far the art of what's possible in terms of trade policy has been clouded by that country's steadfastly ambiguous stance toward the FTAA. Of these four key countries, only Chile and Mexico had articulated cohesive export-led development strategies that bolstered participation in subregional and multilateral schemes. This is reflected in Table 4.2, where these two countries' exports as a percentage of GDP in the 1990s towered over those of Argentina and Brazil, a point I return to in the following section.

Still, the progress that Latin America has made in shifting to an outward development model driven by subregional integration schemes is reflected in the figures, which show that the region's commercial exchange with the rest of the world has doubled since 1990. Similarly, the larger subregional groupings such as NAFTA and MERCOSUR have seen average annual export growth rates of 11 percent to 16 percent among the respective members

Table 4.1 FTAA Negotiating Partners

Country	Population (million)	GDP in US$ (billion)	GDP in US$ (1,000 per capita)	Average Tariff (%)
United States	272.9	9,299.2	34.1	2.5
Canada	30.6	644.7	21.1	3.6
Mexico	97.4	483.5	5.9	12.5
NAFTA	400.9	10,472.4	26.1	
Brazil	168.1	542.0	3.1	16.6
Argentina	36.6	283.1	7.8	12.9
Uruguay	3.3	21.8	6.4	10.0
Paraguay	5.4	11.7	2.1	8.7
MERCOSUR	213.4	858.6	4.0	
Venezuela	23.7	102.2	4.3	10.9
Colombia	41.5	86.4	2.2	12.4
Perú	25.2	56.0	2.1	20.2
Ecuador	12.4	13.6	1.1	10.4
Bolivia	8.1	8.4	1.1	9.7
Andean Group	110.9	266.6	2.4	
Guatemala	11.1	18.0	1.6	5.7
Honduras	6.3	5.4	0.8	5.7
El Salvador	6.2	12.2	1.9	4.3
Nicaragua	4.9	2.3	0.5	8.5
Costa Rica	3.6	15.2	3.9	4.3
Dominican Republic	8.4	17.0	1.8	13.6
CACM	40.5	70.1	1.8	
Jamaica	2.6	7.9	3.1	19.2
Trinidad/Tobago	1.3	6.9	5.0	20.4
Guyana	0.9	0.8	1.0	N.A.
Suriname	0.4	1.1	2.5	N.A.
Bahamas	0.3	4.6	15.0	N.A.
Barbados	0.3	2.5	9.8	N.A.
Belize	0.2	0.7	3.1	N.A.
St. Lucia	0.2	0.6	3.7	N.A.
Antigua/Barbuda	0.1	0.6	9.4	N.A.
Dominica	0.1	0.3	3.7	N.A.
Grenada	0.1	0.4	3.8	N.A.
St. Vincent/Grenadines	0.1	0.3	2.9	N.A.
St. Kitts/Nevis	0.0	0.3	7.2	N.A.
CARICOM	6.7	27.0	4.0	
Chile	15.0	67.4	4.6	10.9
Haiti	7.8	4.3	0.6	N.A.
Panama	2.8	9.6	3.4	8.0
Total	798.0	11,731.0	14.7	

Note: Population and GDP for 1999; average tariffs, latest year available.

Source: Carmichael (2001): 13.

Table 4.2 Macro versus Micro Performance in Four Countries, 1990–2000

		Argentina	Brazil	Chile	Mexico
GDP (growth)	1991–2000	4.7	2.7	6.6	3.5
GDI (GDI/GDP)	1990–1998	17.7	20.8	25.3	22.9
EXGDP (EXP/GDP)	1990–2000	9.2	8.8	30.0	22.9
INF	2000	–0.9	7.0	3.8	9.5
RW	1990–2000	0.0	0.4	3.7	0.8
EMP	1990–1999	1.3	1.7	2.1	3.0
LPRO	1990–1995	4.1	–0.1	3.3	–2.2
URUN	1990–2000	12.2	5.8	7.7	3.5
EDGAP	1994	1.9*	4.7	1.5	3.1
DIST: poorest 40%	1986	16.2	9.7	12.6	12.7***
DIST: poorest 40%	1990	14.9	9.6	13.4	11.7**
DIST: poorest 40%	1994	13.9	11.8	13.3	10.8
DIST: poorest 40%	1998	14.9^	8.2	NA	NA
DIST: richest 10%	1986	34.5	44.3	39.6	34.3***
DIST: richest 10%	1990	34.8	41.7	39.2	39.0**
DIST: richest 10%	1994	34.2	42.5	40.3	41.2
DIST: richest 10%	1998	35.8^^	44.3*	39.1	42.8^

* 1996; ** 1989; *** 1984; ^ 1995; ^^ 1997.

GDP, gross domestic product; GDI, gross domestic investment as percent of GDP; EXGDP, ratio of exports of goods and services to GDP; INF, percentage change in consumer prices over previous year; RW, annual growth rate of real wages; EMP, annual growth rate of employment; LPRO, annual growth rate of labor productivity; URUN, average annual rate of urban unemployment; EDGAP, average years behind in school for ages 15–18; DIST, percent of national income accruing to specified group.

Sources: GDP and INF: ECLAC (2001b); GDI: World Bank (2001); EXGDP: calculated from national accounts in IMF (2001); RW, EMP, LPRO, URUN: ECLAC (2001b); EDGAP: data presented by Behrman et al. (1998); DIST: Chilean and Brazilian data based on urban areas and Argentine data based on Buenos Aires, from ECLAC (1997); Mexican data from INEGI (2001). Most recent distribution figures: ECLAC (2001b) and World Bank (2000).

of each bloc over the past decade.[6] Just since 1994, U.S. FDI in Latin America has increased by 50 percent and U.S. exports to the region (excluding Mexico) by 52 percent; in fact, U.S. trade with Latin America is growing twice as fast as with countries outside of the Western Hemisphere. Within the region, even under conditions of severe external volatility, total intra-regional trade grew at an average rate of around 20 percent during 1997–1999 (CEPAL News 2001). Nevertheless, wide economic disparities within Latin America (see Table 4.1), and the varying levels of readiness to commit fully to the FTAA's ultimate liberalization goals have also slowed the march toward full hemispheric integration.

This was made apparent by the divergent attitudes and stances that surfaced at the Second Summit of the Americas held in Santiago, Chile, in April

1998. With the United States arriving empty-handed (i.e., without fast-track authority) in Santiago, the Clinton team sought to focus the summit on related issues such as education policy, democratic governance, and civil society participation. Understandably, Latin American participants were more anxious to specify both the design and the content of the planned negotiations (Haggard 1998). Would the FTAA negotiations move forward at the level of the five main subregional integration schemes depicted in Table 4.1? Or, would they be conducted at the level of the nine working groups that had been created as part of the FTAA process? It is this latter option that prevailed, along with Brazil's preference for approaching the FTAA as one sweeping agreement to be adopted in its entirety, or a "single undertaking."

Uncertainties over negotiating strategies and U.S. leadership aside, the FTAA's nine designated negotiating groups (market access; agriculture; antidumping, subsidies, and countervailing duties; competition policy; services; investment; intellectual property rights; government procurement; and dispute settlement), have made vitally important, if halting, progress in laying the groundwork for hemispheric integration. These groups, along with a consultative committee designed to address the concerns of smaller economies, and two additional committees dealing with the participation of civil society and with electronic commerce, have articulated a sophisticated and comprehensive negotiating agenda that simply has no precedent in the Western Hemisphere (Schott 2001). Apart from the development of crucial institutional capacities, as well as the increased opportunities for political learning and collegial exchange, the current negotiating group format directly lends itself to the achievement of consistency and complementarity between the FTAA and the WTO.

Perhaps the greater challenge since the formal launching of the FTAA negotiations at the 2001 Quebec City Summit lies in the need for state leaders and policymakers across the region to reconfirm the political economic rationale for a hemispheric integration scheme. While the potential for further hemisphere-wide gains in trade and investment are estimated to be considerable (Hinojosa-Ojéda et al. 1997), those who initially pushed for the FTAA seem to have periodically lost sight of this earlier rationale. Nowhere is this more so than in the United States, the country that accounts for some 75 percent of hemispheric output. Certainly the growing U.S. reliance on Latin American markets for trade and investment provides a structural logic for the FTAA that, in the end, cannot be ignored. In Latin America, despite strong trade performance against the backdrop of the Asian, Russian, and Brazilian financial shocks of 1997–1999, the prospect of further liberalization without clear-cut reciprocity by the United States is being met with the utmost of caution. The fact that Latin American trade regimes have resisted the kinds of protectionist policies that U.S. trade fell prey to in the lead-up to the 2002 TPA vote is a reflection of the extent to which the FTAA project is still a key reference point for the southern hemisphere. Nevertheless, collective action dilemmas continue to distract policymakers across the hemisphere from the FTAA and these still require more careful attention.

Domestic Challenges to Collective Action: The Need to Tackle Asymmetries Head-on

In Latin America, the current collective action challenges stem from the sweeping programs of market reform that have been implemented since the mid-1980s and, for the most part, the lack of cohesive or consistent government responses in the way of adjustment support and productive investment in human capital. When growth was sound through the mid-1990s, Latin American voters and consumers supported market reform within the confines of regional integration, with the prospect that their own vulnerable economic position would eventually improve (Seligson 1999: 129–149). With growth plummeting since the late 1990s, the electorate's mood has turned decidedly distributional. Indeed, while trade liberalization, in particular, has correlated with an increase in the real incomes of the lower 60 percent of the population in a large sample of Latin American countries (Londoño and Székely 1997), it has also inflicted considerable economic stress on workers and producers alike. Thus, for regional integration to advance, its proponents must consistently convey the following: first, how the costs of a thwarted FTAA in terms of sluggish growth and loss of dynamism would far outweigh the benefits; and second, hemispheric policymakers must display a much stronger commitment toward bridging the asymmetries that appear in Table 4.1.

While the actual trade reforms embraced by the majority of Latin American countries conform closely to the liberalizing prescriptions of the "Washington consensus," closer scrutiny of the track record reflects the diversity of those policies that have been pursued under the banner of market reform. In Argentina, for example, until the recent crisis, policymakers had relied on a hands-off approach to liberalization that assigned the task of economic adjustment primarily to market forces. In contrast, since the mid-1980s Chile has relied on a competitive liberalization strategy, which means that public policy (e.g., tax and credit incentives for producers engaging in higher value-added production, affordable credit and technical assistance for smaller trading companies, public support for export diversification and promotion, and a strong emphasis on educational reform and job training programs) has been actively used as part of a development model based on free trade and export-led growth.[7] Mexico, in the aftermath of the December 1994 peso crisis, has followed suit with a Chilean-style competitive strategy. Brazilian policymakers have also leaned toward a competitive strategy, although the continued propensity of the government to readily concede to private sector demands for protectionism suggests that it would still be premature to classify Brazil's strategy as a "competitive" one. What do these differing approaches suggest in terms of the path forward for trade integration in the Western Hemisphere?

Table 4.2 reflects the overall progress that has been made at both the macro- and micro-economic levels in these four countries, while highlighting the comparative success of Chile's competitive strategy. On the macroeconomic side, there is no denying the success of economic liberalization in halting the chaotic inflation that prevailed, for example, in Argentina, Brazil, and Mexico. Under the thrust of lower inflation, growth rates similarly improved. In 1997, for the first time in some twenty-five years, average regional growth surpassed five percent of GDP, and per capita gains approached four percent (ECLAC 1997).[8] Yet, only Chile, with an average annual growth rate of 6.6 percent of GDP from 1991 to 2000, closely approximated the 6-to-7 percent growth threshold that economic theory holds as necessary for triggering higher sustainable income gains; the remainder of the cases averaged growth rates between 2.7 percent (Brazil) and 4.7 percent (Argentina) over this same time period. Total gross investment as a percent of GDP has followed a similar trend, whereby Chile has seen a gradual increase in total investment, averaging 17.6 percent of GDP in the 1980s compared with 23.7 percent in the 1990s, while the remaining three cases have registered declines during this same timeframe. Net FDI has been more responsive to the stabilization signals that all four countries have succeeded in sending, with the four-country total rising from about $10 billion in 1992 to a projected $65.8 billion for 1999 (ECLAC 2001a: 95).

If Chile's higher growth and investment rates offer compelling justification for a more assertive reliance on public policy, as defined above, evidence to support the pursuit of a Chilean-style competitive strategy is equally convincing at the microeconomic level. On balance, and setting aside the question of distributional trends for the time being, Chile stands out as having

achieved higher gains in growth, productivity, and wages than any of its Latin
American counterparts in the 1990s. One could point to Chile's longer timeline with trade liberalization, which preceded these other countries by at
least a decade, as ample justification for its relative success. Yet, comparative analysis of the actual trade and development strategies employed by the
other countries in Table 4.2 suggests that the timing variable alone does not
suffice as an explanation for differential economic performance in the region. The erratic microeconomic performance of the other three countries
can be explained by variations in policy choices.

In the case of Argentina, for example, the painful lesson of the 2001 collapse of the country's ten-year convertibility program based on peso–dollar
parity was the government's failure to pursue a broader mix of policies (fiscal and labor market reform, antitrust), and to more clearly articulate a role
for trade policy as part of a larger development strategy (Pastor and Wise
2001: 60–72). The hands-off management approach based on comparative
advantage and primary exports produced respectable aggregate growth rates
during the 1990s; however, at the level of the real economy (i.e., everyday
economic returns for the average worker), wage gains and employment
expansion virtually stood still. The country's comparatively high labor productivity rates were offset by similarly high levels of unemployment, which
reflected the extent to which productivity gains in Argentina stemmed from
downsizing the labor force (Pastor and Wise 2003b). At the same time, increasing levels of currency overvaluation under a fixed exchange rate regime
fostered a pattern of trade (led by low value-added primary exports) that directly hampered further job creation. To date, MERCOSUR trade has been
dominated by just two partners (Argentina and Brazil), both of which have
experienced severe economic crises since 1998. This has limited this venue
as a source of more dynamic employment expansion and export-led growth
for Argentina.

For Mexico, the low growth rates that appear in Table 4.2, in terms of
aggregate GDP, real wages, and labor productivity, are testimony to the
high price that the country has paid for the reckless economic management
errors that led up to the December 1994 peso crisis. The latter includes a
$100 billion-plus bailout of the domestic banking system, largely at taxpayer
expense. The unexpectedly rapid turnaround of the Mexican economy in the
aftermath of the peso's devaluation, spurred by high value-added industrial
exports and more privileged access to the U.S. market under NAFTA, reflects the enormous amount of restructuring that has occurred since the
onset of trade liberalization, and the importance of a competitive exchange

rate for unleashing the country's new productive potential. By 1997, as real growth rates had rebounded to 7 percent of GDP, the government had firmly committed itself to a new "program of industrial policy and international trade." Similar to Chile's shift a decade earlier, Mexican policymakers, under heavy pressure from the domestic private sector, have now opted for a flexible exchange rate and "active government participation, in the form of highly effective public policies that promote industrial growth" (SECOFI 1996). This shift has also been accompanied by a more carefully targeted social strategy, one that seeks to aggressively direct healthcare and education spending in ways that will better position Mexican workers to succeed in the country's rapidly changing labor markets.[9]

Although Brazil has expressed an affinity for a Chilean-style competitive model (Motta Veiga 1997), the microeconomic track record has yet to reflect this policy preference. As with Mexico, the Brazilian recovery in the wake of the January 1999 devaluation was more rapid and dynamic than expected, and this hints at the tremendous potential that a restructured Brazil would have in the context of the FTAA. Yet, Brazil's low level of exports as a percent of GDP suggests the lack of an explicit trade strategy beyond MERCOSUR, as well as policymakers' continuing ambivalence toward deeper integration. As economic volatility continues to feed the country's ambiguity toward the FTAA, Brazil's microeconomic fate now lies in the hands of policymakers who find themselves increasingly torn between private sector demands for government assistance in the face of recession and external competition and a growing mass of poor Brazilians whose social status continues to deteriorate in the wake of the 1999 devaluation. Hence, Brazil tends to waver between policies that are clearly market supporting (monetary and fiscal reform), and those that are market distorting (unilateral tariff hikes, for example, on consumer durables and some vulnerable nondurable sectors such as apparel).

Finally, what explains the universally disappointing distributional trends that appear in Table 4.2, and why haven't these been more aggressively tackled over the past decade? Although econometric evidence from 1985 to 1995 points to a positive relationship between macroeconomic stabilization/ trade liberalization and distributional gains (Londoño and Székely 1997), why aren't these trends more robust for the 1990s, especially for earlier liberalizers like Chile and Mexico? This distributional deterioration is doubly puzzling when the generally higher levels of spending on healthcare and education in the 1990s, representing some 2 percent of regional GDP, are taken into account. Apart from the unevenness with which trade liberalization and market reforms have been applied in Latin America, two interrelated explanations stand out for the tenacity of income inequality and distributional stress in the region: (1) continued levels of asset concentration since the onset of liberalization; and (2) a widening gap in skill differentials, itself a product of the poor quality and access to training and educational opportunities.

While the failure of wages and income distribution to improve accordingly is still not entirely understood, economic theory points to asset concentration, both productive and human assets, as a main culprit (Birdsall and Londoño 1997: 32–38). Productive assets refer to land, companies, and other financial holdings. Although land tenure patterns in the region are still highly skewed, the low percentage of the population now living in the rural sector, and the small share that agriculture contributes to regional GDP, suggests that the main bottleneck stems from concentrated ownership patterns of other productive assets. For example, in all four countries in Table 4.2, despite the implementation of ambitious market reform packages, long-standing oligopolistic ownership patterns have prevailed. The degree of concentration is such that, on average, three to six firms still account for as much as 70 percent of market share in the most dynamic sectors of these economies (Baer and Maloney 1997: 320). While all four countries now have formal antitrust legislation on the books, enforcement has clearly lagged.

The causal link between these continued patterns of asset concentration and regressive income distribution is the following: for the larger and more globally integrated companies in the region, a dynamic process of microeconomic restructuring is underway, based on intraindustry trade, increasing specialization, rapid productivity gains, and the professionalization of technical and managerial networks. These top conglomerates have further consolidated their market position since the mid-1980s, but in ways that are capital-intensive and offer limited employment opportunities outside the higher skilled niches of the labor market. The remaining mass of productive sector firms are mostly small- and medium-sized ventures that have traditionally produced nontradeable goods for the domestic market, and provided the main impetus for the expansion of less skilled employment. Although in other regions, such as East Asia, these smaller enterprises have been an integral part of a competitive production strategy—from the provision of supply flexibility to the innovation of products, labor practices, and worker skills—the lack of know-how and financial resources has made it much more difficult for this second group of Latin American firms to adapt to new levels of competition. It is this increasing heterogeneity of the region's productive structure, and the compression of income shares within this burgeoning lower tier of smaller, weaker firms, that has perpetuated higher levels of inequality in the 1990s.

It could be argued that this contradictory dynamic just described, where dynamism and innovation have gone hand-in-hand with stagnation and regressive income distribution, is simply a new fact of economic life for all countries operating within a fully integrated global economy. Although Latin America's struggle with income inequality is not unique on this count, the data suggest that the region's disproportionately higher international ranking on regressive distribution stems from major deficiencies in human capital formation. For example, the evidence on educational investments and achievement show that, while Latin America actually spends more on education than East Asia (3.7 percent of regional GDP versus 3.4 percent, respectively), the average Latin American worker today is no better educated than the average East Asian worker was in 1970 (Birdsall and Londoño 1997). These dramatic qualitative differences reflect East Asia's educational emphasis on universal school access and job skill acquisition, policies that have reaped much higher income returns. For example, the annual growth of per capita GDP in East Asia averaged 6.7 percent from 1980 to 1992, versus –0.5 percent for Latin America over the same time period (Stallings 1995).

With an average educational level of just 5.2 years as recently as 1995, Latin America's shallow human asset base and poor skill acquisition has placed its adult working population at a startling disadvantage. This unfavorable lag reflects, first, the extent to which Latin America's educational systems have failed to forge dynamic links between schools and labor markets under a trade-driven economic model that demands increasingly higher skills; and second, the insidious ways in which cumulative human capital inequalities have compounded in the 1990s, like daily interest accumulation on a high-interest loan, as the demands for higher work skills are quickly outpacing the capacity of the educational system to meet the supply.

Whereas Chile and Mexico have designed comprehensive programs in the 1990s that directly target these problems, Argentina and Brazil have yet to generate credible policy responses. In Argentina, it was those patterns of downward mobility for the poorest 40 percent of the population (Table 4.2) that set the tone of the 1999 presidential campaign (Pastor and Wise 2003b). Yet, the Brazilian devaluation shock and the exigencies of fiscal restraint under the convertibility program quickly derailed these political commitments. In Brazil, where downward mobility has been even more acute, similar macroeconomic pressures have led to short-term safety net strategies that do not begin to penetrate the human capital deficiencies that appear in Table 4.2. Given the importance of these two countries as the core of the MERCOSUR bloc, and the essential role that a Brazil-led MERCOSUR must play in completing the FTAA negotiations, these social deficits will most likely fuel domestic ambivalence on trade integration until they are more credibly addressed.

Returning to the question of why so little overall progress has been made in bridging these asymmetries within countries in the region, even this brief review of the most recent research findings confirms that the policy tools are now there for the taking: universal education that links training and skills to restructured job markets; a more carefully enforced competition policy and antitrust regime; and, an explicit trade-led strategy that assertively offers tax and credit incentives for producers to shift to higher value-added exports that offer more in the way of employment creation. Obviously, the lingering weaknesses in the political/institutional setting in most Latin American countries have impeded the attainment of these seemingly straight-forward goals. While the onus for completing the necessary political and institutional reforms falls on the domestic front, the FTAA process could offer an important framework for the kinds of policy debate, institutional overhaul, and political learning that will be necessary for whittling away at these collective action dilemmas. More importantly, it offers the most direct route toward economic recovery in Latin America and the restoration of growth to levels that can make an authentic difference for absolute and relative income gains.

The FTAA and Regional Challenges to Collective Action

This final section explores the ways in which economic asymmetry and the kinds of adjustment stress reviewed above have converged to slow the expansion and weaken the affinities for deepening integration at the sub-regional and hemispheric levels. The United States, for instance, had announced on behalf of its NAFTA partners at the 1994 Miami Summit that Chile would be the first candidate for NAFTA entry, but those negotiations completely stalled until the outgoing Clinton team hastily revived them in the form of a U.S.–Chile FTA that did not see the finishing touches until December 2002. Given the simultaneous launching of the FTAA negotiations, a logical next step would have been for the United States to turn its attention steadfastly on Brazil (JP Morgan 2002: 3), as the hammering out of considerable trade policy conflicts between these two hemispheric giants is clearly a necessary condition for the timely completion of the FTAA. Instead, the U.S. trade policy team opted to launch negotiations with the Central American bloc that, like the Chilean negotiations, raises few of the domestic hackles that bilateral negotiations with Brazil are guaranteed to trigger. While by no means fatal to the FTAA, the U.S. propensity to negotiate with smaller countries where the stakes and returns are so much lower, while also raising protectionist barriers against the larger Latin American traders, continues to raise pressing questions about U.S. leadership and commitment toward the FTAA.

Yet, MERCOSUR, the other main player at the FTAA negotiating table, has likewise pursued the path of less resistance up to this point. By the end of 1994, the MERCOSUR countries had established a tariff schedule meant to converge into a customs union, and by 1996 they had negotiated "associate status" FTAs with Bolivia and Chile. However, since the Brazilian devaluation of January 1999 and Argentina's subsequent crises, MERCOSUR has continued to struggle with compliance and enforcement of some of its most basic liberalization initiatives. While definitely on a gradual track, gradualism itself has also allowed these countries some breathing space, for example, with the negotiation of a separate FTA with the European Union, and it has enabled the MERCOSUR bloc to extract some key concessions from the United States. In the absence of TPA, and with Brazil emerging as the counter-hub and leader of the South, the United States ultimately agreed to both the process for negotiations proposed by MERCOSUR (regional negotiations versus earlier U.S. designs of an FTAA based on NAFTA accession), and some important matters of content (the creation of a special agricultural negotiating group, and the exclusion of labor and environmental issues from the core text of the FTAA) (Masi and Wise 2003).

Despite the various difficulties and unexpected turns for the FTAA, all thirty-four countries and nine working groups continue to plod along at the negotiating table and, as of May 2002, the FTAA's crucial market access negotiations moved into so-called "high gear." While ongoing debates about the need to bridge hemispheric asymmetries by adopting European Union kinds of initiatives (social adjustment funds and FTAA institutions proper) have been repeatedly rejected by the United States and deemed by some to be overly idealistic,[10] the FTAA is still regarded as the most viable vehicle for tackling the vast intrahemispheric differences summarized in Table 4.1. In terms of the FTAA's future potential, it may help to recall that the prospect of NAFTA among Canada, the United States, and Mexico was deemed equally unrealistic in the early 1980s when former President Ronald Reagan proposed it. Although to speak now of the "FTAA era" would clearly be premature, the same was said of the NAFTA agreement as recently as a decade ago. Moreover, while still struggling with its own deficiencies in domestic adjustment support, Mexico's transformation under NAFTA has rendered it the only country in the region to have competitively restructured in ways that approximate the earlier experience of the East Asian trading states (Pastor and Wise 2003a). Below I review some of the main unresolved tensions within and between subregions, the resolution of which could help to grease the wheels of the FTAA process and ostensibly render this a more transformative project.

NAFTA

As mentioned earlier, political conflicts over NAFTA expansion in Canada and the United States have stemmed from (1) societal demands for the enforcement of labor standards and worker rights; and (2) the need to tighten guidelines and compliance procedures that would guarantee stronger environmental protection. In light of its dominant economic weight and leadership role in the hemisphere, the more vociferous expression of anti–free trade attitudes within the United States, and by organized labor in particular, warrants further attention, since this has heretofore constituted a main bottleneck in the pursuit of the FTAA. Two main forces appear to be at work. First, although total reported job losses related to NAFTA have not surpassed 200,000 since the agreement's implementation on January 1, 1994, even this limited labor market stress has been exacerbated by insufficient adjustment support. Unlike Canada, where the safety net is much thicker and income distribution more equal, the heavy reliance on market forces to assist workers in transition has prompted former AFL-CIO president George Meany to declare U.S. labor adjustment support programs the equivalent of "burial insurance" (Destler 1997: 46).

Second, underpinning today's longer-term patterns of income erosion and shorter-term labor market disruptions in the United States are an increasingly unequal human asset structure not unlike that of the Latin American cases explored in the previous section. As recently as 1989, for example, just 14 percent of the U.S. workforce held a college degree, while 40 percent had graduated from high school (Cline 1997: 23–26). Although the "wage penalty" for not attending college in the United States had hit 60 percent by 1979, college grads earned as much as 140 percent more than those without a college degree by 1995. At once, these data reflect the dynamic effects of rapid technological change and modernization of the U.S. workplace over the past two decades, and the extent to which the U.S. education system has fallen behind in increasing the quality and opportunities for improving human capital skills (McMurrer and Sawhill 1998: 39–44). It was in recognition of these counterproductive trends that candidate George W. Bush declared himself the "education president" during the 2000 presidential election, a commitment derailed by the events of September 11 and the security concerns that have subsequently eclipsed it.

As absolute and relative losses in income position have continued to accumulate in the United States, opposition to "free trade" has become a convenient, if misplaced, scapegoat for expressing dismay about much larger distributional challenges and public policy failures over time. This is evident with the chronic delays in education and health reform over the past decade and the serious ratcheting down of social welfare benefits since the 1998 "welfare reform" bill. Tellingly, the deal-breaker for the Democratic Party leadership in the U.S. Senate's TPA bill was the expansion of trade adjustment assistance to include a federal health insurance subsidy, wage insurance, and longer coverage periods for those U.S. workers who are displaced by trade competition. At least on the domestic front, U.S. policymakers are coming around to the notion that more credible signals concerning social adjustment will be essential for the effective pursuit of further trade deals. Although the United States continues to resist the idea of an FTAA social fund that could similarly dissipate obstacles to collective action at the trade negotiating table, the resurgence of intense political instability in Latin America, including the chaotic rotation of the Argentine executive five times in late 2001, followed by a 2002 coup attempt in Venezuela, could force rethinking on this front.

In Mexico, distributional stress has indeed been acute for those workers and self-employed producers who lack the skills and resources to participate successfully in a more competitive export-oriented industrial model (Pastor and Wise 2003a). But at the same time, as NAFTA completes its first decade, Mexico's dynamic gains from increased integration with the North American bloc are indisputable. Like a textbook example of the importance of scale economies and technical specialization, the top twenty U.S. imports from and exports to Mexico now flow across the border within the same manufacturing subsectors (e.g., automotives, telecommunications, and electrical machinery) (Weintraub 1997: 34–38). It is this increased opportunity for intraindustry specialization and rapid advances in competitiveness that prompted U.S. and Mexican producers to lobby so aggressively for an agreement like NAFTA that would further facilitate these dynamic gains. Thus, whereas distributional conflict has divided the perceived "winners" and "losers" in the United States to the extent that TPA authority was blocked until 2002, in Mexico steep adjustment costs have worked to heighten that government's commitment to a more targeted and aggressive social policy that could better capitalize on NAFTA's potential for economic transformation (Pastor and Wise 2003b).

However, as Antonio Ortíz Mena notes in Chapter 9, Mexico's emergence as a regional hub and its post-NAFTA success at negotiating bilateral FTAs with nine different Latin American countries and with the European Union has resulted in an ambiguous stance toward the FTAA. Despite widespread job displacement, wage compression, and persistent income inequality, the majority of Mexican voters have consistently supported those candidates who represent a shift to a more competitive approach where public policy actively promotes educational opportunity, job creation, and income gains, all within the NAFTA framework. More explicitly, broad segments of the Mexican private sector, while supporting these same demands, have voiced strong preferences for a gradualist approach to the negotiation of the FTAA (Rubio 1996: 86–88). To his credit, Mexican President Vicente Fox has repeatedly petitioned the Bush administration to consider seriously socially oriented initiatives that would render NAFTA more viable (social adjustment funds, North American infrastructure improvement, and legally sanctioned guest worker programs). If, down the line, such leadership by Mexico were to be exercised within the FTAA process, this could lend considerable credibility to that endeavor. To put this differently, since Mexico will have little choice but to accept the reality of the FTAA, it would be in its own best interest to play such a leadership role.

MERCOSUR

Like Mexico, the MERCOSUR countries have pursued subregional integration as an extension of earlier unilateral liberalization measures implemented in the context of macroeconomic stabilization programs, and as part of longer-term efforts at microeconomic restructuring. Because Argentina and Brazil represent more than 95 percent of MERCOSUR's combined GDP (approximately $859 billion), to speak of MERCOSUR is to speak of these two dominant countries. Indeed, Argentina and Brazil began their integration process even before the stabilization-related unilateral trade liberalization measures of the late 1980s, mainly with an eye toward cementing each country's recent transition to democratic rule. Since the official launching of the MERCOSUR customs union on January 1, 1995, the common external tariff (CET) now averages 17 percent, and 80 percent of internal trade covered by the agreement has been liberalized. From 1991 until Brazil's 1999 devaluation shock, trade among the four MERCOSUR members grew by some 300 percent, compared with just 60 percent during the 1980s.

Despite these advances, MERCOSUR is still riddled with numerous exceptions. Major sectors, such as automotives, have yet to be incorporated into the agreement, and the capital goods, informatics, and telecommunications sectors are still exempted from the CET. Similar to NAFTA, MERCOSUR trade has rapidly expanded in the 1990s under the impetus of intraindustry specialization and cross-border production,[11] while distributional cleavages within the MERCOSUR countries have been akin to those witnessed in Mexico. But in contrast to NAFTA, the institutional framework for dispute resolution and policy accountability in MERCOSUR is still weak. And, major differences in economic strategy between Argentina and Brazil have increasingly complicated the implementation process, as each country has continued to act out national preferences in a subregional context.

Distributional conflict in both countries has centered on the widening gap between those skilled workers and producers who have successfully positioned themselves within the globalized sectors of the economy, versus those who are still struggling to survive within an increasingly competitive domestic market. Although neither Argentine nor Brazilian policymakers have yet to articulate clearly a role for trade liberalization as part of a broader development strategy (Chudnovsky et al. 1997), those economic agents involved in the expansion of intraindustry trade and specialized production within MERCOSUR quickly came to define it for them. It is this contingent that has been most enthusiastic about accelerating the integration timeline within MERCOSUR. This, however, is where the continuities within MERCOSUR stop, as the preference for markedly different adjustment strategies has divided Argentine and Brazilian policymakers in their attempts to implement the goals that have been set for MERCOSUR.

In Argentina, where a more market-oriented approach to economic management prevailed under the decade-long convertibility program (1991–2001), domestic politics during that time converged in favor of a liberal model that promised to preserve the consumer surplus. Even when faced with double-digit unemployment levels in the wake of the 1994–1995 "tequila shock," or contagion from the Mexican crisis, voters stood by candidates that espoused a fine-tuning of the market model and a social policy that bolstered employment opportunities in that market, rather than a return to protectionism (Pastor and Wise 1999: 34-48). Such was the lesson with the October 1999 election of centrist presidential candidate Fernando de la Rúa (and such were the failures that led to his early resignation in December 2001). At the subregional level, these consumer preferences rendered Argentina the more cautious defender of MERCOSUR's commitment to a liberal trade regime.

This stance changed with the temporary return of Finance Minister Domingo Cavallo in March 2001. Making no secret of his disdain for MERCOSUR, and hard-pressed to fend off a mounting balance-of-payments crisis, Cavallo unilaterally raised tariffs on imported consumer goods and eliminated duties on those capital goods that were essential to maintain domestic production levels. Despite efforts by the subsequent economic team to repair the damage to Argentine–Brazil relations, MERCOSUR has increasingly become a shell of its former self. In recognition of this, and in its search for solutions to an apparently interminable crisis, the Argentine government has more recently proposed an acceleration of the FTAA negotiations and the reform of MERCOSUR into a free trade area without a CET, and some have even called for separate bilateral negotiations with the United States (Masi and Wise 2003). These crisis-driven proposals aside, the longer-run Argentine scenario, say from 1991–2000, was worlds apart from Brazil, where policymakers and the private sector have more consistently displayed a preference for a competitive approach to trade liberalization and regional integration, but also a willingness to resort to old protectionist remedies as entire industries have now felt the pinch from market reform.

On balance, however, and in line with its espoused commitment to multilateralism above all else, Brazil's trade strategy has conformed to GATT/WTO guidelines. Such measures have included the use of various fiscal and financial incentives to promote industrial exports and foster the expansion of integrated intraindustry production networks. Brazil's macroeconomic strategy further distinguishes it from Argentina's hands-off approach in the 1990s, in that the former has insisted on the need for a more flexible exchange rate regime and an active monetary policy (Nofal 1997: 12–17), while until the recent crisis Argentina rejected both as too interventionist. It is these marked differences in economic strategy that contributed to the wild swings in current account balance between the two countries in the 1990s, and this has further heightened tensions within MERCOSUR.

Even prior to the 40 percent devaluation of the real in January 1999, Brazil's comparatively lower levels of per capita GDP and educational achievement, and its much later start in launching market reforms had exacerbated adjustment stress (Dornbusch 1997: 20-37). As a result, voters have been ambivalent, at best, about the deepening of MERCOSUR's liberalization targets. The message thus far has been that public opinion supports Brazil's integration goals, but with the caveat that any further liberalization will be carried out gradually and under the umbrella of an active state policy (Suzigan and Villela 1997). In light of conflicting distributional demands within Brazil, and the lack of consensus between Argentina and Brazil with regard to economic strategy and the pace of liberalization, the MERCOSUR bloc, and its private sector in particular, has yet to display much more than lukewarm enthusiasm for the negotiation of an FTAA.

However, the severe crises that have plagued MERCOSUR since 1999 may render this a moot point. As a cash-strapped Argentina is now taxing all exports, and intermittently resorting to capital controls within the domestic banking system, Brazil can no longer afford the luxury of ambivalence. Faced with a resurgence of political populism and continued economic contagion from the Argentine recession and trade policy reversals, the MERCOSUR countries seem to have little choice but to hitch their star to the FTAA. In Chapter 10, Alcides Costa Vaz notes the unlikelihood that MERCOSUR "countries are willing to give up the political and economic asset it represents in the context of a large multilateral negotiation." Now, with the CET a mere myth, the value of MERCOSUR as such an asset hinges on its nesting within a larger negotiating framework. As MERCOSUR policymakers seek to revolve their worst crisis yet, the FTAA process constitutes an escape valve of sorts, an essential public good for this subregional bloc to draw on during hard times.

FTAA

At face value, the uncertainty that has enshrouded the FTAA process since its inception has stemmed from procedural disputes between the United States and its Latin trade partners over how to approach the FTAA negotiations. At a deeper level, the FTAA process has been bogged down by the same distributional strains that have worked to slow the expansion and deepening of integration initiatives at the domestic level in the countries examined here. Just as politicians and policymakers in Argentina, Brazil, Mexico, and the United States have been hard-pressed to maximize the benefits of trade integration while minimizing the political risks and adjustment costs on the home front, the potential for asymmetrical outcomes between regional groupings has posed further collective action problems. While econometric evidence points to the full multilateral liberalization of Western Hemispheric trade as the most optimal strategy for increasing widespread welfare gains, differences in size and income disparities have worked to shape short-term outcomes that are thus far suboptimal. Chile is a prime example of this trend.

As the earliest liberalizer, and the smallest of the countries analyzed here, Chile is also the most open and trade-dependent economy in this group (total exports equal about 30 percent of GDP, versus 8.8 percent for Brazil or 7.3 percent for the United States). Estimates by Hinojosa-Ojéda et al. (1997) confirm that, in the absence of a full Western Hemisphere FTA, Chile's second most attractive option would be to join NAFTA, and its third most attractive options would be to integrate more closely with the MERCOSUR group. After waiting in the NAFTA queue until it became obvious that the granting of fast-track negotiating authority would be delayed until after the 2000 U.S. presidential election, Chile suddenly found itself staring at the worst possible outcome: exclusion from NAFTA *and* MERCOSUR.

By late 1996, Chilean producers had pushed the government into negotiating a FTA with the MERCOSUR bloc as a whole, thus relegating the question of Chile's accession to NAFTA to the back burner. No matter that Chile posed none of the messy (labor and environmental) problems that arose over Mexico's entry into NAFTA, or that the country's impressive competitive gains over the past decade rendered it a viable candidate for NAFTA accession; the U.S. public's designation of free trade as the economic scapegoat of the 1990s left Chile to pursue its third-best option. Again, although the option was revived by the outgoing Clinton administration in December 2000, it would take another three years for U.S. Trade Representative Zoellick to successfully usher the U.S.–Chile FTA through the U.S. Congress. In the larger scheme of things, it took nearly a decade from the time the United States issued its original invitation to negotiate a bilateral accord, to the actual finalization of the FTA. In the interim, the numerous obstacles that were thrown up on the U.S. side left a sizeable segment of the Chilean policy community to wonder if the FTAA may, in the end, be Chile's better hope for guaranteed access to larger markets in the hemisphere.

Similar conflicts and asymmetries have divided the NAFTA and MERCOSUR blocs. In reality, due to the sheer economic weight of NAFTA ($10.5 trillion GDP) and MERCOSUR ($859 billion GDP) in the Western Hemisphere, and the dominant role that the United States and Brazil play within these blocs, the collaboration of these two main players will be essential for the successful completion of a hemispheric free trade accord. But despite robust evidence demonstrating that Brazil's strongest welfare gains lie, first, at the level of multilateral liberalization and, second, in closer integration with the U.S. economy via NAFTA or a bilateral Brazil-U.S. FTA (Erzan and Yeats 1992: 126–28), complicated collective action problems relegated Brazil to its third-best option: MERCOSUR. Up until the onset of severe Southern Cone economic stress in 2001, at least three main factors worked to convince Brazilian decision makers that, whatever the projected benefits from an accelerated minilateral liberalization timetable that includes the United States, these would still not be sufficient to outweigh the domestic political costs.

The first question concerns tariff reductions and more mutual market access between North and South. Because the average U.S. tariff on Latin American imports is just 3 percent to 4 percent, the burden of tariff reduction falls most heavily on the Latin side. Combine this with the fact that Latin American countries now buy the bulk of each other's products and this means that increased U.S. access to Latin American markets will place some Latin exporters, especially Brazil, at a competitive disadvantage in their own region. A second divisive factor is the differing priorities between the United States and Brazil. As a highly competitive service-based economy, the United States is most concerned with legal issues that reflect this status, such as government procurement and intellectual property rights. In contrast, as more closed and industrial-based economies, Brazil and the remainder of the non-NAFTA countries in the hemisphere are still concerned with sectoral issues that most often hinge on tariff reductions and increased market access.

Third, and perhaps the main reason why Brazil never lined up for possible NAFTA accession, is the reality of fundamental differences in each country's approach to political economic management. While long-standing tensions in the U.S.–Brazilian trade relationship have eased in the wake of Brazil's commercial opening, the country's continued affinities for managed trade and state-led development still symbolize a level of intervention that surpasses the tastes of most U.S. policymakers. The challenges faced by the former Cardoso administration in reconciling these conflicting policy preferences quickly surfaced in the throes of the January 1999 currency crisis, as Brazil's political opposition and local public opinion clamored for policy remedies that directly contradicted the fiscal and monetary adjustments advocated by the United States and its multilateral backers. In terms more specific to the FTAA, since the October 2002 election of left-leaning Luis Inacio Lula da Silva, Brazil's policy establishment and economic elite have more visibly split along the usual sectoral lines: producers who envision sizeable increases in sales to the U.S. market are for the FTAA, while those who will be at a serious competitive disadvantage prefer to stick with a greatly weakened MERCOSUR.

More rational voices, such as Brazilian Ambassador to Washington Rubens Barbosa, insist that the key challenge for Brazil is to revamp a trade strategy that has produced few dynamic gains in the past two decades, and to do so by launching a much deeper and comprehensive set of competitive policies (Barbosa 2001). Although the FTAA offers by far the most compelling opportunities for Brazil's enhanced competitiveness, the Lula administration has sought to simultaneously appease both sides of the domestic debate by declaring its support for a revived MERCOSUR *and* for the FTAA. This is precisely the kind of collective action challenge that the multilateral planners of the Santiago Summit had anticipated, and as such they were prescient in assigning Brazil and the United States joint responsibility for chairing the final stages of the FTAA negotiations from 2003 to 2005. Not only will this force both sides to further concede on differences that already look smaller in the wake of the shocks of 2001, but it also positions leaders from both countries to win domestic support by treating the FTAA negotiation as a two-level game. As Cameron and Tomlin (2000) note with regard to the successful completion of the NAFTA negotiations, it was the ability of policymakers and negotiators to use the threat of domestic restraints to force through compromises at the NAFTA negotiating table, and vice versa with the reference to external pressures and threats intrinsic to that same negotiating table in their quest to win support at home.

What impact will the security and economic shocks of 2001 have in shifting the FTAA calculus in ways that favor greater compromise and concrete progress on the various issues discussed in this chapter? Will current disputes between the United States and Latin America over the former's increasingly protectionist bent derail the FTAA process? In the U.S. Congress, heightened concerns over trade adjustment assistance now compete with a new array of disappointing protectionist concessions made over the past year; within the FTAA process itself, similar tensions continue over the quest to negotiate one single undertaking for all, versus longer timelines and more generous technical support for the smaller, weaker states (Table 4.1). What could tip these trade-offs into greater support for the FTAA? Theory and practice have readily shown that access to large markets and dynamic trade and investment flows are the recipe for more equitable development, and the burden is now on regional leaders to articulate more consistently supplementary policies that will reinforce the position of those weaker actors in the regional market, as well as the notion of integration as a public good for the entire hemisphere.

Conclusion

Although the watershed events of 2001 may make the completion of the FTAA more difficult in practice, in this chapter I suggest that these severe security and economic shocks have simultaneously made its completion more urgent and necessary. Mid-2002 marked the point at which the FTAA negotiations moved into the crucial area of market access. A rough draft agreement is now in circulation and, in the name of transparency, has been posted on the Internet; and, although still quite contentious, civil society's participation, including the incorporation of concerns long expressed by labor and environmental interests, is now firmly embedded in the FTAA process. Earlier doubts about the passage of the TPA bill in the United States have been laid to rest, although there is still uncertainty as to the kinds of limitations that unbridled U.S. trade-remedy laws could place on the FTAA process. However, uncertainties and all, hemispheric participants continue to regard the December 2005 deadline for completing the FTAA as a realistic and obtainable goal.

In this chapter I have argued that the ultimate completion of the FTAA is still intricately tied to two other key matters. First, at the domestic level, more must be done to ameliorate the distributional strains that have come to constitute another main bottleneck for the deepening of trade integration in the Western Hemisphere; and second, at the subregional level, politicians and economic policymakers must reconfirm that there is, indeed, a sound political economic rationale for the FTAA. The data reviewed in this chapter suggest that the rise of regionalism in the Western Hemisphere has fostered a dynamic pattern of FDI, trade creation, and welfare gains, and the evidence points to further trade and investment dynamism under the FTAA. Nevertheless, if frontline policymakers are not able to drum up the same degree of political will that underpinned the creation of NAFTA and MERCOSUR, for example, then the FTAA process may prove to be more gradual and protracted than previously expected.

Notes

Background research for this chapter was supported by the North–South Center at the University of Miami and the U.S. Institute of Peace. I am grateful to John Hipp for his assistance in compiling the database in Table 4.2, and Max Cameron, Tom O'Keefe, Scott Otteman, José Manuel Salazar, Jeff Stark, and the editors for their thoughtful comments on earlier drafts.

1. Trade figures cited throughout this chapter are from the database of the Statistics and Quantitative Analysis Unit, Inter-American Development Bank (IDB), Washington, DC.

2. The most thorough and articulate defense of the FTAA to date can be found in Salazar and Robert (2001).

3. On this point I side with Weintraub (2001).

4. On Chile, see El Mercurio (2002); on U.S.–Central American negotiations, see Becker (2003: C1).

5. To date, the five main subregional schemes in the Western Hemisphere are the North American Free Trade Agreement (NAFTA), including Canada, Mexico, and the United States, implemented on January 1, 1994; the Southern Cone Common Market (MERCOSUR), a customs union that includes Argentina, Brazil, Paraguay, Uruguay, and two associate members—Bolivia and Chile—implemented on January 1, 1995; the Andean Community, a renovated customs union from the 1960s that includes Bolivia, Ecuador, Colombia, Perú, and Venezuela; the Central American Common Market (CACM), also renovated from the 1960s; and the Caribbean Common Market (CARICOM), revived from the 1970s.

6. Database of the IDB Statistics and Quantitative Analysis Unit (see n. 1).

7. For more detail on the Chilean case, see Marcel (1997).

8. All other growth and investment figures cited in this section can be found in World Bank (2000); Inter-American Development Bank website (www.iadb.org), 2000 figures; and International Finance Corporation website (www.ifc.org/economics/data/dataset.htm), 2000 figures.

9. Mexico's social policy reforms are analyzed at length in Giugale et al. (2001).

10. See, for example, the proposals put forth by Pastor (2001).

11. By 1997, over 30 percent of Argentine exports were destined for the Brazilian market, some 45 percent of which were manufactured goods; Brazil's exports to Argentina accounted for 13 percent of its total trade that same year, 80 percent of which were manufactured goods in the same sectors that Argentina exported to Brazil.

References

Baer, Werner and William Maloney. 1997. "Neoliberalism and Income Distribution in Latin America." *World Development* 25, no. 3: 311–27.

Barbosa, Rubens. 2001. "O Impacto da ALCA sobre o MERCOSUR." *Revista Brasileira de Comércio Exterior,* no. 67 (April–June): 22–27.

Becker, Elizabeth. 2003. "U.S. Begins Talks for Trade Pact with Central Americans." *New York Times,* January 9, p. C1.

Behrman, Bere, Nancy Birdsall, and Miguel Székely. 1998. Workshop on Social Mobility. Brookings Institution, Washington, DC, June 4–5.

Bhagwati, Jagdish, and Anne O. Krueger. 1995. *The Dangerous Drift to Preferential Trade Agreements.* Washington, DC: American Enterprise Institute.

Birdsall, Nancy, and Luis Londoño. 1997. "Asset Inequality Matters." *American Economic Review* 87, no. 2: 32–38.

Cameron, Maxwell, and Brian Tomlin. 2000. *The Making of NAFTA: How the Deal Was Done.* Ithaca, NY: Cornell University Press.

Carmichael, Ted. 2001. "Economic Research Note: FTAA Tops Agenda at Summit of the Americas." *Global Data Watch,* April 13, pp. 13–14. (J.P. Morgan Securities Canada Inc., Morgan Guaranty Trust Company, New York.)

CEPAL News. 2001. "Sixth Ministerial Trade Meeting." *CEPAL News* 20, no. 4 (April): 1–3.

Chudnovsky, Daniel, Andrés Lopéz, and Fernando Porta. 1995. "New Foreign Direct Investment in Argentina." In *Foreign Direct Investment in Latin America,* edited by Manuel Agosín, 39–104. Washington, DC: Inter-American Development Bank.

Cline, William. 1997. *Trade and Income Distribution.* Washington, DC: Institute for International Economics.

DePalma, Anthony. 2000. "Latin America Is Priority on Bush Trade Agenda." *New York Times,* December 18, p. C23.

Destler, I.M. 1997. *Renewing Fast-Track Legislation* Washington, DC: Institute for International Economics.

Destler, I.M., and Peter Balint. 1998. *The New Politics of American Trade: Trade, Labor, and the Environment.* Washington, DC: Institute for International Economics.

Dornbusch, Rudiger. 1997. "Brazil's Incomplete Stabilization and Reform." *MERCOSUR Journal,* 8: 20–37.

Economic Commission on Latin America and the Caribbean (ECLAC). 1997. "Macro-economic Performance in 1997." *CEPAL News* 18: 1–3.

———. 2001a. Preliminary Overview of the Economies of Latin America and the Caribbean. Santiago: United Nations.

———. 2001b. Séries Estadísticas Económicas y Sociales. Available at: http://www.eclac.cl/estadísticas. Accessed on September 30, 2003.

El Mercurio. 2002. "Chile Sella Histórico Pacto con Estados Unidos." *El Mercurio,* December 12.

Erzan, Refik, and Alexander Yeats. 1992. "U.S.–Latin American Free Trade Areas." In *The Premise and the Promise: Free Trade in the Americas,* edited by Sylvia Saborio, 117–52. Washington, DC: Overseas Development Council.

Giugale, Marcelo M., Olivier Lafourcade, and Vinh H. Nguyen, eds. 2001. *Mexico: A Comprehensive Development Agenda for the New Era.* Washington, DC: World Bank, 2001.

Haggard, Stephan. 1998. "The Political Economy of Regionalism in the Western Hemisphere." In *The Post-NAFTA Political Economy,* edited by Carol Wise, 302–59. University Park: Pennsylvania State University Press.

Hart, Michael. 1999. "A Matter of Synergy: The Role of Regional Agreements in the Multilateral Trading Order." In *Regionalism, Multilateralism, and the Politics of Global Trade,* edited by Donald Barry and Ronald C. Keith, 25–53. Vancouver: University of British Columbia Press.

Hinojosa-Ojéda, Raúl, Jeffrey Lewis, and Sherman Robinson. 1997. *Convergence and Divergence between NAFTA, Chile, and MERCOSUR.* Integration and Regional Programs Department, Working Paper Series 219. Washington, DC: Inter-American Development Bank.

Instituto Nacional de Estadística Geografía e Informática (INEGI). 2001. Anuários Estadísticos. Mexico City: INEGI (CD-ROM).

International Monetary Fund (IMF). 2001. *International Financial Statistics Yearbook.* Washington, DC: IMF, September (CD-ROM).

JP Morgan Chase Bank. 2002. "A US Move to Restart Latin Trade Liberalization." *Global Data Watch,* December 13, p. 3.

Lawrence, Robert. 1996. *Regionalism, Multilateralism, and Deeper Integration.* Washington, DC: Brookings Institution.

Londoño, Juan Luis, and Miguel Székely. 1997. "Distributional Surprises after a Decade of Reforms: Latin America in the Nineties." Paper presented at annual meeting of Inter-American Development Bank, Barcelona, March.

Marcel, Mario. 1997. "Effectiveness of the State and Development Lessons from the Chilean Experience." In *Chile: Recent Policy Lessons and Emerging Challenges,* edited by Guillermo Perry and Danny Leipziger. Washington, DC: World Bank.

Masi, Fernando, and Carol Wise. In press. "Negotiating the FTAA between the Main Players: The U.S. and MERCOSUR." In *MERCOSUR and the Creation of the Free Trade Area of the Americas,* edited by Marcel Vaillant and Fernando Lorenzo. Washington, DC: Woodrow Wilson International Center for Scholars.

McMurrer, Daniel, and Isabel Sawhill. 1998. *Getting Ahead: Economic and Social Mobility in America.* Washington, DC: The Urban Institute.

Motta Veiga, Pedro da. 1997. "Brazil's Strategy for Trade Liberalization and Economic Integration in the Western Hemisphere." In *Integrating the Hemisphere,* edited by Ana Julia Jatar and Sidney Weintraub, 197–207. Washington, DC: Inter-American Dialogue.

Nofal, Maria Beatriz. 1997. "Why Is There Scant Progress in the Consolidation and Deepening of MERCOSUR?" *MERCOSUR Journal* 8: 12–17.

Pastor, Robert. 2001. *Toward a North American Community.* Washington, DC: Institute for International Economics.

Pastor, Manuel, and Carol Wise. 1999. "The Politics of Second Generation Reform." *Journal of Democracy* 10, no. 3: 34–48.

———. 2001. "Argentina's Dilemma: From Poster Child to Basket Case." *Foreign Affairs* 80, no. 6: 60–72.

———. 2003a. "A Long View on the Mexican Economy." In *The Mexican Economy and Politics in Transition,* edited by Joseph Tulchin and Andrew Selee, 179–213. Boulder, CO: Lynne Rienner Publishers.

———. 2003b. "Picking up the Pieces: Comparing the Social Impacts of Financial Crisis in Mexico and Argentina." Paper presented at Financial Trends in Latin America conference, sponsored by Institute for Global Conflict and Cooperation, University of California–San Diego, and Institute for International Economics, University of California–Santa Cruz, Santa Cruz, CA, April 11–12.

Rohter, Larry, and Jennifer Rich. 2001. "Brazil Takes a Trade Stance and Offers a Warning to the U.S.," *New York Times,* December 19, p. W1.

Rubio, Luís. 1996. "Mexico, NAFTA, and the Pacific Basin." In *Cooperation or Rivalry?* edited by Shoji Nishijima and Peter Smith, 76–93. Boulder, CO: Westview.

Salazar, Manuel, and Maryse Robert, eds. 2001. *Toward Free Trade in the Americas.* Washington, DC: Brookings Institution.

Schott, Jeffrey. 2001. *Prospects for a Free Trade Area of the Americas.* Washington, DC: Institute for International Economics.

Secretaría de Comercio y Fomento Industrial (SECOFI). 1996. *Mexico: Program of Industrial Policy and International Trade.* Mexico City: SECOFI, May.

Seligson, Mitchell A. 1999. "Popular Support for Regional Economic Integration in Latin America." *Journal of Latin American Studies* 31, no. 1: 129–49.

Stallings, Barbara. 1995. "The New International Context for Development." In *Global Change, Regional Response,* edited by Barbara Stallings, 349–87. New York: Cambridge University Press.

Suzigan, Wilson, and Annibal Villela. 1997. *Industrial Policy in Brazil.* Campinas, São Paulo: Universidade Estadual de Campinas.

Weintraub, Sidney. 1997. *NAFTA at Three: A Progress Report.* Washington, DC: Center for Strategic and International Studies.

———. 2001. "Hemispheric Free Trade: The Possibilities." *Foreign Affairs en Español* 1, no. 3: 61–66.

World Bank. 2000. *World Development Indicators.* CD-ROM. Washington, DC: World Bank.

———. 2001. *World Development Indicators.* CD-ROM. Washington, DC: World Bank.

5

The Proliferation of Regional Trade Agreements in the Americas: An Assessment of Key Issues

José M. Salazar-Xirinachs

Latin America has been one of the most active regions in the world in the recent proliferation of regional trade agreements (RTAs) among members of the World Trade Organization (WTO). The region has used multiple paths to trade policy reform and the enlargement of its markets, including unilateral liberalization, multilateral engagement in the WTO, and subregional and bilateral trade agreements. The region is also facing important challenges in the next stage of competitive insertion in the international economic system. Given its long experience with traditional RTAs and the reactivation of regionalism under new principles in the 1990s, Latin America is a source of important evidence and lessons, particularly for other regions such as Asia-Pacific where trade agreements are beginning to proliferate (Scollay and Gilbert 2001; Dutta 1999).

In this chapter, I provide an overview and analysis of the proliferation of RTAs in Latin America and the Caribbean, and assess the evidence from the region regarding the following key analytical and policy issues: Has trade diversion been a serious problem in the RTAs and free trade agreements (FTAs) established by Latin American and Caribbean countries? Have RTAs facilitated liberalization better than multilateral negotiations, or allowed member countries to integrate more deeply? Has proliferation in Latin America diverted attention away from multilateral negotiations? What problems have been created by overlaps between RTAs and how significant have these problems been? Have RTAs contributed to domestic policy reform and, if so, how? What has been the role of macro- and microeconomic policies in RTAs? Finally, I summarize the main conclusions and challenges posed by proliferation of RTAs in Latin America.

Proliferation and Diversity of RTAs in the Western Hemisphere[1]

As Table 5.1 shows, there has been a dramatic increase in the number of trade agreements negotiated by Latin American and Caribbean (LAC) countries in the last ten years, with countries both inside and outside the Western Hemisphere. The table classifies agreements into customs unions and FTAs.[2] There are four customs unions in the Americas: the Central American Common Market (CACM), created in 1961; the Andean Community, created in 1969; the Caribbean Community and Common Market (CARICOM), created in 1973; and the Southern Common Market (MERCOSUR), created in 1991. The first three, originally created under the old inward-looking strategy of industrialization, were significantly restructured and relaunched in the 1990s with a much lower common external tariff (CET) and new and deeper disciplines, while MERCOSUR was conceived under principles of "open regionalism" since its inception.

As regards FTAs, starting with Mexico's participation in North American Free Trade Agreement (NAFTA), created in 1994, there was an explosion in the negotiation of FTAs by LAC countries following more or less closely the NAFTA model. These so-called "new-generation" agreements go beyond liberalization of trade in goods to include liberalization of new sectors such as services and agriculture, and new areas of discipline, such as investment, competition policy, intellectual property rights, and dispute settlement mechanisms. LAC countries have negotiated twelve FTAs among themselves since 1990 and are in the process of negotiating eight more. One of the most notable developments of this trend is that since 1998 the thirty-four countries of the Western Hemisphere (with the exception of Cuba) have been formally negotiating the Free Trade Area of the Americas (FTAA).

Countries in the Western Hemisphere also have been negotiating new-generation agreements with countries outside the hemisphere. Five of these agreements were completed in the last three years: Canada–Israel, Mexico–European Union, Mexico–Israel, United States–Jordan, and Mexico–European Free Trade Association (EFTA). Another nine are under negotiation: Canada–EFTA, Canada–Singapore, Chile–European Union, Chile–South Korea, United States–Singapore, MERCOSUR–European Union, MERCOSUR–South Africa, and Mexico–Singapore.

Table 5.1 Customs Unions and Free Trade Agreements in the Western Hemisphere

	Signed	Entered into Force
Customs Unions		
CACM (Central American Common Market)	1960	1961[a]
Andean Community	1969[b]	1969
CARICOM (Caribbean Community and		
Common Market)[c]	1973	1973
MERCOSUR (Southern Cone Common Market)[d]	1991	1995
Free Trade Agreements		
NAFTA (North American Free Trade Agreement)[e]	1992	1994
Costa Rica–Mexico	1994	1995
Group of Three (Colombia, Mexico, Venezuela)	1994[f]	1995
Bolivia–Mexico	1994	1995
Canada–Chile	1996	1997
Mexico–Nicaragua	1997	1998
Central America–Dominican Republic		1998[g]
Chile–Mexico	1998[h]	1999
CARICOM–Dominican Republic		1998[i]
Central America–Chile		1999[j]
Mexico–Northern Triangle (El Salvador,		
Guatemala, Honduras)	2000	2001
Costa Rica–Canada		2001
Andean Community–MERCOSUR	In negotiation	
Central America–Panama	In negotiation	
CA-4–Canada	In negotiation	
Chile–United States	In negotiation	
Mexico–Ecuador	In negotiation	
Mexico–Panama	In negotiation	
Mexico–Peru	In negotiation	
Mexico–Trinidad and Tobago	In negotiation	
Agreements with Countries Outside		
the Hemisphere		
United States–Israel	1985	
Canada–Israel	1997	
Mexico–European Union	2000	2000
Mexico–Israel	2000	2000
United States–Vietnam	2001	
United States–Jordan	2000	2001
Mexico–EFTA	2000	2001
Canada–EFTA	In negotiation	
Canada–Singapore	In negotiation	
Chile–European Union	In negotiation	
Chile–South Korea	In negotiation	
Chile–EFTA	In negotiation	
United States–Singapore	In negotiation	
MERCOSUR–European Union	In negotiation	
MERCOSUR–South Africa	In negotiation	
Mexico–Singapore	In negotiation	

See table footnotes on facing page.

The new agreements in the Americas embody much more than trade barrier reduction at the border for goods. There is an important diversity in terms of the additional disciplines included as well as in institutional arrangements. The main distinction to be made is between customs unions, on the one hand and FTAs, on the other. As mentioned, customs unions have been progressively deepened during the 1990s by the inclusion of disciplines in services, investment, intellectual property, and technical standards. Each custom union has specific characteristics and a history, which is beyond the scope of this paper to analyze.[3]

The FTAs negotiated in the 1990s present important similarities, partly due to the fact that most of them have been modeled on the NAFTA in terms of their structure, scope, and coverage. Table 5.2 presents an overview of the main chapters and disciplines in nine of these agreements. However, even among these agreements there are important differences. For instance,

---

[a] The agreement entered into force on this date for El Salvador, Guatemala, and Nicaragua; on April 27, 1962, for Honduras; and on September 23, 1963, for Costa Rica. With the signing of the Tegucigalpa Protocol in 1991 and the Guatemala Protocol in 1996, the countries of the Central American Common Market—El Salvador, Costa Rica, Guatemala, Honduras, and Nicaragua—restructured and revitalized their regional integration efforts.

[b] With the signing of the Trujillo Protocol in 1996 and the Sucre Protocol in 1997, the five Andean countries—Bolivia, Colombia, Ecuador, Peru, and Venezuela—restructured and revitalized their regional integration efforts under the name Andean Community.

[c] The members of the Caribbean Community are Antigua and Barbuda, The Bahamas, Barbados, Belize, Dominica, Grenada, Guyana, Jamaica, St. Kitts and Nevis, St. Lucia, St. Vincent and the Grenadines, Suriname, Trinidad and Tobago, and Montserrat (an overseas territory of the United Kingdom). The Bahamas is an associate rather than a full member of the Common Market. Haiti will become the fifteenth member of CARICOM once it deposits its instruments of accession with the group's secretary general. The British Virgin Islands and the Turks and Caicos Islands count as associate members of CARICOM.

[d] Members are Argentina, Brazil, Paraguay, and Uruguay.

[e] Before signing NAFTA, Canada and the United States had concluded the Canada–U.S. Free Trade Agreement, which entered into force on January 1, 1989.

[f] Chapters III (national treatment and market access for goods), IV (automotive sector), V (Sec. A, agricultural sector), VI (rules of origin), VIII (safeguards), IX (unfair practices in international trade), XVI (state enterprises), and XVIII (intellectual property) do not apply between Colombia and Venezuela. See Article 103 (1) of the agreement.

[g] This agreement applies bilaterally between each Central American country and the Dominican Republic. In October 2001, it entered into force between El Salvador and the Dominican Republic.

[h] On September 22, 1991, Chile and Mexico had signed a free trade agreement within the framework of the Latin American Integration Association (ALADI).

[i] A protocol to implement the agreement was signed on April 28, 2000.

[j] This agreement applies bilaterally between each Central American country and Chile. The Chile–Costa Rica bilateral agreement entered into force on February 15, 2002.

Source: Updated from Salazar-Xirinachs and Robert (2001): 4.

Table 5.2 Main Chapters in NAFTA-Type Agreements

	NAFTA	Costa Rica–Mexico	Mexico–Nicaragua	Mexico–Northern Triangle	Group of Three	Bolivia–Mexico	Canada–Chile	Chile–Mexico	Central America–Dominican Republic	Central America–Chile
Objectives, general definitions[a]	x	x	x	x	x	x	x	x	x	x
National treatment, market access for goods	x	x	x	x	x[b]	x	x	x	x	x
Rules of origin	x	x	x	x	x	x	x	x	x	x
Customs procedures	x	x	x	x	x	x	x	x	x	x
Energy[c]	x	...	...	...	...	...	...	...	...	...
Agriculture, sanitary, and phytosanitary measures	x	x	x[d]	x[d]	x	x	...	x[e]	x[e]	x[e]
Standards	x	x	x	x	x	x	...	x	x	x
Government procurement[f]	x	x	x	...	x	x	...	...	x	x
Investment	x	x	x	x	x	x	x	x	x	x[g]
Cross-border trade in services	x	x	x	x	x	x	x	x	x	x
Temporary entry for business persons	x	x	x	x	x	x	x	x	x	x
Financial services[h]	x	...	x	x	x	x	...	...	...	...
Air transportation	...	...	...	...	...	...	...	x	...	x
Telecommunications	x	...	x	x	x	x	x	x	...	x
Safeguards	x	x	x	x	x	x	x	x	x	x
Competition policy	x	...	...	...	x	...	x	...	x	x
Unfair trade practices/anti-dumping and countervailing duty matters[i]	...	x	x	x	x	x	x[j]	...	x	x
Review and dispute settlement in anti-dumping and countervailing duty matters	x	...	...	...	...	...	...	...	x	...

Intellectual property	X	X	X	X	X	X	···
Publications, notification, and administration of laws	···	X	X	X	X	X	X
Administration of the agreement[k]	X	X	X	X	···	X	X
Dispute settlement	X	X	X	X	···	X	X
Exceptions	X	X	X	X	X	X	X
Final provisions	X	X	X	X	X	X	X

[a] Most agreements also include a preamble.

[b] There is a chapter on automobiles in this agreement.

[c] Energy is covered under market access in most free trade agreements.

[d] Agriculture and sanitary and phytosanitary measures are in two separate chapters.

[e] The chapter covers sanitary and phytosanitary measures. Agriculture is covered under market access.

[f] Eighteen months after the entry into force of the Mexico–Northern Triangle free trade agreement, parties must start negotiating an agreement on government procurement. In the case of the Chile–Mexico, parties must do so one year after the agreement becomes effective.

[g] The investment rules are those of the bilateral investment treaties signed by each Central American country with Chile. Article 10.02 states that parties may at any time decide—but must within two years of the entry into force of the agreement analyze the possibility—to broaden coverage of these rules.

[h] Chile and Mexico agreed to start negotiations on financial services no later than June 30, 1999.

[i] Chile and Mexico agreed to start negotiations on the elimination of anti-dumping one year after the entry into force of their free trade agreement.

[j] Parties exempt each other from the application of anti-dumping duties when a tariff on a good reaches zero or on January 1, 2003, whichever comes first.

[k] The issue of the administration of the agreement is addressed in the section on dispute settlement in NAFTA and in the Canada–Chile Free Trade Agreement.

Source: Robert (2001).

only some of them include significant issues in financial services, government procurement, competition policy, and air transport. While most included the telecommunication sector, this is not the case in the Costa Rica–Mexico and Central America–Dominican Republic agreements.

FTAs in LAC have also been a fertile ground for experimentation both in traditional issues and in linking trade and non-trade objectives. For instance, the Canada–Chile agreement eliminates the use of antidumping among the parties. Several agreements have moved beyond the General Agreement on Tariffs on Trade (GATT)/WTO into such areas as environment and labor standards. NAFTA contains two side agreements on labor and environmental cooperation that envisage the possibility of trade sanctions. The Canada–Chile FTA also includes side agreements in these areas, but eliminates the possibility of trade sanctions and instead introduces a system of monetary fines in case of violations. The Canada–Costa Rica FTA also includes side agreements but does not include sanctions nor monetary fines, only transparency and a series of institutional instances for cooperative actions.

MERCOSUR incorporates a "democratic clause" that has at least once been used quite successfully to exercise pressure on Paraguay when the constitutional order was about to be permanently broken in that country. There are ongoing discussions in the context of the Summit of the Americas process as to how to strengthen the democratic provisions in the inter-American system, including a possible cross-reference to the FTAA.

Why Have RTAs Proliferated in Latin America?

As Ethier (1998: 1149) has pointed out, there is a notable absence of research on the fundamental question of why the new regionalism has emerged.[4] As a practical matter, a wide range of considerations enter into a country's decision to negotiate an RTA. In LAC countries, as in other countries around the world, objectives include market access; investment attraction; strengthening domestic policy reform and positive signaling to investors; increased bargaining power vis-à-vis third countries (a particularly strong motivation in the case of MERCOSUR); political, security or strategic linkage objectives (an important motivation from the U.S. perspective in the negotiation of the FTAA); and the actual or potential use of regional agreements for tactical purposes by countries seeking to achieve multilateral objectives.

A brief historical review helps to clarify the specificities, significance, and nature of modern regionalism for Latin America. The idea of integration has deep roots in the region's political, economic, and intellectual culture. Dreams and projects of economic and political integration have been a constant in Latin American history since colonial times. In fact, right at the birth of the new Latin American republics and their independence from Spain and Portugal in the early 1800s, Andean region independence leader Simon Bolívar had the most ambitious of these dreams: to create a pan-American union based on democracy and the rule of law. Even though Bolivar saw his dream collapse during his own lifetime by the assertion of local interests and nationalistic forces, ideas of political integration and common destiny continue to appeal to Latin Americans and to reappear intermittently in different contexts up to the present. A tradition of political thinking favorable to integration interacts in complex ways within the new regionalism in Latin America; however, today there are more basic economic and strategic rationales guiding the process.[5]

Perhaps the most fundamental reason for the new regionalism in Latin America is that it is consistent with and helps to consolidate market-oriented policy reforms and participation in the world economy. Again, placing the policy reform process in historical perspective is helpful. During the nineteenth century, Latin America developed strong economic links with Europe and the United States based mostly on the export of primary commodities in agriculture and mining. National infrastructure systems were built to serve the needs of this export trade, which meant railways and roads from major cities to ports, and little physical integration among countries in the region.

During the first half of the twentieth century, the medium-sized Latin American countries began experiencing a significant degree of industrialization. After World War II Latin American governments adopted a more proactive development approach and set out to pursue policies of industrialization behind high tariffs, inspired by faith in the ability of government policies to secure growth and improve social welfare conditions. Economic and physical integration was seen as an essential ingredient of this strategy in order to expand the limited size of national markets, and this led to the creation of the CACM, CARICOM, and Andean Community in the 1960s and early 1970s.

The pursuit of industrialization and economic integration policies was provided a strong rationale by a number of young economists led by Raúl Prebisch and linked to the U.N. Economic Commission for Latin America and the Caribbean (ECLAC).[6] During the three decades following its creation in 1948, ECLAC provided conceptual and institutional support to the growing consensus in Latin America about the importance of industrialization and economic integration. Latin America entered the postwar era with great optimism. Foreign direct investment in import substitution and basic industries was assigned, and in fact played a major role, as a source of growth for most Latin American economies during this period.

However, after the first oil shock of 1973 the development model followed by Latin America became increasingly unsustainable. Growth dynamics came up against the limited size of domestic markets, a growing percentage of capital accumulation was financed with foreign borrowing, the state enterprise sector grew disproportionately, and a maze of distortions and regulations stifled private enterprise.

The 1982 debt crisis and its impacts, as well as the contrast with the policies and performance by East Asian economies, played an important role in reshaping policy views in Latin America. As the 1980s unfolded, country after country, often under pressure from international financial institutions, but also actively led by a new generation of local political leaders, adopted a new vision of economic policy based on market forces, international competition, and a more limited role for the state in economic affairs.[7]

In the 1990s, the reform process intensified and generalized. On the trade front, most countries not only deepened their unilateral liberalization measures, but also engaged in a three-tiered trade strategy. Those that were not already members joined the GATT/WTO and participated actively in the Uruguay Round (1986–1994). They revitalized subregional agreements under new principles and also proactively engaged in bilateral free trade agreements.

The shift by the United States toward regionalism and the initiative by Mexico to join the United States and Canada in NAFTA posed a major challenge to Latin American countries. The rationale for traditional style integration envisaged benefits for countries at similar levels of development, but high costs for the relatively less developed partners when they joined with larger, more competitive economies. Mexico's move turned this view on its head. A new cost-benefit logic of linking up with the largest and most competitive markets in the world emerged. In fact, one of the defining characteristics of the new regionalism is that it typically involves small countries linking up with larger countries (Ethier 1998).

Unilateral liberalization and successive rounds of multilateral tariff reduction have substantially lowered global and regional tariffs; however, the proliferation of RTAs in Latin America suggests that they are perceived to offer important additional advantages. What are these advantages? The new logic for regionalism in Latin America is based on a number of interrelated factors.

First and foremost, it is related to the new global production paradigm wherein reduced transport and communications costs have made global co-ordination possible for multinational companies, and has opened new opportunities for comparative advantage for developing countries. As Ethier (1998), Lawrence (1997), and others have argued, the instrumental role of the new regional integration is dramatically different from that of the old schemes. Agreement design and rules are more focused on being functional for attracting investment, rather than on the traditional export expansion motive. They also focus on reforming domestic regulations and rules with a view to facilitate the participation of the subregion in the global organization of production and to facilitate regionwide sourcing.[8] From this perspective, RTAs are means by which countries, particularly small countries, try to develop a competitive edge over others to attract foreign direct investment. One of Mexico's objectives for joining NAFTA and also becoming the hub of a complex network of bilateral agreements can be understood in terms of this investment logic. A very similar path of negotiating numerous bilateral agreements has been followed by Chile and can be explained in the same terms.

In some respects, the motivations of smaller economies and larger emerging markets differ. Several smaller economies tend to give priority to signaling and ensuring continuing market access with the objective of becoming export and service platforms for larger markets. For instance, Costa Rica was a pioneer in Central America and the Caribbean in negotiating with Mexico (1995), and then with Chile (2000) and Canada (2001), as well as having a proactive role in the FTAA negotiations. At the same time, the country has had an aggressive investment attraction strategy. These and other fundamental factors of the investment climate explain its recent success in attracting major world-class investments from high-technology companies.[9] In large emerging markets, such as MERCOSUR, the interest of investors is not mainly production for export, but the benefits and competitive advantages of domestic presence to increase market share. Thus, for different reasons large regional blocs allow member countries to better attract international investment.

The investment-driven logic of the new regionalism also helps to understand why the recent vintage of RTAs contemplate new disciplines and

deeper integration in aspects such as investment, services, product and production process standards, competition policy, and other disciplines. Agreement design takes into account the need to facilitate the development of
regional production systems and international outsourcing. This is one of
the reasons why Latin American and Caribbean countries have been deepening arrangements such as the CACM, CARICOM, Andean Community,
and MERCOSUR, and why new bilateral agreements include disciplines in
all these areas.

The new regionalism, however, is based on political and strategic rationales as much as economic. How this applies depends on the precise
grouping of countries. The key original rationale for MERCOSUR was the
diffusion of long-standing tensions between Argentina and Brazil and the
fostering of better relations between the two countries. MERCOSUR is also
based on much more than a desire to liberalize trade. It is part of a vision to
enhance the international political roles of its members, Brazil in particular, both within the Western Hemisphere and as global players.[10] In Central
America, some intellectuals and political leaders have tried to steer the
process beyond economic integration and toward a more political project.
Although this project has not yet been successful, it is one reason why the
region has evolved to have a relatively heavy framework of integrative
institutions, including a parliament and a Central American court of justice.

The efforts to create a FTAA have strong political, strategic, and security dimensions. From the beginning, the FTAA was conceived as part of a
broader effort of rapprochement and interdependence within the context of
the Summit of the Americas process. This new agenda of hemispheric cooperation addresses a range of issues from the protection of democracy and
human rights to the fight against corruption and drug trafficking, and from
the development of hemispheric infrastructure to the promotion of sustainable development and labor issues. Future FTAA members are already parties to the set of principles, rules, and legal and diplomatic instruments of
the inter-American system and the Organization of American States.[11] It is
likely that one of the effects of the tragic events of September 11, 2001 will
be to strengthen the link between geopolitical and security considerations
and the prosperity components of the Summit of the Americas agenda, particularly trade policy.

In short, the proliferation of bilateral and regional trade agreements in
Latin America, and their diversity in terms of coverage and institutional
arrangements, are the result of a complex interaction of economic, political, and security objectives. First, this proliferation is grounded in the de-

cisive shift in development and trade policy towards outward-oriented, market-friendly policies, where integration into larger markets and foreign direct investment are seen as the keys to higher growth. Second, in terms of sequencing, the typical pattern has been for countries to engage first in unilateral liberalization and in joining the GATT/WTO as part of the process of economic reform. Unilateral liberalization was subsequently taken further in the direction of deeper integration with the neighboring countries. From this perspective as Ethier (1998) has argued, national liberalization (both unilateral and that generated by the multilateral system) has promoted the revitalization of regionalism in Latin America. Bilateral agreements and RTAs have also induced additional liberalization.

Third, the fact that national competitive strategies are based to a great extent on the attraction of foreign direct investment provides a new logic to subregional integration efforts and to the role of trade agreements in the global repositioning of countries. In a number of smaller economies in LAC, a strong motivation to engage in bilateral and other RTAs, particularly with larger and relatively more developed countries, has been to develop a competitive edge in attracting investment. Finally, there are also important political and strategic rationales for the LAC countries' engagement in RTAs that depend on the specific groupings and level of aggregation of countries.

Analytical and Policy Issues Raised by Proliferation

The proliferation of RTAs raises numerous analytical and policy issues. This section reviews some of the existing evidence from LAC as regards the following key questions:

- Has trade diversion been a serious problem in the RTAs and FTAs established by Latin American and Caribbean countries?
- Have RTAs been more successful than multilateral negotiations at promoting liberalization, or allowed member countries to integrate more deeply?
- Has the proliferation of RTAs in Latin America diverted attention away from multilateral negotiations?
- What problems have been created by overlaps between RTAs and how significant these problems have been?
- Have RTAs contributed to domestic policy reform and, if so, how?
- What has been the role of macro- and micro-economic policies in RTAs?
- Finally, how can proliferation be harnessed and oriented in order to maximize its role as a building block for a more open trading system?

Table 5.3 Rates of Growth for Intraregional and Extraregional Imports: Western Hemisphere, Latin America, and Subregions, 1990–1999

	Western Hemisphere		Latin America and Caribbean		Andean Community		CARICOM[a]	
	Extra	Intra	Extra	Intra	Extra	Intra	Extra	Intra
Average growth rate, 1990–1999 (%)	7.0	10.1	11.2	11.6	7.6	14.9	8.0	10.4
Total imports, 1990/1999[a] (US$ millions)	442,285/810,801	301,864/720,001	95,346/248,297	16,424/44,173	16,139/31,081	1,176/4,095	5,056/8,647	469/937

	CACM		MERCOSUR		NAFTA	
	Extra	Intra	Extra	Intra	Extra	Intra
Average growth rate, 1990–1999 (%)	11.5	15.7	11.1	15.4	6.8	10.8
Total imports (US$ millions)	5,897/15,674	641/2,374	25,053/64,383	424/15,418	449,865/810,449	227,104/569,945

[a] For CARICOM, the time period is 1990 to 1997.

Has Trade Diversion Been a Problem in Latin America?

A comparison of the magnitude of trade flows in the main RTAs in Latin America in the 1990s provides a rough assessment of the issue of trade diversion and creation. Of course, raw data are of limited value because the impact on trade flows of other concurrent shocks and economic changes are not accounted for. But the raw data are revealing of some important trends.

Table 5.3 presents the absolute numbers and growth rates of intraregional imports and extraregional imports for the period 1990 to 1999, for the Western Hemisphere as a whole, for LAC as a group, and for the five main RTAs: the Andean Community, MERCOSUR, CACM, CARICOM, and NAFTA. The typical behavior observed in this period is an impressive expansion in trade both within these groups and in imports from the rest of the world. This expansion provides no evidence of trade diversion, but it also suggests that if any trade diversion does exist, these largely static costs are exceeded by dynamic gains from trade. Extraregional imports in all cases increased by more than 7 percent annually in the Andean Community and CARICOM and by more than 11 percent annually in the case of the CACM and MER-COSUR during the 1990s, and typically included much higher trade volumes than intraregional flows. Evidence emerging from studies of the various subregions is reviewed below.

MERCOSUR. A 1997 study of MERCOSUR by Yeats attracted a great deal of attention. The study concluded that MERCOSUR had resulted in a significant amount of trade diversion and that much of the increase in trade between MERCOSUR countries was in the "wrong" products, that is, in capital-intensive products. Several researchers questioned these results. A paper by Nagarajan (1998) observes that in focusing on exports, Yeats's analysis failed to capture the importance of growing imports from non-member countries. Using the same index of regional orientation, but adapted to imports, Nagarajan finds that only in a few products does there seem to be trade diversion, and that even for these products there has been an impressive increase in extraregional imports. Given the upper-middle income ranking of MERCOSUR countries, the notion that MERCOSUR countries should be exporting labor-intensive products, rather than the mix of capital-intensive products found in reality, is also questioned. Nagarajan notes that from 1988 to 1996, European Union exports to Argentina and Brazil grew by annual average rates of 19 percent and 17 percent, respectively, suggesting that the formation of MERCOSUR does not seem to have seriously constrained European Union exports to the region.

A more recent study by Estevadeordal et al. (2000) also finds no evidence of trade diversion and argues that MERCOSUR is not just a traditional RTA but a case of "new regionalism," where preferential liberalization is accompanied by aggressive unilateral trade reform by its members, leading to trade expansion and improved welfare for both members and nonmembers.

Thus, there is no clear evidence of trade diversion in MERCOSUR, and even considering the few sectors in which trade diversion has occurred, the increasing multilateral openness of MERCOSUR coupled with dynamic effects greatly outweigh any static welfare losses. It could be argued, however, that it is inappropriate to pass definite judgment on MERCOSUR, or on other agreements in Latin America, as the newer agreements have data for only a few years and are still evolving toward freer trade.

Andean Community. Fewer studies are available in the case of the Andean Community. Rodriguez Mendoza (1999) applies some simple tests to both the Andean Community and MERCOSUR and concludes that far from suffering as a consequence of these two RTAs, the outside world has continued to enjoy increased market access to both regional blocs. This study also analyzes the issue of how the formation of the Andean Community and MERCOSUR affected the level of tariffs against non-member countries. It shows that the average level of the CET of both MERCOSUR and the Andean Community in 1998 was lower than the average level of the tariff schedules of each member country in the year preceding the implementation of the agreements. Echevarría (1998) focuses on trade between Colombia and Venezuela, which comprise 70 percent of intra-Andean trade, and finds that trade creation exceeded diversion.

NAFTA. A recent survey of studies on NAFTA by Burfisher et al. (2001) shows that virtually all studies on NAFTA show trade creation greatly exceeding trade diversion. Krueger (1999a) examined data at the three-digit SITC level, and finds few sectors in which imports of any NAFTA country from the rest of the world fell while rising within NAFTA. She concludes that "changes in trade flows to date do not give much support to the view that NAFTA might be seriously trade diverting" (Krueger 1999: 3).

While this may be true on aggregate, this is not to say that NAFTA did not have impacts on trade and investment flows with nonmembers in specific sectors. For instance, the potential growth of investment and exports in the textile and apparel sector in Central American and Caribbean countries was negatively affected by NAFTA. As Table 5.4 shows, after a period

*Table 5.4 Market Share of Apparel Imports to the United States:
Selected Countries*

	1990	1991	1992	1993	1994	1995	1996	1997	1998	1999
Costa Rica	2.1	2.6	2.9	3.2	3.2	3.2	2.8	2.7	2.4	2.5
El Salvador	0.5	0.6	0.8	1.3	1.9	2.6	3.0	3.8	3.7	4.3
Honduras	0.7	1.2	1.7	2.0	2.5	3.6	5.5	6.4	6.2	6.7
Guatemala	1.1	1.6	1.8	2.1	1.9	2.0	2.1	2.1	2.2	2.2
Nicaragua	0.0	0.0	0.0	0.0	0.1	0.2	0.4	0.4	0.4	0.5
Dominican Republic	4.2	5.1	5.9	6.5	6.5	6.8	6.8	7.0	6.5	6.1
Mexico	2.9	3.5	3.8	4.3	5.7	8.4	11.4	13.7	15.4	16.4

Source: Gitli and Arce (2000), based on data from the U.S. Department of Commerce.

of rapid growth in market share in the United States, in the early 1990s this market share stabilized or diminished in some cases for Central American and Caribbean countries, while Mexico's market share increased drastically. In this area, "NAFTA parity" with Mexico was extended throughout the Caribbean Basin with the approval and enactment of the Caribbean Basin Trade Partnership Act of 2000.[12]

Have the RTAs Liberalized Faster or Deeper?

Does the evidence from LAC support the argument that regional agreements have a capacity to liberalize beyond what can be accomplished multilaterally and to achieve "deep" integration?

As regards trade in goods, one of the characteristics of most of the new RTAs in Latin American and the Caribbean is that, following in many respects the NAFTA model, they contain tariff phase-out programs based on preprogrammed schedules at the outset, which are relatively quick, automatic, and nearly universal. This contrasts quite sharply with the laborious step-by-step development of positive lists that characterized most of the old style trade agreements in the region. In most agreements, the base rate for the liberalization program coincides with the most-favored-nation applied rates (Devlin and Estevadeordal 2001). It is estimated that more than 80 percent of all trade conducted in the hemisphere is now conducted under the framework of one liberalizing agreement or another (Mackay et al. 2001). Two recent studies show that most programs among LAC countries will eliminate tariffs for almost all products by 2006 and that most of the bilateral trade in these agreements becomes fully liberalized, in terms of tariffs, within a ten-year period (Devlin and Estevadeordal 2001; Rodriguez Gigena 2000).

These studies also show that the list of exceptions has been significantly reduced and at present represents between 5 percent and 10 percent of bilateral trade. In the case of MERCOSUR, the main exceptions to the liberalization schedule are automotives and sugar, which are covered under special regimes. In Central America, the list of exceptions has been reduced to three products (roasted coffee, alcoholic beverages, and petroleum products). In the Andean Community, trade has been totally liberalized among Bolivia, Colombia, Ecuador, and Venezuela, and since 1997 Peru joined the FTA under a tariff reduction schedule that would lead to free trade in goods by 2005.

Thus, the RTAs in LAC have indeed shown a capacity for faster liberalization than that at the multilateral level, and to include nearly universal coverage of trade liberalization in industrial goods. However, there are some areas of weakness in the market access picture under the new RTAs. First, they have also introduced selective procedures and discretionary application of rules of origin. Second, nearly all agreements fail to adequately cover the agricultural sector. Exceptions for agriculture reflect the particular sensitivities of each participating country.

"Deep integration" and positive rule making behind the border is a central defining feature of the new regionalism in LAC. Deep integration involves aspects such as investment, services, product and production process standards, and mutual recognition issues. There is very scarce empirical research in Latin America on these questions. Stephenson (2001b) examines what has been done by members of regional trading arrangements in the Western Hemisphere to promote firmer commitments to domestic regulation and recognition agreements in the area of trade in services. The author compares the disciplines on domestic regulation contained in four subregional agreements in the Western Hemisphere—NAFTA, the Andean Community, MERCOSUR, and CARICOM—to those contained in the General Agreement on Trade and Services (GATS) Article VI on domestic regulation, and a similar comparison is done in the area of recognition of qualifications for foreign service providers with GATS Article VII.

Stephenson's (2001b) hypothesis is that because members at the regional level have similar preferences and face fewer costs when designing more detailed common rules on services trade than in the multilateral context, then one might expect to find more detailed commitments to nondiscriminatory regulatory measures affecting trade at the subregional level. With respect to domestic regulation, the analysis provides mixed results in the sense that while some RTAs adopt principles that have a higher degree of generality than those of the GATS, other RTAs, most notably NAFTA and MERCOSUR, apply more stringent disciplines than GATS. With respect to recognition agreements, the analysis shows that the subregional integration schemes examined go beyond GATS.

These conclusions, however, relate to the nature of the disciplines or standards contained in the agreements, not to the actual progress in changing national legislation or enforcement. It can be argued that it is too early to assess the impact of standards on services in the RTAs in Latin America because the new commitments and disciplines in these areas entered into force only very recently.

As explained above, FTAs in LAC have also been fertile ground for experimentation both in traditional disciplines and in linking trade and non-trade objectives. For instance, the Canada–Chile agreement substitutes safeguards for antidumping measures. In doing so, the agreement seeks to reduce the onerous economic costs associated with the use of antidumping as a policy instrument to address the market disruptions resulting from sudden import surges. Such costs result not only from the decline in imports that follows the imposition of antidumping duties, but also from the threat that antidumping investigations pose to exporters (Messerlin 1989; Prusa 1999; Finger 1993). Safeguards are generally considered to be a less costly import relief mechanism than antidumping duties, because they "force" governments to address the domestic factors that may be hindering the competitiveness of the industry affected by increased quantities of imported goods, rather than simply assigning the blame for an industry's hardships to the exporters from another country (Tavares et al. 2001). Institutional experiments such as these might, over time, percolate through to multilateral trade negotiations, shifting the focus of the WTO agenda toward more cost-efficient mechanisms.

Trade negotiations in the Americas support the view that RTAs play a role in expanding the liberal trade order by allowing a smaller group of countries to reach agreement on a larger number of issues. The FTAA negotiations include three areas that are not fully integrated in multilateral negotiations: investment, competition policy, and government procurement. Treatment of these issues in the FTAA might provide important lessons as to how these issues might play out in the new WTO round.[13]

Has Attention Been Diverted Away from Multilateral Negotiations?

Is there evidence in LAC countries for the argument that their proactive pursuit of regionalism in the 1990s has been to the detriment of their commitment or attention to multilateral negotiations? There seems to be no evidence of this. In fact, the opposite seems to be the case. One piece of evidence is related to the increased participation of LAC countries in the GATS after the Uruguay Round. Twenty LAC countries participated and made specific commitments in the Agreement on Basic Telecommunications, and all of these but Brazil also committed to adopt in whole or in part the Reference Paper on Pro-Competitive Regulatory Principles (Stephenson 2001a).

Similarly, seventeen LAC countries submitted improved schedules in the Financial Services Agreement that entered into force in January 1999. LAC countries also made numerous submissions on services and other issues during the months preceding the Seattle WTO ministerial meeting. They have also been quite engaged in both the services and agricultural negotiations since early 2000. From February 2000 to July 2002, LAC countries have made twelve of a total forty-five proposals in the agricultural negotiations. In the services negotiations, they have presented sixteen of a total 110 proposals. This is a good track record of participation considering that the number of proposals presented by other key countries: European Union, 16; Canada, 15; United States, 15; Australia, 11; Switzerland, 11; Korea, 7; New Zealand, 5; and Japan, 3. Finally, most LAC countries supported the launching of a new multilateral round in Doha.

Renewed doubts about a potential "distraction effect" have been raised in relation to the negotiations to create an FTAA. As a practical matter, concurrent WTO and FTAA negotiations can easily stretch the resources of even the largest countries. It is easy for governments of small economies, with limited state budgets and bureaucracies, to reach a level of "negotiation fatigue" or "overload." However, it can be argued that rather than diverting attention and energy from the new round, regional negotiations by LAC countries, particularly the FTAA negotiations, have generated important positive externalities and learning effects that benefit engagement in the multilateral system. Moreover, there is a positive angle to concurrent FTAA and WTO negotiations.

First, as an established practice, many bilateral and subregional meetings are organized on the margins of the FTAA meetings not only for consultations on the subject matter of the meeting itself, but for other bilateral consultations and negotiations. Consultations on a WTO round could also be organized on the margins of FTAA meetings. For small economies, this might be a cost-effective system for gathering information, pooling resources, and developing their own positions.

Second, there is substantial overlap of issues between the WTO and the FTAA talks, which supports complex interaction in substantive issues. This means that the FTAA exercise generates significant preparatory work, including comprehensive hemispheric databases and inventories of national legislation, as well as progress in understanding and negotiating substantive issues, that can also be used effectively in other negotiations.

Third, the FTAA has also generated a significant amount of additional trade-related technical assistance from a variety of sources. Several international and hemispheric organizations have increased their trade-related technical assistance activities, and the same is true of bilateral aid agencies. But perhaps the most important element is that, as Weintraub (1999: 5) learned in a series of interviews, "[P]articipation in the FTAA negotiation process itself has been the most valuable teacher." For a number of countries this is the first opportunity they have had to participate in the negotiation of a modern, state-of-the-art free trade agreement. Because of these "learning-by-negotiating effects," and because of the increased technical assistance it has generated, the FTAA has already strengthened and will continue to strengthen the readiness of countries in this hemisphere to negotiate in the new round.

Finally, an additional positive externality of the FTAA for the WTO is the fact that it has helped to focus attention and generate additional pressure toward timely implementation of WTO commitments. For many countries in the hemisphere, the Uruguay Round commitments constitute the first set of demanding external trade obligations in their history. In many areas, implementation is about creating infrastructure and institutional capacities. As a result of the FTAA experience and the associated technical assistance efforts, many countries will be better placed to implement their existing obligations. Participation in the FTAA also increases a sense of ownership of the rules that is important for effective implementation.

Overlapping Agreements and Spaghetti Bowls

What problems have been created by overlaps among RTAs? How significant have these problems been? To what extent has there been a "spaghetti bowl" problem in Latin America "with a multitude of tariffs and quotas applying to particular products, all depending on administratively defined and inherently arbitrary definitions of the product's 'nationality'" (Bhag-wati 1997)? This section focuses on two areas: rules of origin and dispute resolution.

Rules of Origin

Preferential rules of origin are the sine qua non of RTAs that do not involve the harmonization of tariffs among their members. Rules of origin ensure that non-member countries do not unduly benefit from the preferential treatment that members of a RTA grant to one another. In the absence of rules of origin, non-member countries could act as free riders by simply deflect-ing trade, that is, exporting a particular product to the member of the RTA with the lowest tariff and subsequently selling the product throughout the RTA without facing the trade restrictions that would otherwise apply to them in accessing these markets. Accordingly, the larger the tariff differential between members of a RTA, the greater the incentives that non-member countries have to deflect trade, and therefore the higher the degree of re-strictiveness of the RTA's rules of origin. In contrast, whenever the tariff differential among members of a RTA is small, rules of origin will tend to be less stringent or even nonexistent.

Besides being tools to avoid free riding, rules of origin are also potent instruments to protect domestic producers from import competition and to attract foreign direct investment. Krishna and Krueger (1995) have shown how the existence of rules of origin could afford protection to suppliers of intermediate goods located within a RTA, as producers faced with restric-tive rules of origin and the prospect of benefiting from preferential tariffs turn away from low-cost foreign suppliers of intermediate inputs and toward high-cost suppliers located within the RTA. At the same time, a restrictive origin scheme might provide foreign suppliers of intermediate goods with an incentive to relocate their production facilities to the lower-cost country participating in a RTA, even though the new location might result in higher production costs.

Protection afforded to domestic producers by rules of origin will usually come at a high cost, however. For one, the operation and administration of origin schemes requires significant resources, especially in light of the growing internationalization of production, which is making it increasingly difficult for customs authorities to determine the "nationality" of a good. Likewise, producers will face higher costs as a result of seeking to comply with rules of origin. More importantly, certain rules of origin can cause trade and investment diversion and may, under certain circumstances, introduce monopoly or monopsony (James 1997).

From a theoretical perspective, then, two opposing forces, both driven by the progressive decline of most-favored-nation tariffs in the context of unilateral trade liberalization and successive rounds of multilateral trade negotiations, will determine the significance of rules of origin in the future. On the one hand, lower and more homogeneous tariffs among members of an RTA will erode the scope for trade deflection and therefore, the significance of origin schemes as mechanisms to prevent free riders from enjoying the benefits derived from membership in an RTA. On the other hand, lower tariffs are likely to lead to increased calls for protection, which in turn might foster the formulation of increasingly complex and protective origin schemes, usually based on a value-added approach.[14] Depending on which of these two forces predominates, rules of origin might well accelerate the transformation of the world trading system into a spaghetti bowl. "The systemic effect is to generate a world of preferences with all its well-known consequences, which increases transactions costs and facilitates protectionism" (Bhagwati et al. 1998: 1139).

Empirical evidence on the specific impact of rules of origin in LAC, while scarce and inconclusive, points to the use of rules of origin in the hemisphere not only as tools to prevent trade deflection, but also as protectionist instruments that allow countries to pursue certain strategic objectives. In a recent attempt to explain the structure of NAFTA's origin scheme, for example, Estevadeordal (1999) found that sectors with more restrictive rules of origin were also those with longer phase-out periods for tariff liberalization. This result suggests that NAFTA's rules of origin are primarily used as policy instruments to afford protection. With respect to origin schemes in the rest of the hemisphere, Garay and Cornejo (1999: 277) have pointed out that a majority of free trade areas "have not tended to use rules of origin to compensate for the differences in member countries' national tariffs vis-à-vis third countries in order to prevent trade deflection; instead their design appears to have been more in response to different strategic goals."

Anecdotal evidence also exists on the effects of rules of origin, particularly on investment patterns. Moran (1998), for example, notes that many of the domestic-content rules in NAFTA successfully diverted investment to North America. As specific examples, Moran cites the cases of AT&T, Fujitsu, and Ericsson in the field of telecommunications equipment, and

Hitachi, Mitsubishi, Zenith, Sony, and Samsung in the area of consumer electronics as examples of companies that shifted part of their investments from Asia to North America after NAFTA went into effect.

A central, open question in the debate about the impact of rules of origin on multilateral trade liberalization is the possible role of expanded regional trade agreements in reducing the spaghetti-bowl effect of different origin schemes embedded in RTAs. The negotiations toward an FTAA open the possibility for designing a new institutional structure that reduces the costs associated with the web of rules of origin existing in the hemisphere. The construction of such an institutional structure, however, will have to overcome numerous hurdles, notably the large differences existing among the origin schemes in force in the hemisphere. Perhaps a first step in the direction of a new structure on rules of origin in the context of the FTAA could consist of agreeing on a set of principles aimed at enhancing the transparency and predictability of hemispheric origin regimes. For example, countries could agree to minimize the number of criteria for determining origin, or develop specific disciplines to make the process of origin certification more transparent. Such measures could be complemented by voluntary efforts on the part of members of an RTA to move toward more homogenous tariff structures vis-à-vis third countries, thus reducing the incentives for trade deflection. Rules of origin have the potential to turn world trade into a spaghetti bowl. At the same time, however, they are intrinsic parts of a majority of RTAs and as such, they are here to stay. The relevant question, therefore, is how to minimize their trade- and investment-distorting effects. The current FTAA negotiations offer a unique opportunity to find innovative answers to this question.

Dispute Resolution

In the area of dispute resolution, the proliferation of bilateral and subregional agreements poses serious potential risks to judicial cohesion and judicial economy in the resolution of trade disputes. This is especially so when similar substantive provisions are replicated in the several agreements as in NAFTA and NAFTA-like agreements. The issue can best be illustrated with a hypothetical example. Assume that country A has bilateral trade agreements with countries B and C. Countries B and C claim that country A is violating an obligation under each respective agreement, which reads the same in both, as a result of the same measure by country A. Each agreement contains dispute settlement provisions to deal with disputes that arise under that agreement. Each agreement is discrete, as is its dispute settlement mechanism. Under most systems, the decision to pursue recourse to a neutral body to resolve a legal dispute lies with the complainant who chooses the defendant and defines the scope of the legal inquiry. Assume that countries B and C both decide to seek the establishment of a panel, which is provided under their respective agreements. Already there is a loss of judicial economy, as lawyers would call it, or efficiency, as economists might label it, since overlapping agreements have generated two separate processes with ensuing costs for all concerned because not everyone involved in the dispute is together to resolve it.

This situation might be exacerbated if it is assumed that the panel in the A–B dispute concludes that there is a violation and that the panel in the A–C dispute concludes there is not. This would be a worst-case scenario of lack of judicial cohesion. Honest jurists, however, certainly may disagree. This hypothetical situation is not altogether implausible, since some agreements provide for rosters composed exclusively of nationals of the parties while others provide for non-nationals, and perhaps this different composition may affect how panels view the matter.

If the A–B agreement is NAFTA or Canada–Chile, and if the parties cannot agree on how to resolve the dispute within thirty days, country B may automatically retaliate against A. Country A can only dispute whether the level of B's retaliation is "manifestly excessive" but the retaliatory measure may continue while its amount is litigated. Country C of course has no right to retaliate and continues to feel the adverse effect of the country A measure. Assume the A–C agreement has a choice of forum provision as do NAFTA and NAFTA-like agreements, whereby a complaining party may choose whether to pursue a claim either under the agreement or the WTO, and C's decision on forum, once initiated, is exclusive to the other. C is thus barred from requesting a panel under the dispute settlement agreement (DSA). Assume, however, that C decides to bring the dispute anyway. Can A refuse dispute settlement under the DSA on the grounds that the matter was litigated already under A–C agreement? It would not appear that A could do so without violating its obligations under the DSU. One could imagine a WTO panel on the A–C dispute going on while A sues C under the A–C agreement for breach of the choice of forum provisions. But what if C argues that its case under the WTO is based on a different cause of action or different grounds than available under A–C?

As this example illustrates, proliferation of bilateral agreements and RTAs pose systemic risks and rather than facilitating the resolution of disputes, might make dispute resolution more complex and costly. How to reduce these risks and costs is an open question and one of the major challenges posed by proliferation. Most of the NAFTA-like agreements in LAC are very new and even those that are older have not had much activity in terms of dispute settlement. So the complications suggested by the example are more theoretical possibilities than a matter of historical record. On the other hand, there might be some positive aspects in the proliferation of dispute settlement systems. In particular, these might reduce some of the burden on the WTO and expand institutional capacity to cope with a rapidly expanding caseload of trade disputes.

Have RTAs Contributed to Domestic Policy Reforms, and How?

As suggested above, LAC countries have engaged in the new RTAs to pursue a number of different objectives, and they see these agreements as an important instrument for development. RTAs contribute with domestic policy reform in a number of ways.

Commitment Mechanisms

First, as frequently pointed out in the literature, RTAs allow countries to "lock in" reforms, both in trade and non-trade areas, and therefore function as good commitment mechanisms that enhance the credibility of policy reform and send positive signals to global markets. This issue was recently reviewed in a report on trade blocs by the World Bank (2000), which concludes that in the trade area, RTAs have indeed worked well as commitment mechanisms in practice.[15] The impact of NAFTA in locking in not only a broad range of economic reforms but democracy as well has been widely recognized. NAFTA was instrumental in determining the policy response of both the Mexican and the U.S. governments to the 1995 peso crisis. Mexico maintained the reforms and increased its credibility as a location for international investment, and the U.S. response demonstrated that NAFTA meant more than just trade policy. MERCOSUR has been instrumental in creating interdependencies that reduce historical rivalries and promote cooperation. It also helped to discipline the economic response of its members to financial instability. The democratic clause of MERCOSUR was effectively and successfully used at least once during the Paraguayan political crisis.

Of course, how effective RTAs can be as commitment mechanisms depends on the value of belonging to the group and on the credibility of the threat of action if rules are broken. Thus, not all RTAs are equally effective in this sense. From this perspective, the FTAA, by allowing Latin America to link up with the United States and other industrialized nations, will probably be a particularly effective commitment mechanism for most countries in Latin America for a broad range of economic policies and in other non-trade but related areas. This provides the FTAA with a strategic value that has been widely recognized.

Price Effects

A second type of positive link between RTAs and domestic reforms occurs to the extent that RTAs accelerate domestic reforms that reduce price distortions because countries can no longer maintain substantial price differentials when they open up their economies. In other words, RTAs put pressure on countries to eliminate domestic distortions that are incompatible with free trade, and in this sense they serve as building blocks toward multilateral liberalization. A clear example of this in Latin America is the impact of the FTA between Central America and the Dominican Republic in the latter. Free trade with Central America has forced a national debate in the Dominican Republic about the need to rationalize the whole tariff structure. Producer lobbies in the Dominican Republic successfully pressed the government to reduce tariffs on intermediate goods, so that local firms can compete with Central American imports.

Political Economy Effects

A third type of positive influence of RTAs on domestic policy reform, for which there is a fair amount of anecdotal evidence, is that these agreements have induced positive behavioral changes in the traditionally rent-seeking behavior by business communities. In many countries, the prospect and reality of increased import competition has led the local business communities to be more interested in reducing domestic distortions in transportation costs, telephone costs, electricity rates, and interest rates that hinder their ability to compete with firms from other member countries. Of course, the interaction of RTAs with local interest groups is complex. There are also instances in which the negotiation of RTAs in LAC has been resisted and used by some political leaders and/or nongovernmental organizations as part of a more general anti-globalization, anti-U.S., or anti-"Washington consensus" discourse.

Role of Macro- and Micro-economic Policies
in Regional Agreements

Technological obsolescence leading to competitive disparities, exchange
rate instability, and fiscal imbalances are well-known obstacles to regional
integration projects. The first obstacle engenders protectionist pressures
that usually lead to antidumping actions, exception lists, safeguards, and
other mechanisms that delay the trade liberalization process. Exchange rate
instability undermines confidence in international transactions based on
long-term contracts, which are the main source of steady intra-industry
trade flows. Exchange rate instability also raises the uncertainty of business
strategies focused on the regular use of imported inputs and frustrates the
restructuring initiatives that would allow industrial modernization. Fiscal
imbalances impose restrictions on governments' capacity for economic reform, partly because in many economies, particularly in smaller ones, trade
taxes constitute a relatively large proportion of total fiscal revenue, and
partly because they create difficulties for the financing of social investment,
which is essential to legitimate further trade liberalization and economic
adjustment. Thus, the interaction of macro- and micro-economic policies
with RTAs raises some of the most important analytical and policy issues
confronting countries in their regional economic integration efforts, and
Latin America has a rich experience in this area. As regards exchange rate
regimes, for instance, several regimes coexist, ranging from the Chilean and
Costa Rican heterodoxies, to the Brazilian float, Argentina's convertibility,
and dollarization in Ecuador and El Salvador (Fanelli 1999, 2000, 2001;
Markwald and Machado 1999; Hausmann et al. 1999; Salazar-Xirinachs
and Tavares 1999).

Membership in an RTA exacerbates the weight of external constraints,
making it more difficult for countries to act "defensively" against shocks
originating in other RTA members and to deal with their own macroeconomic disequilibria.[16] Moreover, because in an RTA tariff cuts are deeper
and irreversible in contrast with unilateral trade liberalization, the need for
fiscal restructuring to replace foregone trade revenues is also more pressing.
To the extent that intraregional trade flows grow within an RTA, the issue
of the costs and benefits of some degree of macroeconomic policy coordination emerges. In this respect, the influence of the monetary union in
Europe has also had a strong influence.

In the FTAA, the presence of a dominant trading partner places particular constraints on macroeconomic management. While the United States coordinates some aspects of its macroeconomic policy with other members of the Group of 7, which jointly account for about 80 percent of world trade, the United States could not realistically be expected to assume similar commitments with countries in Latin America. The difference in incentives for macroeconomic policy coordination reflects the fundamental asymmetry between the United States and Latin American countries in terms of economic size, openness, and reciprocal importance as trading partners. In general, larger, less open countries are under less pressure to coordinate macroeconomic policy than their smaller, more open trading partners. Moreover, the incentive to harmonize macroeconomic policies with particular trading partners is a function of the relative importance of trade flows. On all these grounds, Latin America would have far more interest in policy coordination than the United States. It seems reasonable to argue that in the FTAA, Latin American countries will be "policy takers" in the sense that they would need to accommodate their policies with whatever U.S. policy happens to be, rather than expect significant policy coordination.

In the absence of coordinating or compensatory mechanisms, and given the vulnerability to external shocks and contagion effects, from time to time these countries are likely to be confronted with episodes of financial instability, which mark fiscal constraints to further trade liberalization and economic integration. These and other concerns led several Latin American countries in the last few years to seriously consider whether to embark on a dollarization of their economies. Indeed, by 1999–2000 the monetary debate in the hemisphere seemed to be on the verge of a paradigm shift in favor of dollarization. However, the Argentine meltdown of 2001 under the currency board system will probably lead to some reassessment of the costs and benefits of dollarization, and to a reassertion of the need for sound fiscal and financial policies.

The issue of policy harmonization has also been discussed within subregional groups (MERCOSUR, Andean Community, Central America, CARICOM). To the extent that within each of the subregional groups, intragroup trade remains low relative to total trade, so too are the incentives for macroeconomic policy coordination within the group. Yet, the less policy convergence there is, the more difficult it will be for intragroup trade to develop. Ultimately, therefore, to maximize benefits of RTAs this vicious circle will have to be broken, and macroeconomic policies will need some degree of convergence. Needless to say, there is no consensus in the economic literature as to the optimal exchange rate and monetary policy regime or about the desirable level of macroeconomic policy coordination that a country should aim for in an RTA.

In Latin America, the failure to reform fiscal structures has been, for many decades, a common trait of the region's economies, where the aspirations for economic development have amplified the demands on public resources while the tax base has remained extremely small or even shrunk. Not by chance, import-substituting industrialization strategies had a long-lived popularity in the region, since they generated innumerable stratagems for circumventing the fiscal challenge. Even today, years after abandoning import substitution policies, and despite severe fiscal adjustment programs that have included privatization, public sector restructuring, and trade reforms, some Latin American and Caribbean countries are still far from the contemporary standards of public finance management. The problem is compounded by the fact that trade taxes constitute a relatively large proportion of total fiscal revenue in many Latin American economies. Thus, resistance to further trade liberalization and integration into larger markets may come not only from technologically obsolete sectors and perceived competitive threats, but from governments that find it difficult to modernize tax systems to meet both the demands for social investment and the need to finance the fiscal cost of further trade liberalization. In the FTAA process, this issue has received some attention in the Advisory Group on Smaller Economies. However, despite its critical importance for hemispheric integration, it is an area that has been left entirely as a matter of internal national coordination between trade and finance authorities, and has not, at least to date, been brought within the scope of formal hemispheric cooperation efforts.

Multilateralism versus Regionalism: A False Dilemma?

From a pragmatic point of view, the regionalism versus multilateralism controversy is, to a certain point, a false dilemma. It is false, not because (1) RTAs cannot create trade diversion, because they clearly can do this; (2) RTAs cannot create a "spaghetti bowl" phenomenon that could hinder rather than facilitate business, as they can clearly also do this; and (3) scenarios of the world going down a path of RTAs while neglecting or diverting resources and political capital away from the multilateral system are unimaginable, as this would be very negative and welfare reducing indeed.

It is a false dilemma for three fundamental reasons. First, because there are many plausible trajectories where pursuing a multiple-track strategy—multilateral, regional, and bilateral—might get countries to free trade quicker than relying just on one track. In what is called in the literature the "dynamic time-path" question, there is evidence of patterns of mutually reinforcing interdependence where the pursuit of regionalism triggers or induces the pursuit of multilateralism.[17] In addition, the multilateral system is far from being as quick and efficient as is sometimes portrayed. It is slow to achieve results, and it is weak in a number of fundamental areas. Still, it is a major achievement in the area of global governance of the twentieth century and must be protected and strengthened.

Second, the evidence from Latin America shows that these countries did not adopt the new regionalism as an alternative to multilateralism. The typical sequence was that countries first engaged in unilateral liberalization as part of the process of economic reform in the 1980s and early 1990s. The new regionalism was a consequence of this process of reform. Countries also participated actively in the Uruguay Round, and it was in the climate of protracted negotiations and uncertainty about the results of the round that they simultaneously engaged in the revitalization of their customs unions and in the negotiation of FTAs. Also, the evidence reviewed in this chapter from LAC does not support the view that the new bilateral agreements and RTAs negotiated in the region have been seriously trade diverting.

Finally, it can be argued that it might even be counterproductive to portray regionalism and multilateralism as mutually exclusive alternatives, because in practice governments will most likely continue to pursue both simultaneously. In fact, in Doha RTAs obtained increased legitimacy. Paragraph 4 of the Ministerial Declaration recognizes "that RTAs can play an important role in promoting the liberalization and expansion of trade and in fostering development."

So, if regional trade agreements are here to stay, some useful questions for research are: How can regionalism be harnessed and oriented so that it maximizes its role as a building block for a more open world trading system? How can RTAs achieve faster and deeper results in areas where the multilateral system is slow or shallow? Given the failure of the GATT/WTO mechanisms for examining the consistency of RTAs with the conditions of Article XXIV of GATT and Article V of GATS, how can these articles and mechanisms be strengthened or reformed to bring more discipline and more WTO consistency in RTAs? However, dealing with these questions is beyond the scope of this chapter. In this regard it is worth noting that in Doha, ministers agreed "to negotiations aimed at clarifying and improving disciplines and procedures under the existing WTO provisions applying to regional trade agreements. The negotiations shall take into account the developmental aspects of regional trade agreements."

Conclusions and Challenges

Explaining proliferation. Latin American and Caribbean countries have pursued a multiplicity of objectives in negotiating RTAs: market access; investment attraction; strengthening domestic policy reform; positive signaling to investors; increased bargaining power vis-à-vis third countries; political, security, or strategic linkage objectives; and the use of regional agreements for tactical purposes in seeking to achieve multilateral objectives. The hallmark of the new regionalism in the region is, however, interest in linking up with the United States and Canada, the larger and most developed economies in the hemisphere. From this perspective, RTAs are an instrument by which economies, particularly smaller ones, compete to improve their investment climate and to attract foreign direct investment. Political and strategic rationales have also guided the LAC countries' engagement in RTAs, with variations depending on the specific groupings and level of aggregation of countries.

Trade diversion and creation. A review of the existing studies on trade creation and diversion in the different agreements in LAC suggests that there is no evidence of trade diversion or that if any, trade diversion was far inferior to dynamic effects. The typical behavior observed in this period is an impressive expansion in both trade within the group and in imports from the rest of the world. This is largely due to the fact that RTAs have occurred simultaneously with very significant unilateral trade liberalization.

Similarity and diversity in agreements. There is important diversity in the agreements in LAC in terms of disciplines and institutional arrangements. There are four customs unions and almost twenty free trade agreements in force or under negotiation between countries in the Americas, plus twelve negotiated or under negotiation with countries outside the hemisphere. The FTAs negotiated in the 1990s present important similarities associated with the fact that most of them were modeled on the NAFTA in terms of their structure, scope, and coverage. However, even among these some significant differences exist. The combination of different strategic and economic rationales in each case has ensured that not all agreements are created equal, and that pragmatism has been a key component of the LAC experience.

Extent of liberalization. The evidence from RTAs in LAC suggests that these agreements have indeed shown a capacity to liberalize faster than at the multilateral level and to include nearly universal coverage of trade liberalization in industrial goods. Most programs among LAC countries will eliminate tariffs for almost all products by 2006 and most of the bilateral trade in these agreements will become fully liberalized in terms of tariffs over a ten-year period. One weakness in this market access picture is that nearly all the agreements fail to adequately cover the agricultural sector. Exceptions for agriculture reflect the particular sensitivities of each participating country.

Rules of origin. Another weakness of the new RTAs is that they have introduced selective procedures and discretionary application of rules of origin. Several studies suggest an important degree of use of rules of origin not just to avoid trade deflection, but for protectionist and strategic goals. There is also evidence of use of rules of origin to influence investment patterns. One lesson to draw in this area seems to be that as an intrinsic part of most RTAs, rules of origin are here to stay and that the relevant question is how to minimize their trade- and investment-distorting effects. A useful hypothesis is that a broader plurilateral agreement such as the FTAA offers an opportunity to "clean up" to some extent the spaghetti bowl effect of different origin schemes in the Americas.

Dispute resolution. In the area of dispute resolution, the proliferation of bilateral and subregional agreements poses serious potential risks to judicial cohesion and judicial economy in the resolution of trade disputes. Dispute resolution could become more complex and costly. How to reduce these risks and costs is one of the major challenges posed by proliferation. On the other hand, there might be some positive aspects in the proliferation of dispute settlement systems. In particular, it might reduce some of the burden on the WTO and expand the institutional capacity to cope with a rapidly expanding caseload of trade disputes.

Depth of integration. There is very scarce empirical research in Latin America on the question of the extent that RTAs have promoted deep integration beyond what has been achieved at the multilateral level. In the area of domestic regulation in services sectors, one study provides mixed results: while some RTAs adopt more general principles than GATS, other RTAs, most notably NAFTA and MERCOSUR, apply more stringent disciplines than GATS. With respect to mutual recognition, a number of RTAs do go beyond GATS in encouraging the formation of recognition agreements. These conclusions relate to the nature of the disciplines in the agreements, not to actual progress in changing national legislation or enforcement. Most of the new RTAs in LAC do expand the liberal trade order in that they include areas that are not fully integrated in multilateral negotiations: investment, competition policy, and government procurement.

Innovation, experimentation, and linkage issues. FTAs in the Western Hemisphere have been a fertile ground for innovation and experimentation, both in traditional disciplines and in linking trade and non-trade objectives. For instance, the Canada–Chile agreement eliminates the use of antidumping among the parties. Several agreements have moved beyond the GATT/WTO into such areas as environment and labor standards, with some using a sanctions approach, others monetary fines to punish violators, and others based strictly on cooperation in these areas. LAC countries almost unanimously reject a trade sanctions approach to labor and environmental concerns. Regarding the trade–democracy nexus, MERCOSUR incorporates a "democratic clause," and there are ongoing discussions as to how to strengthen the democratic provisions in the inter-American system, including possible cross-reference to the FTAA. There seems to be a growing consensus in the Americas to strengthen the trade–democracy nexus. It is likely that one of the effects of the tragic events of September 11 will be to strengthen the link between geopolitical and security considerations on the one hand, and trade and prosperity components of the inter-American system on the other.

Distraction from multilateral negotiations. This chapter argued that there is no evidence in LAC that the proactive pursuit of regionalism in the 1990s has been to the detriment of the countries' commitment or attention to multilateral negotiations. In fact, the opposite seems to be the case. There is concrete evidence of increased participation in the WTO process by LAC countries in the 1990s. Regional engagement has generated positive externalities and learning effects that benefit engagement in the multilateral system.

The contribution of regional trade agreements to domestic policy reforms. RTAs contribute to domestic policy reform in a number of ways, including by acting as commitment mechanisms enhancing the credibility of policy reform and sending positive signals to global markets, particularly when the agreement includes a larger, relatively more developed country that acts as enforcer; by putting pressure on countries to eliminate domestic price distortions that are incompatible with free trade; and by inducing positive behavioral changes in the traditionally rent-seeking behavior of business communities.

Macro- and micro-economic policies and RTAs. Competitive disparities, exchange rate instability, and fiscal imbalances are well-known obstacles to regional integration projects. To the extent that intraregional trade flows grow within a RTA, the issue of the costs and benefits of macroeconomic policy coordination emerges. Resistance to further trade liberalization and regional integration may come not only from technological obsolescence and perceived competitive threats, but from governments that find it difficult to modernize tax systems to meet both the demands for social investment and the need to finance the fiscal cost of further trade liberalization.

What to do about proliferation? Although the academic controversy on multilateralism versus regionalism has provided many useful insights, an understanding of the economic, political, and historic contexts of trade policy strongly suggests that governments will most likely continue to pursue both simultaneously, and that RTAs are here to stay. They have too many benefits and attractions for governments to give them up. The appropriate and pragmatic response is rather to orient and discipline this proliferation, partly through reinforced multilateral procedures but also through other means, in order to reduce the opportunities for discrimination and to maximize their role as building blocks for a more open trading system.

Notes

This paper is reprinted by permission of the *Journal of Asian Economics* (13, March–April, 2002: 181–212), published by Elsevier Science Inc. The views expressed in this chapter are mine and should not be attributed to the Organization of American States or to its member countries. I am grateful to Jorge Mario Martinez and Soonhwa Yi for their valuable research for this chapter, and to Karsten Steinfatt and Rosine Plank-Brumback for their contributions to the last section. The chapter also benefited from comments from Geza Feketekuty, Gary Hufbauer, and Brian Staples.

1. Throughout this paper the term regional trade agreements (RTAs) is used to include bilateral, multilateral, and regional agreements, including customs unions and free trade agreements (FTAs). Where necessary, the relevant distinctions are made in the text.

2. Note that the table does not include nonreciprocal trade agreements of which there are five in the Americas: the Caribbean Basin Initiative, the Andean Trade Preferences Act, CARIBCAN and the agreements between CARICOM and Venezuela and CARICOM and Colombia. It also does not include the "partial scope" agreements negotiated under the Latin American Integration Association (ALADI). For an analysis of the nonreciprocal agreements in the Western Hemisphere, see Steinfatt (2001).

3. For history, characteristics, and recent evolution of these agreements, see Salazar-Xirinachs et al. (2001).

4. Important discussions of country objectives in pursuing RTAs are Perroni and Whalley (1994) and Whalley (1996).

5. An original analysis of the role of culture in shaping Latin American policies and institutions and its relationships with the United States is Harrison (1997).

6. For a brief history of the role of ECLAC, see Thorp (1998).

7. For a history of Latin America's experience with adjustments and market-oriented reforms during the 1982–1993 period, see Edwards (1995).

8. The point is important because to the extent that the new regionalism in Latin America and elsewhere is about these deeper aspects of integration, the traditional analyses of costs and benefits of RTAs, which focus mainly on barriers at the border while ignoring differences in national institutions and domestic regulations, are seriously deficient.

9. Perroni and Whalley (1996) observe that several of the recently negotiated RTAs contain significantly fewer concessions by the large countries to smaller countries than vice versa. Yet, it is small countries who have sought them and see themselves as the main beneficiaries. The authors explain this apparent paradox by interpreting such agreements as insurance arrangements for smaller economies, which partially protects them against uncertainty in market access. Some of these agreements appear to produce little or no benefit relative to the status quo for smaller countries, but if they are evaluated relative to a postretaliation tariff equilibrium, the value of these agreements to small economies is large because they help preserve existing access to larger foreign markets. This logic helps to explain why, even though they enjoy a quite satisfactory degree of access to the U.S. market based on the Generalized System of Preferences and Caribbean Basin Initiatives, the Central American countries are interested and eager to negotiate a reciprocal FTA with the United States.

10. For recent statements of MERCOSUR's trade objectives, see Lafer (2001) and Barbosa (2001); for an American perspective on Brazil's trade policy see Kissinger (2001).

11. Presidential Summits of the Americas were held in Miami in 1994; Santiago, Chile in April 1998; and Quebec, Canada in April 2001. For analyses of the political, strategic, and security objectives of countries in the Americas and of the summit process, see Gaviria (2001), Weintraub (2000), Franco (2000), Feinberg (1997), and the Leadership Council for Inter-American Summitry (2001).

12. For an analysis of the impact and opportunities of the Caribbean Basin Trade Partnership Act of 2000 on Caribbean Basin economies, see Leon and Salazar-Xirinachs (2001).

13. Also significant is the fact that one objective of the FTAA negotiations is to eliminate agricultural export subsidies affecting trade in the hemisphere. At the Toronto ministerial meeting in November 1999, one month before the Seattle ministerial conference, participants further agreed to work toward reaching agreement in the WTO on eliminating agricultural export subsidies.

14. Rules of origin in the Americas are based on one of two approaches: value added and tariff shift. The implications of adopting each approach are highlighted in Mackay et al. (2001): 129): "The value added approach generally defines a maximum percentage of third country processing or components that can be included for a good to qualify for preferential tariff treatment. This approach suffers from severe limitations because it is highly dependent on fluctuations in a wide range of factors that determine the prices and cost of a good. It is also administratively very burdensome for customs administrations that must audit the cost of these materials because accounting methods vary widely throughout the world. Moreover, low-wage countries are at a disadvantage when using this method because they must use a higher percentage of originating components to qualify for the preferences.

"The 'tariff shift' model requires a determination that a party has modified a good or product enough to change its classification in the [harmonized system], thus making it eligible for preferential tariff treatment. This method is not without problems. It does not always ensure that there will be a substantial transformation in the production of a good."

15. Fernández (1997) contains a useful analysis of the conditions under which a regional agreement will enhance the credibility of policy reform.

16. MERCOSUR provides one of the clearest examples of how different macroeconomic rules can undermine regional integration efforts. See Fanelli (2001).

17. On the dynamic time path question, see Bhagwati and Panagariya (1996). Many trade experts have argued that the creation of the European Economic Community led directly to the Dillon and Kennedy Rounds. Others point to the 1982 shift to regionalism by the United States as having been instrumental in persuading the European Union and developing countries to launch a new round. The WTO (1995) argued that the failed Brussels ministerial meeting in December 1990 and the spread of regional integration agreements after 1990 were major factors in eliciting the concessions needed to conclude the Uruguay Round. In 2001 many seemed to be concerned that the new Bush administration would give priority to the FTAA and not to the new round, and this acted as an additional incentive for the repeated European and Japanese calls for a new round.

References

Barbosa, Rubens. 2001. "The FTAA that Is in Brazil's Interest." *Gazeta Mercantil,* November 5, 2001.

Bhagwati, J. 1997. "Fast Track to Nowhere." *The Economist,* 18 October.

Bhagwati, J., David Greenaway, and Arvind Panagariya. 1998. "Trading Preferentially: Theory and Policy." *The Economic Journal* 108, no. 449 (July).

Bhagwati, J., and Panagariya, A. 1996. "Preferential Trading Areas, and Multilateralism: Strangers, Friends or Foes?" In *The Economics of Preferential Trading Agreements,* edited by J. Bhagwati and A. Panagariya, 1–78. Washington, DC: American Enterprise Institute Press.

Burfisher, Mary E., Sherman Robinson, and Karen Thierfelder. 2001. "The Impact of NAFTA on the United States." *Journal of Economic Perspectives* 15, no. 1 (winter): 125–144.

Devlin, R., and A. Estevadeordal. 2001. "What's New in the New Regionalism in the Americas?" INTAL-ITD Working Paper 6. Buenos Aires: Instituto para la Integración de America Latina y el Caribe, Integration and Trade Division, Inter-American Development Bank, May.

Dutta, M. 1999. *Economic Regionalization in the Asia-Pacific: Challenges to Economic Cooperation.* Cheltenham, UK, and Northampton, MA: Edward Elgar.

Echevarría, Juan José. 1998. "Flujos Comerciales en los Países Andinos: ¿Liberalización o Preferencias Regionales?" *Coyuntura Económica* (Fedesarrollo, Bogotá, Colombia), (September): 87–118.

Edwards, Sebastian. 1995. *Crisis and Reform in Latin America: From Despair to Hope.* Washington, DC: Oxford University Press for World Bank.

Estevadeordal, A. 1999. "Negotiating Preferential Market Access: The Case of NAFTA." INTAL-ITD Working Paper 3. Buenos Aires: Instituto para la Integración de America Latina y el Caribe, Integration and Trade Division, Inter-American Development Bank, June.

———. 2000. "Negotiating Preferential Market Access—The Case of the North American Free Trade Agreement." *Journal of World Trade* 34, no. 1 (February).

Estevadeordal, A., J. Goto and R. Sáez. 2000. "The New Regionalism in the Americas: The Case of MERCOSUR." INTAL-ITD Working Paper 5. Buenos Aires: Instituto para la Integración de America Latina y el Caribe, Integration and Trade Division, Inter-American Development Bank, April.

Ethier, Wilfred J. 1998. "The New Regionalism." *The Economic Journal* 108, no. 449 (July).

Fanelli, José María. 1999. *Macroeconomic Regimes and the Trade Agenda in Latin America.* Buenos Aires: Latin American Trade Network.

———. 2000. *Coordinación Macroeconómica en el MERCOSUR: Marco Analítico y Hechos Estilizados.* Buenos Aires: Centro de Estudios de Estado y Sociedad, November. Available at: www.redMERCOSUR.org.uy. Accessed October 2002.

———. 2001. "Coordinación Macroeconómica en el MERCOSUR: Balance y Perspectivas." In *El Desafío de Integrarse para Crecer: Balance y Perspectivas del MERCOSUR en su Primera Década,* edited by Daniel Chudnovsky and José María Fanelli. Buenos Aires: Red MERCOSUR, Siglo XXI, Inter-American Development Bank.

Feinberg, Richard. 1997. *Summitry of the Americas: A Progress Report.* Washington, DC: Institute for International Economics.

Fernández, Raquel. 1997. "Returns to Regionalism: An Evaluation of Nontraditional Gains from Regional Trade Agreements." Policy Research Working Paper. Washington, DC: World Bank. Available at: http://econ.worldbank.org/docs/342.pdf. Accessed October 2002.

Finger, J. Michael, ed. 1993. *Antidumping: How It Works and Who Gets Hurt.* Ann Arbor: University of Michigan Press.

Franco, Patrice. 2000. *Towards a New Security Architecture in the Americas: The Strategic Implications of the FTAA.* Washington, DC: Center for Strategic and International Studies.

Garay, L.J., and R. Cornejo. 1999. "Rules of Origin in Free Trade Agreements." In *Trade*

Rules in the Making: Challenges in Regional and Multilateral Negotiations, edited by M. R. Mendoza, P. Low, and B. Kotschwar, 261–79. Washington, DC: Brookings Institution and Organization of American States.

Gaviria, Cesar. 2001. "Integration and Interdependence in the Americas." In *Toward Free Trade in the Americas,* edited by José M. Salazar-Xirinachs and Maryse Robert, 303–15. Washington, DC: Brookings Institution Press/General Secretariat of the Organization of American States.

Gitli, Eduardo, and Randall Arce. 2000. *¿Qué Significa la Ampliación de Beneficios para los Países de la Cuenca del Caribe?* Heredia, Costa Rica: Centro Internacional de Política Económica.

Harrison, Lawrence. 1997. *The Pan-American Dream: Do Latin America's Cultural Values Discourage True Partnership with the United States and Canada?* New York: Basic Books.

Hausmann, Ricardo, Michael Gavin, Carmen Pages-Sierra, and Ernesto Stein. 1999. "Financial Turmoil and the Choice of Exchange Rate Regime." Washington, DC: Inter-American Development Bank, Office of the Chief Economist. Available at: www.iadb.org/res. Accessed October 2002.

James, W.E. 1997. "APEC and Preferential Rules of Origin: Stumbling Blocks for Liberalization of Trade?" *Journal of World Trade* 31, no. 3 (June).

Kissinger, Henry. 2001. "Brazil's 'Destiny': An Obstacle to Free Trade?" *Washington Post,* May 15.

Krishna, K., and A.O. Krueger. 1995. "Implementing Free Trade Areas: Rules of Origin and Hidden Protection." In *New Directions in Trade Theory,* edited by A. Deardorff, J. Levinsohn, and R. Stern. Ann Arbor: University of Michigan Press.

Krueger, Anne. 1999a. *Trade Creation and Trade Diversion Under NAFTA.* Working Paper 7429. Cambridge, MA: National Bureau of Economic Research.

———. 1999b. "Are Preferential Trading Arrangements Trade-Liberalizing or Protectionist?" *Journal of Economic Perspectives* 13, no. 4 (Fall): 105–124.

Lafer, Celso. 2001. "Brazil at the Inter-American Dialogue." Speech by Ambassador Celso Lafer, Minister of Foreign Affairs, Inter-American Dialogue, Washington, DC, March 1.

Lawrence, Robert. 1997. "Preferential Trading Arrangements: The Traditional and the New." In *Regional Partners in Global Markets: Limits and Possibilities of the Euro-Med Agreements,* edited by Ahmed Galal and Bernard Hoekman, 13–34. London: Centre for Economic Policy Research.

Leadership Council for Inter-American Summitry. 2001. *Advancing Toward Quebec City and Beyond.* Policy Report 3. Miami, FL: North-South Center, University of Miami.

Leon, Rene, and José M. Salazar-Xirinachs. 2001. "The New Caribbean Basin Initiative: Impact and Opportunities." *Integration and Trade* 5, no. 13 (January–April): 113–24.

Mackay, D., M. Robert, and R. Plank-Brumback. 2001. "Trade in Goods and Agriculture." In *Toward Free Trade in the Americas,* edited by José M. Salazar-Xirinachs and Maryse Robert, 125–40. Washington, DC: Brookings Institution Press/General Secretariat of the Organization of American States.

Markwald, Ricardo, and João Bosco Machado. 1999. "Establishing an Industrial Policy for MERCOSUR." In *MERCOSUR: Regional Integration, World Markets,* edited by Riordan Roett, 63–80. Boulder, CO: Lynne Rienner Publishers.

Messerlin, Patrick A. 1989. "EC Antidumping Regulations: A First Economic Appraisal, 1980–85." *Weltwirfschaftliches Archiv* 125.

Moran, Theodore H. 1998. *Foreign Direct Investment and Development.* Washington, DC: Institute for International Economics.

Nagarajan, Nigel. 1998. *MERCOSUR and Trade Diversion: What Do the Import Figures Tell U.S.?* Economic Papers 129. Belgium: European Commission Directorate-General for Economic and Financial Affairs, July.

Perroni, Carlo, and John Whalley. 1994. *The New Regionalism: Trade Liberalization or Insurance?* Working Paper No. 4626. Cambridge, MA: National Bureau of Economic Research.

Prusa, Thomas J. 1999. *On the Spread and Impact of Antidumping.* Working Paper 7404. Cambridge, MA: National Bureau of Economic Research.

Robert, Maryse. 2001. "Free Trade Agreements." In *Toward Free Trade in the Americas,* edited by José M. Salazar-Xirinachs and Maryse Robert, 87–107. Washington, DC: Brookings Institution Press/General Secretariat of the Organization of American States.

Rodríguez Gigena, Gonzalo. 2000. *La Normativa Comercial en los Acuerdos Regionales del Hemisferio.* Buenos Aires: Latin American Trade Network, May.

Rodriguez Mendoza, Miguel. 1999. "Dealing with Latin America's New Regionalism." In *Trade Rules in the Making: Challenges in Regional and Multilateral Trade Negotiations,* edited by Miguel Rodriguez Mendoza, Patrick Low, and Barbara Kotschwar, 81–105. Washington, DC: Organization of American States and Brookings Institution Press.

Salazar-Xirinachs, José M., and José Tavares. 1999. "The Free Trade Area of the Americas: A Latin American Perspective." In *The World Economy, Global Trade Policy 1999,* edited by Peter Lloyd and Chris Milner, 75–90. London: Blackwell Publishers.

Salazar-Xirinachs, José M., Theresa Wetter, Karsten Steinfatt, and Daniela Ivascanu. 2001. "Customs Unions in the Western Hemisphere." In *Toward Free Trade in the Americas,* edited by José M. Salazar-Xirinachs and Maryse Robert, 45–86. Washington, DC: Brookings Institution Press/General Secretariat of the Organization of American States.

Scollay, Robert, and John Gilbert. 2001. *New Regional Trading Arrangements in the Asia Pacific?* Washington, DC: Institute for International Economics.

Steinfatt, Karsten. 2001. "Preferential and Partial Scope Agreements." In *Toward Free Trade in the Americas,* edited by José M. Salazar-Xirinachs and Maryse Robert, 108–22. Washington, DC: Brookings Institution Press/General Secretariat of the Organization of American States.

Stephenson, Sherry. 2001a. *The Growing Participation in Multilateral Services Liberalization by Latin America and the Caribbean.* OAS Trade Unit Studies. Washington, DC: Organization of American States, March.

———. 2001b. *"Deeper" Integration in Services Trade in the Western Hemisphere: Domestic Regulation and Mutual Recognition.* OAS Trade Unit Studies. Washington, DC: Organization of American States, March.

Tavares de Araujo, José, Jr., Carla Macario, and Karsten Steinfatt. 2001. *Antidumping in the Americas.* OAS Trade Unit Studies. Washington, DC: Organization of American States, March. Available at: http://www.sice.oas.org/tunit/pubinfoe.asp#tustudies. Accessed November 2002.

Thorp, Rosemary. 1998. *Progress, Poverty, and Exclusion: An Economic History of Latin America in the 20th Century.* Washington, DC: Inter-American Development Bank.

Weintraub, Sidney. 1999. *Technical Cooperation Needs for Hemispheric Trade Negotiations.* Washington, DC: Organization of American States.

———. 2000. *Development and Democracy in the Southern Cone: Imperatives for U.S. Foreign Policy in South America.* Washington, DC: Center for Strategic and International Studies.

Whalley, John. 1996. *Why Do Countries Seek Regional Trade Agreements?* Working Paper No. 5552. Cambridge, MA: National Bureau of Economic Research.

World Bank. 2000. *Trade Blocs.* World Bank Policy Research Report. Oxford and New York: Oxford University Press.

World Trade Organization (WTO). 1995. *Regionalism and the World Trading System.* Geneva: WTO Secretariat.

Yeats, Alexander. 1997. "Does MERCOSUR's Trade Performance Justify Concerns About the Effects of Regional Trade Arrangements? YES!" Washington, DC: World Bank. Modified version available at: www.worldbank.org/forum/non_govt/academic/mrod_e1.htm. Accessed October 2000.

Part III

Comparing Trade Strategies
in the Americas

6

Argentina's Foreign Trade Strategy: The Curse of Asymmetric Integration in the World Economy

Eduardo R. Ablin and Roberto Bouzas

In Argentina, as in most countries, foreign trade policy has traditionally been a divisive and hotly debated issue in which consensus has been slow to emerge. Yet what makes the Argentine case special is how difficult it has been for a consistent foreign trade strategy to prevail over time. Despite the fact that import substitution industrialization (ISI) dominated policymaking for most of the postwar period, trade and exchange rate policies were typically very volatile. At the outset of the new century, and after nearly two decades of far-reaching policy reform, the debate on Argentina's foreign trade strategies remains unsettled. The divide has been made more apparent by the economic crisis that accompanied the collapse of its currency board in 2001. Behind this volatile historical pattern and the current policy impasse there is an unbridged divide over preferences and interests.

Historically, the integration of Argentina into the world economy followed two distinct paths. During the period of outward orientation (1870s to 1930s), Argentina implemented open trade policies. However, even in the context of an export-oriented development strategy and sustained real income growth, a lively debate on the appropriate level of protection to be conferred to domestic producers took place (Hora 2000). The collapse of the international division of labor in which Argentina's static comparative advantages fit so well during the Great Depression opened the door to an inward-oriented development model. Initially adopted as a response to adverse external circumstances, ISI became an explicit development strategy after World War II, as urban and domestic market-oriented sectors gained more leverage in trade policymaking at the expense of export-oriented agricultural interests. However, the role of the latter as a key foreign exchange earner maintained it as an influential player. For nearly half a century, export-oriented sectors struggled to protect their share in national income by supporting more open trade policies and a market-determined exchange rate. The result of this conflict was a volatile structure of incentives that followed the ebbs and flows of the leverage that each of these groups had on policymaking.

By the mid-1970s, the shortfalls of inward orientation had become quite evident. Argentina's macroeconomic performance worsened severely and the country steadily lost ground in international trade. The first comprehensive attempt to overhaul the inward-oriented trade regime (and the ISI model) was implemented in the late 1970s, to be followed by a severe financial and balance of payments crisis in 1980–1981. The external debt crisis and the ensuing acute foreign exchange shortage led to a period of "forced" protection that in practice restored the trend toward autarky. The democratic government elected in 1983 inherited an economy largely closed to foreign trade and completely severed from world capital markets. In the foreign trade realm, its major initiatives were a bilateral cooperation program with Brazil and a timid trade reform as of 1986. The administration that took office in 1989 went much further and adopted a radical and ambitious structural reform program that characterized the 1990s. In the realm of foreign trade, the reform combined a three-pronged strategy of unilateral, preferential, and multilateral liberalization that radically altered the face of Argentina's trade regime. However, a rigid currency board and a succession of external shocks (among others, the appreciation of the U.S. dollar in the late 1990s and the devaluation of the Brazilian real in January 1999) raised protectionist pressures again and challenged trade liberalization and the functionality of the strategic partnership with Brazil. Eventually, a full-fledged financial crisis in December 2001 placed all economic policies in a state of flux.

In this chapter, we discuss Argentina's recent trade strategies. In the first section, we review the basis of (and the obstacles to) unilateral trade liberalization during the 1990s. Next, we present the rationale behind Argentina's more active role in the multilateral trading system during and after the General Agreement on Tariffs and Trade (GATT) Uruguay Round, as well as the emerging frustration over its results. In the following section, we briefly address the debate on preferential trade negotiations, focusing on the tensions posed by Argentina's membership in the Southern Common Market (MERCOSUR) and other (real or imaginary) competing trade partnerships. Lastly, in the final section we draw some conclusions from the preceding analysis.

Unilateral Trade Liberalization and Structural Reform in the 1990s: Trade Liberalization or Outward Orientation?

During the postwar period Argentina's trade policies were basically shaped by domestic considerations: neither multilateral nor regional commitments, both very feeble, placed significant constraints on policy design. The absence of external (multilateral or regional) constraints, combined with the division characteristic of Argentina's domestic political economy, laid the foundations for a volatile trade policy regime. Although ISI provided the dominant paradigm for nearly half a century, policies shifted at regular intervals between the interests of (agricultural) export-oriented sectors and those of (industrial) domestic market–oriented activities. This trade policy pattern went hand in hand with endemic macroeconomic instability, high inflation, and large real exchange rate fluctuations, which in turn led to volatile and often contradictory signals for resource allocation.

During this period trade policy was usually designed and implemented in a context in which "urgency" and "political expediency" superseded almost any other consideration. Instead of providing long-term signals for resource allocation, trade policy was often used to achieve short-term objectives, such as combating price inflation or raising revenues for the public sector (Lucángeli 1989). This policy pattern was accompanied by a very limited exposure of politicians, government officials, and businesspeople to the strengths and limitations of the GATT system. Based on urgency considerations, Argentina typically missed the potential benefits of reciprocity: tariff reductions were usually undertaken autonomously and disconnected from GATT negotiations. Characteristically, they were followed by policy reversals (Ablin and Lucángeli 2000).

The first comprehensive departure from the inward-oriented model was the trade-cum-capital-account liberalization program implemented in the late 1970s. This reform initiative included drastic tariff cuts and a pre-fixed crawling peg to bring inflation down. This combination placed severe pressure on producers of tradeables and exposed domestic industry to severe competitive pressures, leading to a first wave of de-industrialization. Parallel liberalization of the capital account created additional strains, as large capital inflows (attracted by high domestic interest rates) further appreciated the domestic currency. Eventually, this ill-structured program proved un-sustainable and led to an external debt crisis and a financial meltdown in the early 1980s (Bouzas and Keifman 1987).

The subsequent "forced" protection proved intense, but transitory. In 1985 the Alfonsín administration launched a new stabilization program (the Plan Austral) and one year later a timid trade reform. The new policies (supported by two World Bank structural adjustment loans) envisaged only limited and progressive liberalization, but were indicative of a growing con-sensus on the need to reduce nominal protection as a prerequisite for non-inflationary growth. Eventually, the failure of the stabilization plan made Argentina slide toward social unrest, a new balance of payments crisis and, eventually, hyperinflation. Surprisingly, the trade liberalization program launched in the mid-1980s outlived the ensuing turmoil, to be deepened after a more reformist-minded administration, headed by Carlos Menem, took office in 1989 (Damill and Keifman 1993).

Between 1990 and 1993, the trade policy regime was overhauled through the elimination of practically all quantitative restrictions, reduction of the average tariff rate and dispersion of nominal tariff rates, the streamlining of foreign trade procedures, and the abrogation of most export taxes (Makuc and Ablin 1994). The average tariff rate fell from 28.9 percent at the be-ginning of 1989 to 9.5 percent by 1991. The standard deviation and the per-centage of tariff headings taxed at the maximum rate also contracted from 13.9 percent to 9.4 percent and from 40 percent to 22 percent, respectively. Only a handful of products (motor vehicles, textiles, and footwear) remained subject to special treatment (quantitative restrictions, minimum specific import duties, and export or origin requirements). In order to mitigate the remaining anti-export bias (including that resulting from the real apprecia-tion of the local currency), in December 1992 the government raised export tax rebates to a range of 2.5 percent to 20 percent (Berlinski 1998).

The trade liberalization experiment of the early 1990s was undertaken as part of a structural reform program that included deregulation, privatiza-tion, and adoption of a currency board that pegged the peso to the U.S. dol-lar and made monetary policy fully dependent on the change in international reserves. Simultaneously, all capital account controls and foreign exchange restrictions were eliminated and for the first time in decades the private sec-tor was given full rights over foreign trade earnings. As in the 1978–1981 failed experiment, the fixed nominal exchange rate placed the private sec-tor under heavy pressure to rationalize and exercise price restraints. But this time convergence toward the U.S. inflation rate was much faster than in the late 1970s. Price stabilization and a law-enforced fixed nominal exchange rate reduced uncertainty, stimulating firms to lengthen their planning horizons and to concentrate in promoting higher efficiency. Lower tariffs and the real appreciation of the domestic currency also reduced the relative price of imported capital goods and intermediate inputs, stimulating investment and higher productivity.

Privatization and deregulation of public utilities also raised systemic productivity, as firms benefited from more readily available and higher-quality services (although in some cases at high costs by international standards). In addition, infrastructure was significantly upgraded in areas such as energy transport and distribution, telecommunications, and overland transport as well as ports and river navigation. A liberal regulatory regime, an ambitious privatization program, and a large potential to reap efficiency gains laid the basis for a foreign investment boom that produced a substantial revaluation of domestic assets. However, except for natural resource–intensive activities (such as oil and gas, mining, and forestry) and motor vehicles (benefited by a special promotion regime), the bulk of foreign direct investment was domestic marketing seeking rather than export oriented.

The real appreciation of the domestic currency and the sizable trade deficits that followed rapid aggregate demand growth during the early 1990s eventually led to a surge of claims from import-competing sectors. Rapid import growth of durable and nondurable consumer goods challenged domestic producers and raised demands for a more aggressive enforcement of trade relief measures. Typically, the authorities responded with ad hoc policy initiatives, such as increasing a special import surcharge (the "statistical levy") from 3 percent to 10 percent in 1992, the imposition of specific duties on sensitive products such as textiles and footwear, and more aggressive use of safeguards and trade remedy laws. They also acquiesced to, or even promoted, private sector orderly marketing agreements within MERCOSUR.[1]

The real appreciation of the Brazilian currency and the fast aggregate demand growth that followed the launching of the "Plano Real" in Brazil in 1994 temporarily eased pressure on Argentina's trade accounts. Shortly afterward, a succession of external shocks (the East Asian and Russian crisis, appreciation of the U.S. dollar, worsening terms of trade, and devaluation of the Real in 1999) plunged the economy into depression and made Argentina's competitiveness problems even more apparent. Again, in response to mounting domestic pressures and a shrinking economy, trade policy became hostage to short-term policy objectives rather than part of a long-term and consistent strategy. This was taken to an extreme in 2001, when the administration of President Fernando de la Rua (in power since late 1999) implemented a battery of nontransparent and discriminatory measures aimed to foster price competitiveness in a desperate attempt to save the currency board. This set of measures included unilateral tariff changes that repudiated MERCOSUR's common external tariff (CET), tailor-made "competitiveness" plans for selected sectors (based on discretionary tax exemptions), and a new and cumbersome methodology to set the parity of the peso.[2] Although the tariff hike did not go beyond the maximum GATT-bound rate of 35 percent, the nature of the new parity system raised concerns over its compatibility with multilateral commitments.

At the end of 2001, Argentina experienced a full-fledged financial crisis that eventually led to the collapse of the currency board. The end of the fixed nominal exchange rate and the subsequent free floating of the peso devalued the domestic currency by more than 300 percent. The new exchange rate made the relative price of tradeables skyrocket and, jointly with a sharp aggregate demand contraction, produced a sizable trade surplus. However, the absence of trade and investment finance and the prevailing high uncertainty more than compensated for the impact of the new relative prices. The result was a 5-percent contraction of exports during 2002. Imports fell by a remarkable 60 percent, dragged down by an 11-percent contraction in real output. The higher real exchange rate significantly reduced protectionist pressures, but not for long. As the economy began a modest recovery after mid-2002 and imports from Brazil picked up, renewed demands for protection were raised by the textile industry, among other sectors. If anything, the 2001/2002 crisis confirmed the resilience of inward-oriented sectors, the absence of energetic export-oriented interests, and the fragilities of trade liberalization processes anchored in a low real exchange rate. As the Argentine experience confirms, trade liberalization should not be taken as equivalent to outward orientation, as other policies can counteract the potentially positive effects on efficiency of a more open trade regime.[3]

Argentina and the Multilateral Trading System: Learning to Live with Constraints

Prior to the Uruguay Round, Argentina's participation in the multilateral trade regime and the use of GATT instruments were sporadic. This passive stance towards the multilateral trading system cannot be attributed exclusively to Argentina's autarchic tendencies. On the one hand, until the Uruguay Round, developing countries enjoyed a special status that effectively exempted them from most of the rules and obligations of the GATT. This special status was granted by Article XVIII.B (balance of payments provisions for developing countries) and the principle of special and differentiated treatment (GATT's Part IV). On the other, as a relatively small trading nation, Argentina was not a major participant in the request and offers process through which market access concessions were exchanged by the largest trading nations. In addition, in the case of Argentina a high concentration of exports in primary or processed agricultural products subject to exceptional GATT rules limited the interest in the GATT system. As a result, Argentina made use of GATT provisions only occasionally, typically in reaction to third-party actions affecting its exports rather than as part of a coherent strategy geared to promote its rights and goals in the multilateral trading system. Consequently, most of the benefits that accrued to Argentina from the successive rounds of multilateral negotiations (such as zero tariff rates for soybeans or the expansion of the Hilton beef quota on the occasion of successive accession of new member states to the European Union) were windfall gains rather than the outcome of an explicit bargaining strategy (Makuc and Ablin 1997).

Gradually, the growing share of international trade accounted for by mid-sized developing countries and the potential contribution of exports to economic growth raised developing countries' (LDCs') stakes in the multilateral system. This, plus the explicit inclusion in the Uruguay Round agenda of issues of interest to developing economies (such as trade in textiles and apparel, tropical products, and temperate agricultural goods), stimulated closer engagement of LDCs in multilateral negotiations. In the case of Argentina, the launching of the Uruguay Round in 1986 coincided with a period of domestic trade policy reform that encouraged more active participation in multilateral negotiations. But lack of knowledge and training over the foundations and working procedures of the GATT system conspired against a structured participation (Makuc 1989). When the Uruguay Round started to gain momentum again by 1990, Argentina's domestic trade policy agenda had evolved dramatically toward reform. The coincidence between the shift in Argentine trade policies and a turning point in GATT's history placed multilateral trade negotiations at the highest place ever in Argentina's foreign trade priorities. The country's goals remained too narrowly focused on agriculture, but interest and involvement in the GATT system reached unprecedented levels (Makuc and Ablin 1997).

Membership in the new World Trade Organization (WTO) brought less discretion in trade policy implementation. In 1994, Congress passed legislation incorporating WTO agreements and reformed many domestic regulations that were not in conformity with multilateral provisions. However, except in a few conflictive areas (e.g., intellectual property protection), many of the concessions made by Argentina as part of the final Uruguay Round agreements were undertaken unilaterally, such as in services trade.[4] Similarly, most tariff reductions also preceded the critical negotiating stage of the Uruguay Round, confirming that the Uruguay Round agreements were seen as a "lock-in" device rather than a vehicle to bargain for concessions.

As a result of the Uruguay Round, Argentina bound its entire tariff schedule at a rate of 35 percent as part of MERCOSUR's customs union, adopted formal procedures (including the establishment of an independent body) to determine injury to domestic industry in the course of "unfair" trade or safeguards investigations, and reformed its intellectual property rights legislation in conformity with the Trade Related Intellectual Property Rights agreement. Argentina also committed to phasing out the special promotion regime for motor vehicles after the transition period established by the Trade Related Investment Measures agreement. After 1994, Argentina's trade policies also became more closely scrutinized by other WTO members. The introduction of a more effective dispute settlement mechanism made Argentina a more frequent target of consultations or dispute settlement procedures. On several occasions, the Argentine government had to comply with Dispute Settlement Body rulings on issues related to market access or implementation of trade relief measures. For the first time in history, the multilateral trading system became an effective constraint on policy autonomy, demonstrating to both the public and private sectors the need to take international commitments into account in the course of policy formulation.[5] On balance, except for participation in the Cairns Group, Argentina's renewed interest in the multilateral trading system during the 1990s lacked a "positive" agenda. Rather than a forum to promote its interests in the international trading system, the Uruguay Round negotiations and its final agreements were used as vehicles to consolidate domestic policy reforms.

More recently, a new revisionism of Argentina's participation in the multilateral trading regime emerged, fueled by frustration over the benefits obtained by agricultural exporters (lack of reciprocity) and by concerns over a presumably biased implementation of unfair trade policies in developed and developing countries. The critics argue that the benefits of a rules-based system have been in practice counteracted by a biased agenda built on an asymmetric structure of power. The implication is that Argentina should either play hardball and implement more aggressively its own trade remedy laws or that trade negotiations should pursue alternative bilateral or regional North–South agreements as potentially more expeditious ways to obtain concessions.

Regional Integration: Second Thoughts on Regional Partnerships

The third pillar of Argentina's trade strategies in the 1990s was preferential liberalization. Membership in MERCOSUR and enforcement of a customs union were their driving forces. However, as the decade unfolded, second thoughts over the potential net benefits of playing the role of Brazil's regional partner (in the context of a customs union) became more apparent. The motivations behind the choice of preferential partnerships also changed as the imperative of restoring credibility and access to international financial markets grew more important pari passu with the rising costs of maintaining the currency board.

Argentina had already been an active player in the regional trade agreements of the 1960s and 1970s, the scope of which had been severely constrained by the prevailing inward-oriented model. In the Latin American Free Trade Association (LAFTA) intraregional trade expanded and diversified modestly and almost exclusively in those sectors where multinational firms were able to exploit scale economies and a regional division of labor (such as in office equipment, chemical products, and electronics). In LAFTA, as well as in the Latin American Integration Association (LAIA), market access concessions were carefully drafted to prevent hurting established producers. The result was that after a dynamic initial phase characterized by the exchange of nonconflictive market access concessions, preferential liberalization would lose steam or even come to a halt. A case-by-case approach to the exchange of concessions and the pressure of established producers led to very modest progress in trade liberalization. Apart from that, political tensions conspired against closer trade relations with neighboring countries.

A sea change took place when Argentina and Brazil signed the Programa de Intercambio y Cooperación Económica (PICE) in 1986. On the Argentine side the driving force behind PICE was as much political as well as economic. At the time, the elimination of conflict with Brazil (and Chile) was regarded as a means to strengthen democratic institutions, downsize the military, and reshape their role in political life. On the trade side, the contraction of intraregional commerce after the debt crisis, the perception of common external economic challenges (the debt crisis and the search for a new pattern of integration into the world economy), and the development of convergent policy preferences (gradual trade liberalization) contributed to provide a shared background to bilateral economic cooperation.

The sector-based, gradual and flexible approach to trade liberalization adopted by the PICE reestablished bilateral trade flows to the levels prior to the external debt crisis. Yet a deteriorating macroeconomic environment and the growing difficulties to make headway toward liberalization through a "positive list" approach rapidly placed limits on the liberalizing drive. By the end of the 1980s, the PICE was moribund. The Integration, Cooperation and Development Treaty of November 1988 did nothing to change this course of events. The revival of bilateral cooperation had to wait until new governments took office in Argentina and Brazil in mid-1989. The new administrations revised the methodology of PICE in tune with their more radical approach to economic reform.

In July 1990, a few months after the announcement of North American Free Trade Agreement (NAFTA) negotiations and launching of the Enterprise for the Americas Initiative, the Argentine and Brazilian governments signed the Acta de Buenos Aires, setting new criteria for bilateral economic integration. The major innovation was the abandonment of gradual and selective liberalization in exchange for automatic, across-the-board and linear tariff cuts (with designated exceptions for a limited number of sensitive products). The new understanding left the door open for other LAIA members to join.

In March 1991, Argentina, Brazil, Paraguay, and Uruguay signed the Treaty of Asunción, which established MERCOSUR. The treaty replicated and broadened the objectives, mechanisms, and procedures set bilaterally by Argentina and Brazil in the Acta de Buenos Aires, including a detailed mechanism (the trade liberalization program, TLP) to reach 100 percent preferences over most favored nation tariff rates by the end of 1994 (one additional year was given to Paraguay and Uruguay). The TLP successfully promoted trade liberalization for most of the tariff schedule and, in a context of unilateral liberalization, led to a significant expansion of intraregional trade.

Common external trade policies proved more difficult to negotiate and enforce. Although the general criteria for the CET were established in December 1992, it was much harder to reach agreement on specific tariff rates. Major differences pertained to foodstuffs (where Argentina proposed high tariff rates to compensate for foreign subsidies), and capital goods, electronic and electrical equipment, and intermediate goods (where Brazilian authorities preferred relatively high tariff rates to protect domestic producers). These differences were bridged in 1994 by a compromise that replicated Brazil's structure of protection and allowed for long convergence periods for sensitive sectors. This compromise attempted to accommodate the prevailing differences in domestic production and protection structures by means of a transition period.

But the idea of MERCOSUR as a customs union had never been consensual in Argentina. On the one hand, the authorities responsible for economic affairs feared the loss of autonomy over trade policy formulation implicit in the customs union approach. On the other, business also had an ambiguous stance, as domestic producers felt threatened by the prospect of rapid import liberalization vis-à-vis Brazil rather than encouraged by the prospect of enjoying preferential access to that country's huge and protected market, or by the strategic implications of MERCOSUR. The customs union approach, however, was vigorously espoused by the Brazilian government, which gave great value to its strategic (rather than purely commercial) implications. Argentina's ambiguities were temporarily overcome by the control that the foreign policy bureaucracy held on MERCOSUR issues and, after the Plano Real in 1994, by the export boom that followed Brazil's economic stabilization and the swift recovery of aggregate demand. At the time, the CET was regarded by many as the price to be paid to enjoy the mercantilist benefits of having preferential access to a rapidly growing market (Bouzas 2002).

But the underlying debate was far from settled. When the convergence schedules of the CET started to bite, second thoughts reemerged both in the public and private sectors. As the time to pay the cost of adopting a common structure of protection drew closer, the issue of net benefits of MERCOSUR gained renewed importance. Moreover, by the end of the 1990s the effectiveness of MERCOSUR to reduce trade policy discretion, remove nontariff barriers, deal with policy and structural asymmetries, and enforce more effective institutions and dispute settlement procedures were all clearly in dispute. In addition, after the free trade agreements signed with Chile and Bolivia in 1995, MERCOSUR had failed to maintain a unified position in its negotiations with the Andean Community and Mexico (Bouzas 1999). Disagreement over the desirability and speed of the Free

Trade Area of the Americas (FTAA) versus a plurilateral deal with the United States also became increasingly apparent.

The Brazilian foreign exchange crisis of January 1999 gave renewed energies (and arguments) to MERCOSUR's critics. Many regarded the devaluation of the real as an abrupt change in the rules of the game, despite the fact that MERCOSUR included no formal understandings on exchange rate policy. Argentine import-competing sectors reacted vocally fearing that a flood of "cheap" imports from Brazil (which never materialized except in very few sectors) would wipe out domestic firms from their own market. Export-oriented business, in turn, failed to surge in support of MERCOSUR, hurt by a devaluation that priced them out of the Brazilian (usually their largest) market. The Argentine government dealt with this explosive mix of pressures through ad hoc interventions such as nontariff restrictions, antidumping measures and official acquiescence with (and even promotion of) private sector market agreements in industries such as footwear, paper, poultry, and steel.[6]

By that time, a second brand of criticism against Argentina's participation in MERCOSUR became more vocal. Argentina's fragile financial stance provided a case for influential domestic actors to weigh alternative preferential trade arrangements in terms of their potential contribution to credibility rather than to the expansion of trade. De jure "dollarization" and a faster pace of FTAA negotiations (or even a bilateral trade agreement with the United States) thus came to be regarded as combinations more appropriate than the "protectionist" and "unstable" MERCOSUR to ensure macroeconomic stability and an outward-oriented model. However, the enthusiasm for North–South preferential negotiations was (and is) far from universal. Many businesspeople fear the potential competition of more efficient producers and the possibility of being traded off for relatively minor concessions in areas of traditional interest of Argentina (such as agriculture).

Argentina's Foreign Trade Strategy: An Assessment

In the last decade and a half, Argentina's foreign trade regime underwent a significant transformation. Five decades of inward orientation were left behind and the trade regime shifted toward more openness and transparency. Hand in hand with trade liberalization, free capital movement and the currency board fostered Argentina's closer integration into the world market. Such integration, however, was highly asymmetric—very intense in the financial realm but modest in the area of trade.[7] Argentina's feeble integration into the world trading system has been to a large extent the result of domestic trade (and exchange rate) policies. However, a structure of comparative advantages biased toward sector that exhibit huge international distortions (such as temperate-climate agricultural products) has also been an important factor.

Argentina is a country well endowed with natural resources. Its comparative advantages lie predominantly in agricultural, mining, and energy products. (By the late 1990s, foods and beverages, ores and metals, and fuels accounted for as much as two-thirds of total exports, the bulk of which was traded in undifferentiated markets.) During the 1990s, despite a significant increase in export volume and excluding diversification of exports to Brazil (where manufactures make a more substantial contribution), Argentina's export commodity breakdown experienced no substantial transformation. Behind this export structure there is a relatively small group of commodity exporters, largely concentrated in grains and oil seeds (which account for a third of total Argentine export sales) and energy (contributing almost a fifth).

Although the radical trade reform of the 1990s was a top-to-bottom process as many other failed attempts of the past, it had some distinguishing characteristics. First, it was a reaction to the collapse of inward orientation as a development model. Second, it was part of a broader and more comprehensive reform program that radically altered the structure of incentives prevalent during import substitution. Third, it was enforced by democratic governments, which broke the historic association between trade liberalization and authoritarian rule. All these factors suggest that the new policy regime should have been more resilient than other previous attempts. However, the financial collapse that took place at the turn of the century and the prevailing fatigue with economic reform policies have raised new pressures for policy reversal.

The two major obstacles to a return to protectionist policies are the reforms that took place in the 1990s in production structure and the constraints posed by external factors. The 1990s reforms substantially changed the production structure of local industry by reducing the share of domestic value added in gross output. These reforms significantly increased the opportunities for horizontal and more flexible production schemes based on imported inputs, but they failed to produce enough incentives to alter the predominantly inward-looking orientation of domestic firms, except in traditional export sectors. Thus, industrial modernization contributed very little toward creating an outward-oriented coalition that could join the traditional agricultural and natural resources–based interests to counter the influence of the inward-looking sectors modeled prior to the 1990s. However, it made the economy much more dependent on imported inputs by breaking up production chains.

The potential contribution of external factors to prevent policy reversals is also likely to be very strong. Multilateral trading agreements still offer some room for policy discretion, but the formal reversal of multilateral commitments seems unlikely. Preferential trading agreements may become even more effective constraints on policy discretion. In this respect, MERCOSUR is likely to play a decisive role, since Brazil has become Argentina's largest export market. Other preferential negotiations, such as those underway with the European Union and the FTAA process may also limit the scope for policy reversals, as full withdrawal would be very costly in terms of reputation and "defensive" considerations. Thus, at least in the case of Argentina, over the medium term preferential negotiations are likely to be a complement, rather than an alternative, to outward orientation and trade openness. If more open trade policies experience a reversal, that would take place at the expense of all negotiating arenas.

However, these checks on policy reversal constitute negative rather than positive forces in favor of sustainable trade liberalization. After a decade and a half of poorly designed and implemented reforms, Argentina still lacks an energetic and diversified export-oriented sector that could become the main force behind increased tradeability. For historical reasons, Argentina also lacks a state bureaucracy capable of overcoming temporary political shifts in favor of a long-term, strategic course for trade policy. These fragilities suggest that trade strategies in Argentina will continue to be volatile, thus limiting the opportunities for a beneficial integration into the world economy.

Notes

The views expressed in this chapter do not necessarily reflect those of the Argentine government.

1. Many of these policies were challenged at the WTO and eventually had to be reversed.

2. The new methodology consisted of a peg against a basket of currencies composed of equal shares of U.S. dollars and Euros. In order not to provoke an immediate devaluation of the peso as a result of the new peg, the rule was made conditional on the U.S. dollar–Euro bilateral exchange rate reaching unity. Until then a "convergence factor"

was in effect, equivalent to the difference between the actual quotation of the basket of currencies and the one-to-one parity between the peso and the dollar. The convergence factor acted in practice as a variable levy on imports and a variable subsidy on exports.

3. A successful trade reform needs to raise two relative prices: the price of exportables relative to importables and the price of exportables relative to nontradeables. Tariff cuts and the removal of nontariff barriers achieved the former, but the latter depends on the evolution of the real exchange rate. This means that if the domestic currency experiences a real appreciation pari passu with trade liberalization (as a result, for example, of capital account liberalization cum stabilization), one relative price (exportables/nontradeables) would be shifting in the wrong direction. This would stimulate an inefficient and unsustainable allocation of too many resources into the production of nontradeables. French-Davis (1999) makes a case for a clear difference between trade reforms led by exports (as in East Asia) and those led by imports (as in many Latin American countries). See also Bouzas and Keifman (2003).

4. The commitments undertaken under the General Agreement on Trade in Services (GATS) include bound offers in the third modality of services provision (commercial presence) in areas such as business services, communications and telecommunications, construction and engineering, financial services (except insurance), and travel and tourism.

5. According to December 2001 data, Argentina was the WTO member most disproportionately challenged in the dispute settlement mechanism, as measured by the difference in number of cases in which Argentina was challenged and in which it acted as a plaintiff.

6. Argentina's constitutional arrangements (which place international agreements over and above domestic legislation) were a major factor behind the inability of the Argentine authorities to respond to the devaluation of the real with the reimposition of tariffs. Such a decision would have been challenged in the courts with a high chance of success. See Ablin and Lucángeli (2000).

7. Before the crisis, Argentine external liabilities were equivalent to approximately one-fourth of emerging markets' total capitalization. By contrast, even after the rapid growth recorded in the 1990s, by the end of the decade Argentine exports still accounted for only 0.4 percent of total world trade. Prior to the devaluation, the export/GDP coefficient was also below 9 percent.

References

Ablin, E. R., and J. Lucángeli. 2000. *La Política Comercial Argentina: Evolución Reciente y Limitaciones de los Instrumentos Futuros.* Boletín Informativo Techint 304. Buenos Aires: Centro de Estudios de Estado y Sociedad.

Berlinski, J. 1998. *El Sistema de Incentivos en Argentina (de la Liberalización Unilateral al MERCOSUR).* Estudios de la Economía Real 6. Buenos Aires: Centro de Estudios para la Producción.

Bouzas, R. 1999. "MERCOSUR's External Trade Negotiations: Dealing with a Congested Agenda." In *MERCOSUR. Regional Integration and World Markets,* edited by Riordan Roett, 81–93. Boulder, CO: Lynne Rienner Publishers.

———. 2002. "MERCOSUR After Ten Years: Learning Process or Deja Vu?" In *Paths* to *Regional Integration: The Case of MERCOSUR,* edited by Joseph S. Tulchin, Ralph H. Espach, and H.A. Golding, 115–34. Washington, DC: Woodrow Wilson International Center.

Bouzas, R., and S. Keifman. 1987. *Política Comercial y Tendencias Recientes del Comercio Exterior en la Argentina (1976/1985).* Documentos de Trabajo e Informes de Investigación 58. Buenos Aires: Facultad Latinoamericana de Ciencias Sociales.

———. 2003. "Making Trade Liberalization Work." In *After the Washington Consensus: Restarting Growth and Reform in Latin America,* edited by Pedro-Pablo Kuczynski and John Williamson, 157–79. Washington, DC: Institute for International Economics.

Damill, M., and S. Keifman. 1993. "Trade Liberalization in a High Inflation Economy: The Case of Argentina 1989–91." In *Trade and Growth: New Dilemmas in Trade Policy,* edited by M. Agosin and D. Tussie, 128–42. London: Macmillan.

French-Davis, R. 1999. *Macroeconomía, Comercio y Finanzas para Reformar las Reformas en América Latina.* Santiago: McGraw Hill.

Hora, R. 2000. "Terratenientes, empresarios industriales y crecimiento industrial en la Argentina: los estancieros y el debate sobre el proteccionismo (1890–1914)." *Desarrollo Económico* 40, no. 159: 465–92.

Lucángeli, J. 1989. *Política Comercial y Desempeño Industrial: La Experiencia Argentina de los Últimos Cuarenta Años.* Boletín Informativo Techint 259. Buenos Aires: Centro de Estudios de Estado y Sociedad.

Makuc, A. 1989. *La Ronda Uruguay 1986–90, Negociaciones Comerciales Multilaterales del Acuerdo General, Aranceles y Comercio, GATT.* Boletín Informativo Techint 258. Buenos Aires: Centro de Estudios de Estado y Sociedad.

Makuc, A., and E. R. Ablin. 1994. *Comercio Exterior Argentino: MERCOSUR y Apertura.* Buenos Aires: Errepar.

———. 1997. *Comercio Exterior.* Buenos Aires: Errepar.

7

Regional and Transregional Dimensions of Brazilian Trade Policy

Pedro da Motta Veiga

Brazil's trade agenda became increasingly complex in the second half of the 1990s. A diverse set of external negotiations involving other member-states of the Latin American Integration Association (LAIA) and several developed countries was added to the Southern Common Market's (MERCOSUR) already complex internal agenda.

In December 1994, the Free Trade Area of the Americas (FTAA) was launched as an initiative backed largely by the United States, followed by the signing of an interregional cooperation agreement in 1995 between MERCOSUR and the European Union that covered trade and economic cooperation. In both these processes, MERCOSUR acts as a single economic bloc, which has not been the case in negotiations with other LAIA members, such as the Andean Community nations and Mexico.

In preferential trade negotiations with developed partners, Brazil's prevailing approach has been shaped by caution or, more accurately, by a *defensive* stance. How can we explain this defensive stance when contrasted with, for instance, Mexico's active approach when discussing free trade agreements with its partners in North America in 1994, and recently with the European Union?

A reason traditionally invoked to justify this stance points to the fact that Brazil is a *global trader,* maintaining strong trade relations with diverse regions of the world and hosting foreign direct investments originating in the United States, the European Union, and Japan. The main policy implication of this type of global market insertion would be to reduce Brazil's interest in participating in trade negotiations that would impose trade preferences with one region or another.

In the words of Abreu (1997: 3), "for economies such as that of Brazil whose trade outside the hemisphere is very significant, it is not easy to demonstrate the advantages of a preferential trade zone such as the FTAA as compared to multilateral liberalization." Furthermore, from this stand-point, the option for the FTAA would imply—in terms of the negotiation strategy—that Brazil "would give up the concessions that could be obtained from its trading partners outside the hemisphere through a multilateral ne-gotiation" (Abreu 1997: 3).

This is a relevant argument, and there are certainly significant economic risks for Brazil associated with preferential liberalization initiatives in its relations with the United States or the European Union. However, this does not fully explain the logic of Brazil's negotiating position. Even if this was based solely on an economic rationale, assessment of the costs and benefits associated with different negotiating processes would extend beyond the "Brazil as a global trader" argument, which is based on aggregate data of bilateral trade and investments flows. Therefore, we must consider other factors, including the sectoral composition of bilateral trade and investment flows, presence of intra-industry trade, pre-existence of preferential agree-ments linking the potential partners to third-party countries, and the trade barriers (both tariff and non-tariff) that affect bilateral trade. These are just some of the factors to be taken into account when assessing the potential impacts of a preferential trade liberalization agreement, and particularly when comparing the potential effects of various preferential arrangements.

The core argument of this paper is that Brazil's negotiating position, particularly in its talks with developed countries, is not based on a rational assessment of the costs and benefits associated with these negotiations from an economic standpoint. On the one hand, Brazil's position in its trade nego-tiations is certainly shaped by the interests and lobbying capacity of public and private players. However, it is also grounded on cost-benefit assessments based on implications for the nation's foreign policy—and the paradigm shaping this policy—more than on economic or trade considerations or concerns.

In this chapter, I analyze the factors shaping Brazil's negotiating position, both within MERCOSUR and in the foreign relations of this bloc. In line with the framework presented by Aggarwal and Espach in Chapter 1, Brazil's negotiating position is shaped by both economic and political factors, all packaged within a larger, specific concept of the need for greater insertion into the international system. This view is dominated by political or longer-term strategic concerns.

Brazil's Preferential Trade Negotiations: Conditioning Factors and Rationale

Accounting for some two-thirds of the total GDP of MERCOSUR, Brazil's economic performance, domestic policies, and negotiating stance within this bloc have marked effects on the overall development of the integration process, as well as its methodology and negotiations agenda. Brazil has also played the role of protagonist in MERCOSUR's external relationships, with a strategy of assigning high priority to negotiations as a bloc, particularly when the partner is a major player in international trade, such as the United States and the European Union.

Regarding MERCOSUR's internal agenda, Brazil's negotiating position is certainly one of the key factors shaping the bloc's current profile, one that is halfway between a free trade area and a customs union, with sparse institutionalization and weak tools for disciplining member nations. At the level of its foreign relationships with more developed partners, Brazil's negotiating stance is clearly defensive. This is especially evident within the FTAA, where the aggressive demanding approach of the United States substantiates Brazil's defensive concerns.

What are the factors that shape this negotiating strategy, and the logic behind them? The following two general considerations are important in answering these questions.

- The political economy of Brazil's liberalization reforms, regarding trade policy and politics, has been marked by the supremacy of import-competing sectors over export sectors.
- The dominant paradigm of Brazilian foreign policy over the past four decades is characterized by competition with the United States, and the objective of developing the nation's industrial capacity as a key condition for independent activities within the international system.

Concerning the political economy of the liberalization program, in late 1994 Brazil was completing a triple-pronged trade liberalization drive. At the regional level, MERCOSUR's customs union was coming into effect. At the multilateral level, Brazil was prepared to sign on to the commitments at the completion of the Uruguay Round. Unilaterally, thanks to the foreign exchange policy of the government's economic stabilization plan, the competitive impacts of the unilateral liberalization completed at the end of the previous year were reaching their full potential. Afterward, beginning in 1995, the liberal guidelines of industrial and foreign trade policies in Brazil began to shift. At least two factors (discussed below) lie at the root of this change.

First, Mexico's Tequila Crisis in late 1994 produced an import administration process based largely on tariffs. This was designed to avoid a sharp deterioration of Brazil's trade balance, which slipped into the red in 1995 after over a decade of significant positive results. The deterioration of the trade balance could have undermined the stabilization strategy based on the nominal exchange rate. Common external tariff rates moved—generally upward—in order to discourage imports of durable and non-durable consumer goods.

Second, as the exchange rate appreciated after the introduction of the stabilization program, the impacts of the reduction in tariff protection introduced between 1990 and 1993 were magnified. Hence, less competitive industrial sectors were severely affected, prompting the reappearance of protectionist pressures from these sectors. Some segments (such as toys and apparel) benefited through the introduction of import quotas. The government implemented new trade protection mechanisms (anti-dumping rules and safeguards) in accordance with the Uruguay Round agreements.

Hence, the macro- and micro-economic impacts of the exchange rate appreciation and the rising doubts about the sustainability of Brazil's stabilization strategy converged to make the government gradually adopt new guidelines for industrial and export promotion policies. Fresh incentives were introduced to assist sectors that were being restructured and to attract producers capable of substituting imports (such as telecommunications equipment manufacturers). Regarding exports, government support was expanded through public financing and the phasing out of existing export taxes on semi-processed products, and an export credit insurance system was introduced.

These new trends confirm that, from 1995 onward, a neo-activist stance took shape in the fields of foreign trade and industrial policy, one that extended beyond the emergency measures justified through the macro- or micro-economic conjunctural rationale. This shift set limits on the extent of Brazil's liberalization in the fields of trade and industrial policy. Without a clear-cut reversal in the liberalization process, trade policy increasingly reflected the idea that the negative effects of trade liberalization were significant and had not yet been absorbed by industry. In addition, policymakers recognized sizeable risks in any new measure that could increase the openness of the domestic goods and services markets.

With this change in orientation, policymakers came to agree that, once the unilateral tariff reduction schedule, the MERCOSUR transition period, and the multilateral negotiation cycle of the Uruguay Round were completed, Brazil should take time to "digest" this three-track liberalization movement, pruning from its external agenda any initiatives that might result in any additional commitments to further liberalization. The perception of the competitive fragility of Brazilian industry—and its consequent potential vulnerability—was extremely important to this strategic formulation. In addition, this perception was compatible with a policy agenda shaped mainly by the interests of the import-competing sectors. This hegemony of import-competing sectors in Brazil's trade policy was a distinctive trait of the transformation dynamics that swept through Brazil in the 1990s, when compared to the changes taking place in other major Latin American nations, such as Mexico and Argentina. In Brazil, the resistance that grew among entrepreneurial, trade union, and civil servants' interests consolidated during the long and reasonably successful period of protectionist industrialization, which had marked effects on the implementation of market-based reforms.

The main outcome, in terms of trade policies, of Brazil's gradualist, negotiated style of liberalization, which was interrupted only during the thirty months of the Collor administration, consisted of the survival, even after reforms, of protectionist structures and intersectorally discriminatory incentives. Both of these policy programs benefited these same import-competing sectors that had been privileged by industrial and export policies over earlier decades (auto assembly, chemicals, electrical/electronics and capital goods sectors).

This continuity was also evident in the area of foreign policy, despite major changes in the Brazilian economy. The globalist paradigm that dominated Brazil's foreign policy since the 1960s remained, and framed the political logic behind Brazil's participation in MERCOSUR, as well as in other preferential liberalization initiatives.

What is this "globalist paradigm" that has formed the cornerstone of Brazilian foreign policy for the past four decades? As expressed by Soares de Lima (1994: 35), it is a perspective on Brazil's position in the international system that results from "combining . . . several different intellectual influences," including a nationalist criticism of the pro-U.S. foreign policy matrix produced under the aegis of the Instituto Superior de Estudos Brasileiros, the view of the Economic Commission for Latin America and the Caribbean on center–periphery international dynamics, and the tradition of realist thought in international relations, particularly the concept of the international system as anarchic. According to this view, North–South polarization provides the rationale for Brazil's foreign policy, which aims in part to create conditions for the implementation of an autonomous national industrial strategy.

One of the main components of Brazil's foreign policy paradigm is competition against the United States, particularly within the Americas, with the objective of establishing conditions favorable to the development of the nation's industry.

MERCOSUR

From the beginning, the role of the federal government has been decisive in the design and implementation of Brazil's participation in MERCOSUR. Ultimately, the logic behind subregional integration was essentially political. What were Brazil's motives? At the beginning of the integration process, dating back to the bilateral agreements with Argentina during the second half of the 1980s, this motivation related to the shift from a military to civilian regime. The main motive of Brazil's re-definition of its posture toward Argentina was to overcome the "previous ambivalences of the military governments" (Soares de Lima 1994: 38).

Regional integration represented Brazil's first reaction to the new challenges posed by globalization and the emergence of regional economic blocs. The changing international environment of the 1980s was perceived by Brazil as less permissive for state-led development strategies, which reduced the resources and leverage available to the country from strategic international relationships. The end of the Cold War and the simultaneous consolidation of globalization and regionalization during the late 1980s and early 1990s served only to strengthen these perceptions.

These bilateral projects with Argentina and then regional projects were elements of a broad-ranging foreign policy strategy. The importance assigned to the regional project in Brazil was a function of the perception of MERCOSUR's capacity to contribute to the general objectives of this strategy. This MERCOSUR capacity can be assessed in light of two basic criteria: (1) the level of convergence (or divergence) among the policies that make up the national development projects of the member countries; and

(2) the level of convergence or divergence in the foreign policies of the member countries *strictu sensu* in relation to the rest of the world and, in particular, toward the United States.

Brazil's strategic approach to the MERCOSUR project combines this political logic of the trade bloc's role within the nation's larger objectives with the prevailing perception of economic incentives that are viewed to be few, particularly due to the vast difference in size between Brazil and its partners. This explains the government's lack of interest in proposals for deepening the customs union, or for those viewed as potentially reducing the margins of freedom of the federal and state governments with respect to development policies. This negotiating position of Brazil is certainly the main factor shaping the current profile of MERCOSUR, a flawed customs union endowed with weak institutions, mechanisms, and means for disciplining members who violate their commitments.

From the standpoint of regional integration, it is important to note that the integration process, and MERCOSUR itself, had no major impacts on the design and implementation of Brazil's national industrial development project. This has remained intact, and has been little affected by the elements of a parallel regional industrial project. To the contrary, in intra-bloc negotiations Brazil systematically expresses its affirmation of a national industrial development project under the logic of competition with its partners, and almost never approaches industrial development as a cooperative process among all members.

Brazil and MERCOSUR Negotiations
with Developed Countries

In terms of Brazil's trade negotiations with non-MERCOSUR countries, the convergence in Brazilian trade policy formulation between the foreign policy paradigm and the hegemony of the import-competing sectors in national and regional trade policy has the following implications. First, Brazil's strategic priority is the establishment of preferential links with the other countries of South America, rather than transregional arrangements. Second, transregional agreements (with countries outside South America) do not, in principle, fit the core objectives of Brazil's foreign policy.

Within this context, dominated by the politics of foreign policy rather than economic logic, an agreement with the United States is by definition the less desirable option, particularly if it is viewed as a project urged on by the United States that threatens the survival of the regional political initiative backed by Brazil. Seen from Brasília, this risk concerns not only markets, but also competition for political hegemony.

The FTAA is often seen as an economic project that will generate huge and long-lasting political consequences. Its implementation would permanently shift the balance of power within the hemisphere, and especially in South America. Moreover, as a former Brazilian ambassador put it, "[I]t will expand and legitimate the U.S. preeminence in the Americas, favoring the emergence of a unipolar world. And even if other factors lead to the emergence of a multipolar world, [the FTAA] will place Latin America within the zone under the direct hegemony of the United States, thus leaving [Latin American countries] little space for political maneuvering" (Souto Maior 2000: 6).

According to this view, an agreement with the European Union has political functionality, derived from the "threat" represented by the FTAA. From this standpoint, should the FTAA threat cease to exist, the political incentives behind an agreement with the European Union would fade.

It is interesting to note that, from the point of view of "national industrial strategy," an agreement with the European Union should not suit Brazil's interests. From this perspective, the talks with the European Union are basically a North–South bargaining game based on the hypothesis of a trade-off between opening up Europe's agricultural market to exports from MERCOSUR and opening up the industrial markets of MERCOSUR countries to exports from Europe. Consequently, the interest shown by the Brazilian authorities in terms of the agreement with Europe is essentially explained through a foreign policy—that is, political—rationale, strengthened by the fact that the European Union explicitly favors biregional negotiation between these two blocs (in contrast to the United States within the FTAA). This utility as a legitimate negotiating body gives MERCOSUR an important political role, particularly during recent times of crisis.

Brazil's current dominant outlook on the two negotiation processes highlights the risks associated with them and downplays potential opportunities. From this standpoint, the potential costs of Brazil's participation in the FTAA process and negotiations with the European Union are seen as essentially linked to transitional adjustments, particularly in industrial sectors, and to divergent priorities in the negotiating agendas of Brazil and its partners.

For Brazil, the risks of this divergence in negotiating priorities are mainly linked to the consolidation of arrangements in which the issues stressed by the more powerful countries are dealt with adequately. Brazil has less concern with those issues or interests that are of higher priority to countries with less negotiating clout. This problem is best illustrated by the obstacles to dealing with agricultural matters in both negotiating processes, but particularly in the talks with the European Union.

The core strategy of Brazil in both negotiations has been to protect its national production structure and regulatory regimes as much as possible from the potential adjustment costs triggered by liberalization and negotiation of trade disciplines. These objectives outweigh the role of these agreements as tools for attracting investments and generating new export flows. Consequently, assessments of these agreements in Brazil as a whole tend to be negative, except when one of the talks is perceived as a tool for neutralizing the other one or for increasing the bargaining power of Brazil and MERCOSUR.

Regionalism and Preferential Arrangements: Contrasting Incentives

It is interesting to note that a project such as MERCOSUR, which represents Brazil's first strategic reaction to the challenges of a globalized market, for the most part has emerged in the Brazilian view as a single-pronged approach that excludes other insertion strategies, particularly when involving negotiations with developed partners in an international setting that is not multilateral. How can this single-minded strategic vision be explained? First, the economic risks associated with the regional project are limited, from any standpoint, reducing concerns over the delicate competitive edge of Brazilian industry. The economies of Brazil's MERCOSUR partners are relatively modest, and intra-bloc competition has not prompted significant divestment in any Brazilian sector. Also, at the regulatory level, integration has barely touched the freedom enjoyed by Brazilian policymakers to deploy policy tools considered as domestic in the industrial area. Brazil has clearly emerged as the major beneficiary of regulatory competition to attract foreign investment within MERCOSUR.

However, the dynamics unleashed by MERCOSUR and domestic reforms in member countries are leading towards the consolidation of MERCOSUR as a regional production hub for industrialized goods for the extended domestic market—which still enjoys a reasonable level of protection against imports—and also other South American markets. A number of factors lie at the root of this process, including the following:

• The rise in intra-MERCOSUR trade, particularly in the traditionally import-competing industrial sectors. Brazil has experienced increasing specialization of manufactures exports, especially in scale-intensive industries (including steel, petrochemicals, automobiles), and in sectors ranked as specialized suppliers (essentially mechanical and electrical materials). For some of these sectors, the functional aspect of exports within MERCOSUR is associated less with diversified and aggressive export strategies than with defensive or "compensatory" strategies prompted by the loss of domestic market shares during the import liberalization period. Intra-MERCOSUR preferences allowed these sectors to benefit from privileged access to neighboring markets in order to offset domestic losses.

• The logic of growing market share guided much of the new foreign direct investment channeled to this bloc, as well as mergers and acquisitions involving companies in its member nations. In addition to the trade agreements, joint ventures and other types of arrangements among companies created a private forum for dealing with structural and regulatory asymmetries among the member states. The strategy of leading companies in various industrial sectors was to seize potential gains in scale allowed by the extension of the domestic market and by the maintenance of appreciable levels of tariff and occasionally non-tariff protection against imports from outside this bloc.

The net outcome of this set of trends is the consolidation of MERCOSUR as an industrial pole, with Brazil as its hub, and the other countries in South America as potential additional spokes. In the Brazilian perspective, this gives regional integration functional importance as a tool of its industrial development strategy.

For Brazil, the assessment of the costs and benefits associated with MERCOSUR is quite favorable. The project has imposed negligible constraints on the national industrial development project, and Brazil has benefited greatly from the inflow of investments attracted to the extended market. There is one caveat, however, to this positive assessment: MERCOSUR has not managed to induce its members to line up automatically behind Brazil's foreign policy, which was Brazil's main political objective. However, despite the discrepancies among the foreign policies of MERCOSUR members, particularly between Brazil and Argentina, the consolidation of FTAA negotiations confers a new type of political functionality (a defensive one, certainly) to this regional initiative.

From the standpoint of the private sector, which has benefited from privileged access to an extended domestic market, extending the liberalization project to include other countries, particularly developed ones, is a threat to the market shares of leading companies in the regional market. In addition, it may undermine public and private trade management and regulatory mechanisms consolidated alongside the process of establishing the customs union. This threat of extending MERCOSUR market access to developed nations looms even larger if this agreement should imply any dilution of intra-MERCOSUR trade preferences, as well as among MERCOSUR nations and other LAIA economies, as would be the case if the FTAA comes into effect. From this standpoint, an agreement with the European Union is viewed in Brazil as less threatening than one within the FTAA.

Conclusions

The logic behind the strategies of national and regional policymakers involved in current trade talks is based less on a "rational" assessment of the economic incentives and cost structure theoretically associated with preferential liberalization processes than on prevailing perceptions regarding the nature and content of national political prospects and objectives, as well as the utility of various trade arrangements for the accomplishment of these objectives. The case of Brazil illustrates this hypothesis.

The functional value of the various preferential liberalization projects is assessed in Brazil in the light of their capacity to help strengthen the nation's power—both political and economic (or, better put, "industrial" power)—in the field of international relations, and particularly its objective of boosting Brazil's negotiating clout vis-à-vis the United States within the hemisphere, and particularly in South America.

The uniqueness of Brazil's trade negotiations strategy does not lie in the fact that it is framed by a political vision. It can be argued that the subordination of trade policy to foreign policy occurs in several countries. Perhaps the distinctive feature of Brazil's trade policy formulation is to be found in the "close subordination" pattern that relates trade policy to foreign policy, and the consequent hegemony of political motives over economic considerations when assessing actual and prospective trade negotiations.

Currently, efforts to reinvigorate the regional initiative have been stifled by the deepest crisis in MERCOSUR's history, while Brazil faces the challenge of negotiating broad preferential liberalization programs with its main partners in the developed world. As we have seen, the MERCOSUR project, conceived in the early 1990s within a framework defined by the objectives of Brazil's foreign policy, constituted the first strategic move by Brazilian diplomacy, in parallel with unilateral trade liberalization. This move was in response to a new, emerging international context perceived by Brazil to be less permissive toward development strategies, and one that reduced the power resources available to the country within the international system. Changes in this international environment could prompt, in the near future, the emergence of a second strategic drive in Brazil's foreign policy.

This second strategic move would reflect the need for Brazil to adapt its foreign policy to a new set of constraints, defined by the challenge of preferential trade negotiations with the United States, Brazil's main political competitor in the hemisphere, and with the European Union, a powerful economic competitor. The major outcome of such a move would likely be the revision of the "close subordination" pattern that relates trade policy to foreign policy, making more room for economic and trade considerations in the assessment of preferential trade negotiations with developed countries.

In this "second strategic move" scenario, Brazil's negotiating stance within MERCOSUR would undergo a significant shift. In a situation where the centrifugal pressures on MERCOSUR—generated both by FTAA dynamics and the economic vulnerability of its members—are intensified, Brazil would show greater willingness to discuss within MERCOSUR an agenda that until now it had rejected. This could increase prospects for an enhanced regional dimension to MERCOSUR, a project that by now has been almost exclusively dominated by the logic of national interests and actors.

Under this scenario, which combines the deepening of regional integration in MERCOSUR and a new trade liberalization cycle, tied to the talks underway with the United States and the European Union, the structure of protection and incentives that emerged from liberalization in the early 1990s would likely be redefined. Regarding the private sector, the most probable outcomes of such a scenario would be (1) criticism from entrepreneurs in industrial sectors comfortable in the current situation and potentially threatened by further liberalization; and (2) intensification of pressures urging the government to complete the cycle of reforms designed to reduce domestic production costs and lower export prices, mainly through tax reform.

This scenario, however, is far from becoming a reality. Recently the issue of FTAA negotiations seems to have become increasingly important to the country's domestic policy agenda. During the presidential campaign of 2002, the debate over the FTAA gained momentum and the main candidates criticized the project of hemispheric integration. At the same time, candidates were not precise on their plans for strengthening MERCOSUR, raising doubts about their willingness and ability to deal with the deep crises of the regional integration project.

How is the political economy of Brazil's trade negotiations likely to evolve in the coming years? Clearly the progress of negotiations with the European Union and the FTAA seems to contribute to the emergence of a new liberalization cycle. However, the politicization of domestic discussions on these talks will tend, at least initially, to strengthen the partisans of the hegemonic paradigm of foreign policy, as political debates will concentrate on highly sensitive issues such as the risks associated with increased U.S. hegemony in the hemisphere or asymmetry in the negotiations between Brazil and developed countries.

To sum up, in the 1990s the foreign policy paradigm that provided the framework for Brazil's trade policy over the previous four decades underwent a period of revision, marked both by change and continuity. Economically and especially politically, MERCOSUR was the main component of the changes that brought about Brazil's trade policy. The severe crisis affecting MERCOSUR and its negotiations with the United States and the European Union currently represents a dramatic change from the environment of the 1990s. In response to this new environment, Brazil's foreign policy will certainly change again. This could take the form of either a deepening of this revisionist movement, combining the strengthening of regional integration and preferential trade liberalization with developed partners,[1] or Brazil's strategic vision could return, once again, to its focus on the principles and objectives of a "globalist paradigm," meaning the preservation of the national industrial project and competition with the United States.

Early in its tenure, the recently elected government in Brazil revealed some preference for a strategy combining the re-invigoration of MERCOSUR— mainly through the strengthening of its political and institutional dimensions, along with the setting of trade and cooperation agreements with other South American countries—and the negotiation of a bilateral trade agreement between MERCOSUR and the United States.

While still only generically formulated, such a strategy seems fully compatible with the *regional leader* strategy type set out by Aggarwal and Espach in the introductory chapter: MERCOSUR and South America are given priority, both economically and politically, and bilateral negotiations between MERCOSUR and the United States is perceived as a less risky initiative, in political terms, than the FTAA.

Note

1. Any such potential revision would not imply the adherence to some kind of "peripheral pragmatism" as a new foreign policy paradigm, nor will it mean the abandonment of the project of industrial development.

References

Abreu, M. P. 1997. *O Brasil e a ALCA: interesses e alternativas.* Texto para Discussão 371. Rio de Janeiro: Departamento de Economia, Pontifícia Universidade Católica do Rio de Janeiro, August.
Soares de Lima, M. R. 1994. "Ejes Analíticos y Conflictos de Paradigmas en la Política Exterior Brasileña." *America Latina/Internacional* 1, no. 2: 27–46.
Souto Maior, L. A. 2000. "A Crise do Mercosul e Política Internacional." *Carta Internacional* (Universidade de São Paulo) 8, no. 93: 5–6.

8

Chile's Multidimensional Trade Policy

Osvaldo Rosales

Chile has consolidated significant changes in its international position and production structure over the past decade. Both aspects encourage an active trade policy noted for advancing unilateral trade liberalization while at the same time subscribing a considerable number of bilateral and regional preferential trade agreements.

Chile has become a global economic actor due to the multiple initiatives through which it participates in world trade. Specifically, Chile was one of the first Latin American countries to join the Asia-Pacific Economic Cooperation (APEC) forum, and the first associate country in the Southern Common Market (MERCOSUR) customs union. Furthermore, it has established clear leadership in bilateral free trade agreements (FTAs) with the European Union, South Korea, and the United States.

These manifold initiatives reflect deep changes in Chile's production structure, due to the growing significance of foreign trade in its economic activities, the broad range of products that it exports, and the large number of countries with which it engages in trade. More significant yet are the growing numbers of Chilean entrepreneurs whose business depends directly on the evolution of world markets.

Chile is a small and open economy that is highly dependent on foreign trade. Therefore, it has become vulnerable in the same measure to changes in the world economy and to uncertainties experienced by its economic agents. For these reasons, Chilean trade policy seeks to secure, through bilateral and multilateral means, competitive conditions that Chile would hardly be able to obtain through unilateral measures alone, to facilitate access to new markets and defend the success of its exporters.

Therefore, it is extremely important for Chile to secure an international position that ensures stability through an organized world trade system governed by fair, transparent, and non-discriminatory rules that limit unilateral measures among trade partners as much as possible, particularly to avoid having disparities in size and economic power determine protectionist measures in the markets. For open economies such as Chile's, multilateral channels represent the ideal option. However, this alternative does not necessarily run apace with the urgency required by economic and technological development and, furthermore, not all goals can be pursued and achieved through multilateral means. In such a scenario, progress can be made in bilateral relations or through subregional agreements, provided that the negotiating parties are willing to establish better conditions for competition than those offered at the time by the multilateral system.

In the 1990s, Chile was noted for including the new international trade approaches in its bilateral and regional agreements, taking into account the significant changes brought about by the entry of all Latin American countries to the multilateral system. Chile participated in the debate of the new and complex issues addressed by the Uruguay Round and chose to adopt the new standards of world trade as a benchmark for negotiations with its trading partners. In addition, the government accepted the profound changes that the adoption of the new standards would entail for its own economic organization.

At the regional level, Chile has been a protagonist in the numerous bilateral agreements signed within the framework of the Latin American Integration Association (ALADI) and the launching of the Free Trade Area of the Americas (FTAA). As a means to consolidate its outward-looking development policy, Chile negotiated the ALADI economic complementarity agreements as a first step toward liberalizing trade in a substantial share of goods traded with regional trade partners, with well-defined time frames for tariff reductions.

In a second phase, Chile set out to expand those agreements by incorporating new areas and disciplines, bearing in mind the experience gained by NAFTA and the emergence of MERCOSUR. These two subregional agreements created new opportunities for integration, forcing the governments of the Coalition of Political Parties for Democracy (Concertación) to adapt their hemispheric policies in the trade area. Both regional trade agreements forced changes in Chilean trade policy. Externally, we had to improve both our knowledge of proper negotiations and our skills to carry out the process. Internally, it involved considerable coordination efforts among ministries to deal with the horizontal issues that foreign trade agreements bring up.

Modernization of the institutional framework and the achievement of reasonable levels of coordination among agencies to address foreign trade issues were attained in the process of negotiating the more evolved agreements that Chile subscribed to with MERCOSUR and Canada, and in the negotiations for the FTAA. Negotiations with Canada became an example of coordination because of the way that sanitary and phytosanitary issues were addressed. For the first time, the establishment of a joint committee was proposed to harmonize and monitor compliance with the standards of both countries.

At the same time, the institutional issues that regulate international trade were an increasing cause of concern for Chile. In negotiations with Canada, and subsequently with Mexico, Chile managed to bring into the debate the possible elimination of antidumping measures among trade partners. At the multilateral level, Chile expressed its interest in this issue by participating in a challenge to the Byrd Amendment (passed in October 2000, directs the U.S. government to pay the liquidated anti-dumping and anti-subsidy duties to the companies that have brought forward the cases) because, in our view, it established perverse incentives leading to a multiplication of cases and a distortion of the original intent of antidumping claims.

Chile pursues its external trade objectives by seeking bilateral agreements with its main trading partners, or by improving the conditions for competition guaranteed under the multilateral system. We do so without establishing priority sectors or activities, and without exclusions. At a regional level, Chile follows a policy of consensus among states to strengthen the ability of the governments of emerging economies to influence the process of globalization of economic institutions.

In multilateral issues, Chile seeks legal and institutional protection that will serve as an impartial arbiter of commercial disputes, aimed at expanding—without discrimination—the benefits derived from the elimination of trade barriers. In the multilateral arena, progress can be made in areas where bilateral negotiation is difficult, particularly where there is radical inequality in terms of power. This is the case, for instance, in negotiations with the United States for opening agricultural markets, reducing subsidies, and limiting antidumping legislation.

However, it is also true that subregional negotiations provide room for progress toward liberalization in areas where progress at the multilateral and bilateral levels becomes more difficult. For example, the possibility of advancing in the liberalization of services, investment, and other trade disciplines with neighboring countries—either MERCOSUR or with members of the Andean Community—is enhanced if there is an FTAA that provides a framework for deepening bilateral agreements. Achieving bilateral agreements on these issues will be difficult until the FTAA comes into being.

Chile's experience, gained over more than ten years of active trade policy, shows that it is not possible to rank different negotiating levels according to importance, whether they are bilateral, regional, or multilateral. Each one allows the achievement of objectives that cannot be readily attained at another negotiating level.

The Strategy of Multiple Negotiations

The circumstances described above raise the question of how to advance in a setting of multiple negotiations, based on unilateral liberalization but granting growing importance to bilateral and regional agreements, and also to the progress made in multilateral negotiations. This question can be answered with the propositions that follow.

First, the Chilean case shows that an adequate unilateral liberalization policy is the basis for developing a multiple negotiation program in world trade. Without this base, it would have been impossible to hold simultaneous conversations with such dissimilar partners as the United States, MERCOSUR, the European Union, and APEC. The risk of incoherence and relapsing to a highly differentiated tariff system adapted to the type of trade agreement would have been too high. At the same time, it is also true that unilateral liberalization, by itself, is insufficient because it does not ensure access to other markets. Today, to develop an area for trade is much more complex in terms of institutional density, and must take into account principles such as reciprocity, certainty, and transparency among member countries.

Second, addressing trade issues not covered by a unilateral policy leads a small economy with a large degree of openness into an unpredictable scenario in multilateral negotiations to establish direct bilateral negotiations with the main trading partners. Contrary to what was usually assumed, in the 1990s the implementation of bilateralism showed that it did not run counter to regionalism or to the trend for worldwide liberalization. On the contrary, there is evidence in the hemisphere that the most advanced bilateral policies have given rise to the largest subregional pacts, either along the axis built by the United States and Canada in the North, or by Brazil and Argentina in the South.

Third, bilateral agreements have an expansive effect and they reorganize regional space, creating new policy options and modifying expectations and incentives among a broad range of trading partners. This weakens restrictive trade preferences limited to a few countries and becomes the basis for a renewed hemispheric dialogue. In this case, an explosion of preferential agreements is coupled with competition to avoid being left out or to minimize the costs of trade diversion and redeployment of investment.

The above statements are close to the reflections on the new Latin American regionalism made by Enrique Iglesias, president of the Inter-American Development Bank, who identified the strategy as a process of liberalization that takes place at three levels. In the first level, there is a commitment to unilateral liberalization by the countries. The second level consists of multilateral commitments undertaken under the Uruguay Round and the World Trade Organization (WTO) trade disciplines. The third level involves regional integration agreements that supplement the other two levels and make it possible for them to operate in a continuous and irreversible process.

Evolving Integration Policies

For almost two decades, Chile based the development of a competitive external sector on the unilateral opening of its foreign trade. In the 1990s, although the first Concertación administrations maintained the commitment to the program of unilateral opening initiated under the previous administration, they supplemented this approach with an active trade policy intended to speed up the opening of external markets and avoid exclusion from third-country trade agreements. A third phase is now beginning, in which, as the export-led growth strategy consolidates, the problems of an active trade policy appear more clearly and now require the establishment of an institutional framework which guarantees stable access to foreign markets.

Limits to Unilateral Opening

The strategy of unilateral opening set the basis for a period of prolonged growth of the external sector of the Chilean economy. The implementation of a uniform tariff system coupled with a program of sustained reduction of trade barriers is a strategy that Chilean trade policy favors to this day.

Originally, it was intended to dismantle a protectionist structure that refused to consider the external sector as the engine of economic growth. The expected gains from competitiveness in national industry were sought by aligning domestic with international prices and by greater foreign investment in the export sector, as a way of modernizing the production structure and disseminating new technologies.

Unilateral tariff reduction was accompanied by a set of national policies aimed at ensuring greater integration into world markets based on an economic policy that favored macroeconomic equilibrium, privatization of state-owned companies, foreign investment in the services sector, and capital account opening (capital movement).

The Concertación administrations initiated changes in trade policy, leading to the introduction of a clear regional bias in the pursuit of trade agreements. They also increased unilateral openness in the movement of goods and services. Trade in goods has benefited from the 1991 tariff reduction, which lowered duties to 11 percent from 15 percent, and again in 1997 with a commitment to reduce tariffs by 1 percent per year, from 11 percent in 1998 to 6 percent in 2003. Both legal initiatives were unanimously approved by Congress, thereby confirming a solid political consensus, another major feature of Chilean trade policy.

Regarding the capital account, restrictions to short-term capital movements were removed and foreign access to the financial services sector was expanded. In services, new areas for private investment were opened when concessions for the operation of public infrastructure projects were granted. In telecommunications, deregulation and competition were enhanced; at the same time, the internationalization of banks was broadened.

Although the policy of unilateral openness has been the pillar for growth of the external sector and the guiding principle behind our insertion in the international arena, it turned out to be clearly insufficient, giving rise to a more active trade policy. This greater activity is reflected in the large number of bilateral agreements entered into by Chile and in our increased commitment at the regional level to the quality of our involvement in the FTAA and MERCOSUR.

This new approach values multilateral, plurilateral, and bilateral agreements insofar as they allow supplementing aspects that a policy of unilateral openness cannot address, deal with, and resolve. The new approach, in the first place, seeks to open new markets through mutual concessions with trading partners who otherwise would be unwilling to accept greater trade liberalization. In the second place, it attempts to protect markets that are subject to trade diversion due to preferential agreements between trading partners and third countries. In the third place, it strives to lower transaction costs faced by private agents by reducing the levels of uncertainty, information asymmetry, and lack of transparency, while challenging mechanisms that may lead to a proliferation of protectionist attitudes. An active trade policy of this type is pursued to achieve greater trade liberalization than what is possible by relying exclusively on progress by the multilateral system, to avoid being excluded from the growing number of preferential trade agreements, and to limit protectionist measures through the use of non-tariff barriers.

Regionalism in the ALADI Framework

Chile's first bilateral trade agreements, signed in the early 1990s with Mexico, Venezuela, Colombia, and Ecuador, were negotiated within the framework created by ALADI. Appealing to the formula of economic complementarity agreements, Chile sought to negotiate a substantial portion of reciprocal trade, committing to relatively brief tariff phase-outs (three to six years) in negotiations that could be resolved rapidly in the political sphere. Due to the nature of these agreements, negotiations concentrated basically on trade in goods. Negotiations covering new sectors (services and investment) were left on the agenda; for the more complex technical aspects, such as rules of origin, the regulations established in ALADI Resolution 78 were incorporated.

Negotiations under the ALADI framework involve other benefits, in addition to their simplicity. Since they are part of the Montevideo Treaty (1980), governments are able to choose the "fast-track" option and to negotiate agreements that do not require legislative debate and negotiation. Second, they benefit from the eligibility clause approved in the Tokyo Round (1980), and are recognized by the multilateral system.[1]

A third feature that facilitates negotiating this set of first-generation bilateral agreements is the non-binding nature of the most-favored-nation principle. This led countries to assess more rapidly the mutual benefits of trade liberalization, without having to consider the impact of indirect effects—which are more difficult to measure—that bilateral concessions may generate in favor of third parties.

This ALADI clause, which may be debatable from a doctrinal point of view, is enormously effective since it has been invoked in most of the economic complementarity agreements signed in Latin America. In turn, this set of bilateral agreements enhances regional integration and gives renewed impetus to the integration agenda in the continent. This is an example of how a bilateral policy used for liberalization purposes becomes the basis for stronger regionalism that, in practice, helps to overcome the cumbersome bureaucratic negotiations that Latin American multilateralism employed in the 1960s.

Although the proposal for "open regionalism" in Latin America does not offer a finished model for trade agreements, it marks a shift in unilateral liberalization strategies by placing bilateral trade within the framework of a regional cooperation policy. The integration agenda incorporates the criteria of a trade policy that views the development of foreign trade as the driving force behind a new wave of growth.

In Latin America, the "open regionalism" approach represents a policy of transition from the period of unilateral liberalization to another period marked by the multiplication of economic complementarity agreements. Chile joins this political process of regional integration by flexibly incorporating what each country is willing to contribute, beyond the concessions obtained through the multilateral system, as reflected in the economic complementarity agreements.

Broad Bilateralism with MERCOSUR

In negotiations with MERCOSUR, Chile has declared that its trade agenda is part of the larger challenge of creating a regional foreign policy. For the first time, Chile proposes an integration program that includes the close relationship that exists between opening up the service sector and investment; between macroeconomic stability and trade liberalization; and between the removal of economic boundaries and greater political and cultural integration.

At the subregional level, Chile's new economic interests are reflected in its active participation in the privatization programs of state-owned utilities in neighboring countries, particularly in sectors where Chile has acquired more experience and expertise; in placing on the agenda non-discriminatory export promotion programs; and in the promotion of market deregulation and the elimination of barriers to foreign investment.

The entry of Chile into MERCOSUR as an "associate member" reflected a change in the scope of Chilean trade policy and the economic interests of the Chilean corporate sector, while simultaneously protecting the option of continuing to advance in its unilateral liberalization policy.

The new agenda addresses a series of issues not covered in economic complementarity agreements. In addition to tariff negotiations, the agenda includes a series of complementary goals, such as a stable and consistent economic framework for integration, improvement of infrastructure at border entry points, and the design of inter-oceanic corridors (physical integration protocol). These goals are further supplemented by a cultural agenda with a specific scope separate from economic integration issues.

Unlike the ALADI agreements, the new agenda includes all sectors as the basis for negotiation, while avoiding permanent exceptions for certain products. At the same time, the parties undertake to identify and start removing non-tariff barriers while banning the use of new trade restrictions.

In matters of a more technical nature, the guidelines established in ALADI resolutions are abandoned and, in fact, with respect to rules of origin, Chile adopts the model set by MERCOSUR. Moreover, institutional issues and trade defense mechanisms—such as treatment of non-tariff barriers, safeguards, and provisions governing the application of trade sanctions—are approached according to different criteria.

Negotiations between MERCOSUR and Chile constitute an example of how more advanced rules than those offered by ALADI can be taken to a multilateral level in the region. These rules were discussed for the first time in the framework of the customs union negotiations and set the standards that were lacking in the ALADI agreements. The bilateral formula applied in the case of Chile cleared the way for MERCOSUR negotiations with Bolivia. However, in subsequent negotiations by MERCOSUR with the Andean Community and with Mexico, it has not been easy to replicate the success of the earlier initiatives.

In view of the scope of the negotiations, the Chilean government modified the political treatment given to economic complementarity agreements, which since the Montevideo Treaty (1980) have been exempted from parliamentary approval, and decided to submit the agreement with MERCOSUR to Congress for ratification.

The experience gained after the negotiation has shown the importance of issues not directly related to trade in the pursuit of a policy of economic integration in times of crisis. Perforation of the common tariff and the introduction of administrative measures to regulate trade are part of the major crisis affecting MERCOSUR. The Chilean relationship with MERCOSUR is going through a difficult time, and Chile has turned down full membership to the customs union. In its negotiation agenda, Chile wants to include additional issues and to establish institutional procedures for dispute settlement.

At the same time, macroeconomic stability gains new relevance in the development of bilateral relations, to avoid beggar-thy-neighbor policies associated with fiscal and monetary instability. Moreover, to limit protectionist pressures, it is necessary to pursue the development of institutional mechanisms for dispute resolution and greater transparency in the application of non-tariff measures.

Deep Bilateralism in the New Agenda

From the beginning of the 1990s, Chile expressed its desire to enter into a FTA with the United States. Therefore, Chile followed with great interest the negotiations between the United States and Mexico and the creation of NAFTA. At the First Summit of the Americas, Chile was invited to be a part of NAFTA, and negotiations toward this objective began.

At the time, Chile learned first hand that the ambiguities noted in NAFTA were the result of the lack of definition of U.S. policy, as confirmed by the lengthy and fruitless debate surrounding the fast-track request made by President Clinton. Chile came to the view that, in that scenario, conditions were not suitable for sustaining what were likely to be lengthy, indefinite negotiations, and chose the second best option available by pursuing separate FTAs with NAFTA's member countries.

Beyond the trade benefits that these agreements could generate, Chile saw the regional NAFTA as an opportunity for implementing a general policy on globalization issues through the incorporation of the basic principles of "deep regionalism," which involve an integration agenda that goes beyond the WTO provisions.

During the preparation for its first negotiation with Canada, Chile reviewed and extended its trade policy—which basically revolved around the exchange of goods—by adopting the new rationale of deep regionalism found in NAFTA. Thus, Chile gave renewed priority to three objectives: removal of non-tariff barriers in the areas of services and investment, liberalization of market regulation and competition policies, and development of impartial procedures for trade-related dispute settlement.

Chile adhered to a programmatic regionalism, based on NAFTA's agenda, and incorporated those subjects into the bilateral agreements signed with Canada (1996) and Mexico (1997). To implement this new policy, Chile had already put in place part of the foundations in the early 1990s under the government's program of modernization of its institutional framework. During that period Chile established a new institutional framework to deal with environmental issues that would integrate the efforts of multiple institutions, and made labor reforms one of the pillars of the social consensus for the new decade. At the same time, responding to the commitments of the Uruguay Round, the second administration of the Concertación enacted a miscellaneous law covering a variety of issues not included in foreign trade.

In the context of these initiatives, Chile has played a leading role in the new Latin American regionalism by consistently including in its trade policies all possible forms of integration, from a unilateral reduction of tariffs, through the promotion of economic complementarity agreements in the framework of ALADI and its associate membership in the main regional treaty (MERCOSUR), evolving toward FTAs with a more extensive agenda (Canada, Mexico, and Central America).

Hemispheric Convergence

Since the Initiative for the Americas in the early 1990s, hemispheric regionalism became part of the international policies of all countries in the region. This was a major shift in the relationship between the United States and the rest of the continent.

Chile was not detached from the initiatives of the Bush administration (1989–93). It participated actively, leading a pioneering program in international cooperation that exchanged the payment of foreign debt interest for contributions to an environmental development fund that fosters the participation of civil society (The Americas Fund), prompted by Alejandro Foxley, finance minister during President Aylwin's administration.

The First Summit of the Americas, held in Miami in 1994, was a milestone to showcase the will to achieve hemispheric regionalism. In terms of principles, the Summit's commitment to strengthening democracy in the continent placed the trade agenda within a broader foreign policy framework. This understanding is present in the FTAA to this day, as recently demonstrated in Quebec.

The willingness of American countries—Chile included—to engage in a hemispheric dialogue reflects the Latin American interest in protecting its exports to the United States from the erosion of market share, mainly in favor of East Asian countries. As North American markets were taking the lead in buying up exports from Asian economies, Latin American countries saw the opportunity to realign their export sector toward new markets. The perception of trade disadvantage became more evident for the rest of Latin America with the creation of NAFTA.

Chile hosted the Second Summit of the Americas, which was held in Santiago in April 1998. This meeting set 2005 as the deadline for FTAA negotiations. Chile's goal was to get the negotiations started, seeking uniform progress in all negotiating groups under the *single undertaking* modality.

For Chile the FTAA is an opportunity to achieve greater convergence among the different agreements subscribed in the region, to enhance and improve existing bilateral agreements by extending and incorporating new trade rules and trade disciplines, and to establish negotiations with countries with which Chile does not have trade agreements.

In the second stage of negotiations, during the round held in Buenos Aires in April 2001, Chile led the push to accelerate the timetables set for the implementation of FTAA agreements. Discussions about dates partially revived the confrontation generally used to explain the difficulties encountered by the FTAA, that is, a northern group led by the United States pitted against the MERCOSUR countries who, while advancing in their own integration, prefer delaying the FTAA. Although in this particular case the MERCOSUR countries were notably prudent, an evaluation of the negotiations as a whole reveals other issues underlying the discussions.

The main feature of the FTAA is its evolution toward a multilateral forum (of the GATT–WTO type) at a regional level. Progress in negotiations depends on the initiative of each country, according to its relative weight in trade terms vis-à-vis each relevant issue. Alliances revolve around specific interests, and the aim is to achieve balanced negotiations. The principle of "broad reciprocity" implicit in multilateral forums is also present, since the advantages gained by one country—as the main supplier of a good or service—are necessarily passed on to members of less relative weight. In addition, the benefit of additional time for de-tariffication and implementation of compensatory measures has been accorded to the most vulnerable economies, thus relaxing the principle of strict reciprocity. However, unlike the WTO, the FTAA agenda covers a broader range of issues and, in this sense, the blueprint for negotiations is closer to the "deep regionalism" inaugurated by NAFTA. Another outstanding feature of the FTAA is the determination of member countries to carry on a dialogue with civil society organizations, and convening regular public consultations to achieve this goal.

Among the greatest difficulties faced by the FTAA is the pace imposed by members who are more reticent about the process, either because they absorb the greater trade impacts or because they believe other international fora are more suitable to discuss certain issues. In this respect, the restrictions faced by U.S. negotiators in addressing issues such as antidumping legislation and subsidies clearly add to the difficulties.

Bilateralism in the Asian Pacific

Chile's efforts to open up its economy and expand the gains from open trade are not limited to the Western Hemisphere and Europe. For years now Chile has been expanding its trade in the Asian Pacific region. In particular, Japan is our second most important trading partner after the United States, while Korea ranks among our top five or six export markets. Clearly the Asian market offers tremendous opportunities and Chile wants to be a leading player in gaining access to the potential they represent. In the pursuit of more open trade, the first FTA to succeed in the Asian Pacific region was with South Korea, and conversations with Japan to facilitate the access of Chilean exports are ongoing. In 2002, Chile has initiated negotiations for a trilateral agreement with New Zealand and Singapore. Moreover, to the extent that Chile signs FTAs with other industrial nations, the industrialized nations of Asia tend to lose out to the extent that trade diversion becomes an issue to their exporters. This provides a very practical, if modest, incentive for Asian countries to consider a more liberal approach to trade with Chile. In addition, Chile is interested in obtaining the benefits of increased investments from those nations and in becoming a platform for the expansion of their activity to the rest of South America.

South Korea. In February 2003, Chile and South Korea signed an FTA in Seoul, reflecting the agreements reached in late 2002. It is an historic accord because it is the first FTA between an Asian and a Western country, the first of such treaties for South Korea, and the first trans-Pacific FTA. This is a great achievement for Chile and for the strategy of open regionalism, placing the country among the pioneers in opening and deepening economic ties with the Asian Pacific region.

Through this agreement, Chile will be in a position to become a bridge between Asia and America and will continue to expand export markets, which now reach 480 million consumers, based on the FTAs currently in operation. APEC will facilitate Chilean exports to the Asian markets. To the extent that the FTA with South Korea increases bilateral trade between the two countries, maritime shipping costs will be reduced, making it easier for Chile to ship products at lower costs to other Asian destinations.

South Korea is an important trade partner for Chile. Over the past decade it has fluctuated between the fourth and sixth place among Chilean export markets, competing with Brazil and Mexico as export destinations. The South Korean economy ranks eleventh in the world by size, with 47 million inhabitants and an annual per capita income of US$ 9,400 (ca. 2001). It is one of the world's high-growth economies, achieving average annual growth rates of 8.9 percent in the 1980s and 5.7 percent in the 1990s.

The FTA negotiated between Chile and South Korea provides important competitive advantages to Chilean export products. South Korean import duties are high, varying from averages of 7 percent for industrial products to 50 percent for agricultural products. In the agricultural sector there are many import duties that exceed 40 percent, and many that exceed 100 percent.

As this is the only FTA negotiated by South Korea so far, Chilean exporters enjoy significant and exclusive import duty reductions. The reductions apply to the fishing, mining, forestry, agricultural, and agro-industrial sectors.

Japan. Over the last two decades, Japan has been Chile's most important trading partner in the Asian Pacific region, and the second largest export market, after the United States. Moreover, Japan is an important foreign investor in Chile, especially in the mining and fisheries sectors.

Chile's trade balance with Japan has traditionally been favorable to Chile, generating surpluses that fluctuate between US $1.6 billion and US$1.9 billion, as a result of strong Chilean export performance, and with Chilean exports to Japan growing at an average annual rate of 4.2 percent and reaching over US$ 2.5 billion in 2000.

In 1999, reflecting the interest expressed by the private sector of both Chile and Japan, and an agreement with the Japanese Foreign Trade Organization, a study of the likely impact of an FTA between the two countries was commissioned. The study showed that such an FTA would be highly beneficial for the Chilean economy and for bilateral economic relations. According to the study, an FTA between Chile and Japan would significantly improve the bilateral business environment by consolidating the role of the Chilean economy as a business and an investment platform for launching activities aimed at the rest of South America, and by generating greater benefits for Japanese investments, especially in view of the interest of Japanese investors in increasing their industrial and financial presence in world markets.

Therefore, an FTA with Japan would be an important contribution for the consolidation of a new export phase for the Chilean economy, based on the activities in which the Chilean economy has developed a competitive advantage. In particular, it appears that some enterprises in the mining and mining services sectors could take advantage of recent regional integration treaties. The same is true of retail/wholesale trade, agroindustry, and food processing, which stand out as sectors in which cooperation and exchange could be greatly expanded in the context of an FTA that would facilitate the incorporation of Japan's advanced technology and financial strength with the objective of improving Chilean competitiveness.

Due to the profile of Chilean imports from Japan, intensive in equipment and capital goods, an FTA that lowers import duties would favor the competitiveness of a wide range of industrial activities and thus consolidating Chile's export capabilities.

Free Trade Agreement with the United States

One of the most important agreements that Chile has negotiated on a bilateral level is the FTA with the United States, its leading trading partner and principal foreign investor. These negotiations, opened shortly after the Summit of the Americas in 1992, gained momentum under the Bush administration (2001–5) and reached agreement in December 2002. This negotiation put to the test the abilities of a developed country and a developing country to achieve a mutually satisfactory, comprehensive trade agreement, in which the issues of market access were as important as the institutional issues aimed at preserving fair competition. In an agreement of this type, Chile expected to improve conditions to increase the value added to its exports, encourage investment, improve the depth and internationalization of its capital markets, and establish more impartial and transparent rules for the settlement of trade disputes.

Beyond the willingness of the parties engaged in the negotiation, the FTA with Chile was seen as a dual condition: as a test of the internal consensus that could be achieved in the United States in opening up to the continent, and as a precedent for evaluating its willingness to review the most damaging protectionist mechanisms affecting exports from emerging countries in the hemisphere. The willingness of the United States to reach agreement with Chile was a measure of its commitment to the hemisphere.

In response to those who view this bilateral agreement as a divergence from MERCOSUR, it should be pointed out that for Chile, the FTA with the United States represents continuity of the FTAs negotiated with Mexico,

Canada, and Central America. Chile will also attempt to build on the experience to deepen the initial agreements with other Latin American partners. Furthermore, in 2001 MERCOSUR expressed its wish to negotiate an FTA with the United States.

Without question, the agenda under negotiation between Chile and the United States was not limited to bilateral issues. Both parties recognized that several issues needed to be addressed at the hemispheric level, and others at a multilateral level. Regarding these other levels of negotiation, Chile has a policy of reaching understandings with MERCOSUR, and with trade partners as important as Mexico, to submit to the United States a joint agenda concerning issues such as subsidies, access to agricultural markets, and trade defense mechanisms.

Chile conducted its negotiations by placing on the table previously subscribed agreements. Chile's aim was to make compatible negotiations concurrently conducted at a hemispheric level, so that the experience gained therein and the agreements achieved at each level might be transferred to other levels. Indeed, a significant portion of the progress made in the FTA negotiations would not have been possible without a process of direct consultation between both parties on the main trade issues addressed within the FTAA.

In reviewing the proposals that Chile made in the context of the FTA with the United States, one finds that they did not differ from the proposals made for the FTAA. These include tariff removals to avoid depending on the Generalized System of Preferences, ensuring equal access for Chilean exporters in the North American market, the elimination of tiered tariffs, and certain issues of higher complexity, such as the elimination of agricultural subsidies and antidumping duties.

To each of its trading partners and in all its negotiations, Chile has stated that the application of antidumping measures within the scope of an FTA is illegitimate. This issue is not only evident in the results, but also in the conditions under which the negotiations are conducted. In the course of negotiations, Chile had been affected by the escalation of protectionist measures on behalf of U.S. producers in an attempt to set positions or impose views on negotiators, which called into question the depth of the U.S. commitment.

Chile's interest in eliminating antidumping measures is the result of Chilean exports having been repeatedly affected by the ease with which U.S. producers file dumping complaints. Accusations that lack technical rigor inevitably lead to lengthy and costly judicial proceedings, which greatly affect the export values of emerging economies. If the accusations are found to be groundless, there is no possibility of recovering the financial costs or losses that they caused.

Governments with economic liberalization policies like Chile's lose public support for their negotiations if there is no effective consistency with stated goals. If successful export efforts made by small open economies are subjected to protectionist escalation—in the certainty that there will not be a proportional reaction given the disparity of the powers at play—political conditions are created that may lead to a reversal of liberalization, owing to the lack of reciprocity in the commitment to trade liberalization. This view was shared by the Bush administration, which had frequently expressed that hesitations in the commitment to liberalize trade in the Americas may bring about undesired political effects and a proliferation of protectionist measures.

New Problems in Trade Policy

Greater Institutional Demands

The new issues on the trade agenda, which are not easily amenable to unilateral policy measures, introduce added political complexity to negotiations, demand higher levels of institutional coordination and assume more detailed knowledge about how highly globalized markets work. While the treatment of e-commerce captures the limelight in debates on how technology modifies the boundaries between the national and international spheres in world trade, it is also possible to see this complexity in sectors representing trade disciplines recently added to the multilateral system. Liberalization of the service sector and intellectual property rights, for example, involve a review of public policies that until recently were absent from trade agreements.

The incorporation of services is a source of new controversies in the national treatment of foreign service providers, as evidenced in a sector as sensitive as pharmaceuticals. In this sphere, it becomes difficult to establish the boundary between public policies that are part of a national development strategy and those that merely pursue the creation of a trade advantage. Liberalization of services seeks to replace a state welfare policy with one of improved supply and quality of the services guaranteed by market competition. However, the benefits of such a replacement come with new risks for users, and therefore the negotiation of market liberalization must be supplemented with additional regulations to protect public welfare.

In current negotiations investment protection is an issue that is going

through a tough test to accurately define the concept of indirect expropria-
tion. Trade negotiations should establish a fair balance between the interests of investors and those of civil society, which expect that the regulatory
powers of government agencies will not be curtailed.

In this perspective the new issues of international trade increase the political complexity of the negotiations as new actors arrive on the scene. The
concept of private sector becomes broader, from a strictly entrepreneurial meaning to encompass civil society as a whole—including labor
unions and professional sectors. Civil society has broader interests as well,
including the preservation of specific standards in labor, social, and environmental issues that may be affected by opening the economy to international investors or competition from foreign service providers.

This new generation of trade agreements requires an updated institutional
framework to generate the necessary social consensus that will grant them
legitimacy. In this area, Chile has taken the lead in the region by promoting
an active policy of public consultations and opening negotiations to teams
of legislators, including representatives of pro-government and opposition
parties.

In sensitive areas of negotiation, such as the harmonization of sanitary
and phytosanitary standards, the new boundaries between national and
international spheres put to the test the sectoral approaches by which governments are managed. These issues call for greater coordination among
government agencies, used to working independently and without much
contact with their peers, following the traditional sectoral division of labor
within public administration.

The traditional functional separation of government is called into question in the dynamic areas of foreign trade. For example, the increasing importance of the food industry leads to a review of vegetable, animal, and
human health standards, which not only must meet consistent criteria on a
domestic level but also criteria consistent with new international demands.
The food industry may be one of the sectors where progress toward the
globalization of public institutions is being achieved at a faster pace. An
example of this is the joint committee created under the Chile–Canada
agreement and subsequently under the Chile–Mexico agreement to deal with
sanitary and phytosanitary issues.

The treatment of rules of origin stands out among the technical com-
plexities of tariff negotiation. National product classifications, the components of which are generated by increasingly more globalized production

chains, need to be adapted to a more integrated world economy, changing the notions of distance and time, and the concept of domestic production.

The never-ending task of disaggregating values or reclassifying components with a view to establishing the national origin of a product, encourages new levels of cooperation and consultation between the public sector and the industries affected by those rules, so that technical specifications reflect as accurately as possible the product base.

Finally, the administration of trade treaties needs to be included among the challenges arising from a more demanding relationship with trade partners and from the accumulation of multiple agreements. The rationale employed during the negotiating phase increasingly tends to differentiate itself from that which emerges at the stage of implementation and administration of treaties. In this area, the government of Chile has also decided to strengthen its institutional framework by working jointly with the private sector through a cooperation agreement with the Santiago Chamber of Commerce.

Balanced Objectives

Economic policies typically pursue a combination of equally desirable objectives that also affect each other. If this were not the case, the long debate on how to incorporate environmental and labor issues into an FTA would be unnecessary. Undoubtedly, the application of a multiple-objective policy is not free from difficulties. In the case of emerging economies, trade liberalization policies are dealt with in terms of enhanced competitiveness in the export sector and increased investment, two objectives that are not always mutually compatible in the short term.

Indeed, it has not been easy for Chile to attain a reasonable balance among its multiple objectives. The demands of macroeconomic policy have not always favored trade policy objectives. Similar situations have arisen in relation to financial openness and commercial openness.

In the mid-1990s, this conflict between equally desirable objectives grew increasingly incompatible due to the sustained revaluation of the Chilean peso that adversely affected Chile's export sales momentum. The revaluation was generated by a significant inflow of foreign currency caused by the opening of the service sector to international investment and the growth of exports. At the time, it was said that Chile was the first casualty of its own export success.

Faced with this crisis, reflected in a growing trade deficit and loss of dynamism in the export sector, the country gave a strong signal of its commitment to economic openness. Indeed, rather than curbing imports through administrative measures, domestic demand was contracted by drastically tightening monetary policy. In addition, the commitment to a sustained tariff reduction from 11 percent to 6 percent was renewed.

At the same time, the law on import safeguards was refined and a more proactive and watchful position was taken with regard to the performance of foreign markets. Since then and through 2003—particularly on account of the higher-risk, lower-growth scenario in the world economy—trade policy gained renewed legitimacy in the domestic sphere by identifying itself with the defense and stabilization of existing export markets.

To maintain a sustainable current account deficit in a scenario of recessionary adjustment, with a clear over-valuation of the currency and greater openness in the capital account, foreign direct investment was targeted at public utilities, which were opened to international investment, and attracted a large share of total foreign direct investment during the late 1990s. The public utilities benefiting from the largest volume of foreign direct investment were telecommunications, energy, water supply, and other public infrastructure, such as roads, airports, and ports, which gained much momentum from an extensive plan of public works concessions.

Even though the liberalization of access to public utilities may respond in part to the implementation of commitments made under the Uruguay Round, Chile took an early leadership role in this area, unilaterally modifying a major part of its legislation as a means of encouraging the inflow of capital. The inflows had a dual effect on our balance of payments: on the one hand, they intensified the problem of the over-valuation of the currency, adversely affecting the competitiveness of the export sector and, on the other hand, they transformed Chile into an exporter of capital and entrepreneurial expertise to the rest of the region.

Defending Successful Exports

In a difficult economic environment, trade negotiations necessarily tend to become defensive in nature. Instead of focusing efforts on gaining access to markets, negotiations focus on defending successful exports. Under these circumstances, non-tariff protectionist mechanisms become visible, including administrative measures of questionable consistency with the economic agreements or with proclaimed liberalization policies.

A wide array of trade protection mechanisms is found in the hemisphere, ranging from antidumping duties applied to successful Chilean exporters to the United States and other countries, to "managed trade" measures recently put in place by Brazil and Argentina within the MERCOSUR. Since the 1997 economic and financial crisis in Asia, Chile has faced a larger number of defensive reactions from leading foreign trade partners and, therefore, the Chilean trade strategy has focused on the institutional aspects that govern foreign trade, concentrating on the norms, regulations, and other specific institutions that support foreign trade (subsidies, antidumping duties, and dispute settlement). The strategy addresses many aspects not covered in the first stage of openness, or aspects insufficiently addressed in the second stage, and it aims to establish comparable conditions regarding liberalization, competition, and transparency from trade partners.

Non-tariff measures as a whole may become significant sources of uncertainty and create new costs for exporters in a scenario of greater trade liberalization. In the case of exports to the Unites States, for example, the possible application of antidumping or check-off measures may become a source of permanent discouragement to Chile's export momentum. At the same time, these measures cause economic damages and affect mutual trust due to the circumstantial and unilateral application of sanitary and phytosanitary measures that suddenly modify labeling or certification standards, or demand laboratory tests initially not required.

Chile's policy does not challenge the right of any state to exercise its powers in this field. However, it proposes that governments abstain from using these mechanisms as trade sanctions against partners with whom they have entered into FTAs. Chile seeks a fair, technical, transparent, and impartial treatment that allows the general interests of trading partners to prevail over the interests of any particular economic group or sector. In practice, this means that government powers that react unilaterally should be limited, making it necessary to review and update dispute settlement mechanisms.

Conclusion

The deepening of a unilateral policy of openness has placed Chile in a privileged position to enter into FTAs with its leading trade partners. In other words, through such agreements, the country is interested in exporting, at the regional level, the conditions of competition and openness attained at the domestic level.

This approach is reflected in the conditions proposed by Chile in the more progressive bilateral agreements that it has negotiated, and in the interest of incorporating these advances in the negotiation of economic complementarity agreements during the past decade. In particular, with neighboring countries, Chile seeks to make markets more competitive and open, and to extend and protect Chilean investments abroad, considering that since the mid-1990s the country has become an exporter of capital and entrepreneurial expertise to the rest of the region. The fact that Chile has become an international investor changes the role it plays in the international arena and calls for new approaches to trade policy.

Moreover, due to the principal role played by the external sector in Chile's economic development, the country's trade policy makes increasing demands on international bodies to guarantee fair trade. In other words, the policies call for less discrimination and unilateralism in government decisions and more transparency in the procedures. The needs of Chilean trade policy lead the country to play a more active role in the international foreign trade agenda. For example, Chile joined key U.S. trading partners in questioning the operation of its antidumping measures, and has participated actively in the organization of the Doha trade round, advancing proposals that seek to refine dispute settlement mechanisms.

Despite the privileged economic conditions that deal with the process of hemispheric integration, which is an integral part of trade policy objectives, Chile notes that recent negotiations have not been exempt from difficulties that are beyond its control, related to negotiation scenarios or the political realities of its partners. The difficulties are mostly linked to the heterogeneity of objectives, differences in negotiating capabilities, inconsistencies shown by the major economies, and the lack of political will to develop a regional institutional framework to deal with trade-related issues.

First, the heterogeneity of the continent itself gives rise to a disparity of objectives, just as within the United States one can identify conflicting positions regarding the relationship between trade liberalization and economic integration with the rest of the continent. These various objectives to some extent reflect the short-term interests of specific industries or economic sectors. However, economic integration has to respond also to objectives of different types, be they of the states or civil society. In fact, the two most important hemispheric concessions granted by the United States thus far have been justified in non-economic terms, as in the case of the Caribbean Basin Initiative and the Andean Trade Preferences Act. This exchange of economic and non-economic objectives in the policy of hemispheric integration was aptly reflected in the Quebec Summit and in the defense that President George W. Bush made of U.S. trade policy. He pointed out that the benefits of free trade for the region reduced the greatest threats to hemispheric stability, whether these were natural disasters, political instability derived from extreme poverty, or other complex phenomena, such as those linked to drug trafficking or illegal migration.

Second, the asymmetry of the powers engaged in negotiations means that negotiations move forward at the pace set by the hesitations of the leading actors. The will for integration is dependent on a minimum consensus achieved among the leading political and economic powers. Evidence thereof are the debates in the United States on how to facilitate compliance with its trade obligations (as compared with the European Union), as well as the resistance shown by its own industry to accept competition from successful exporters (as evidenced by the increasing number of antidumping cases). In the case of Brazil, its hesitation became evident when it proposed creating a South American Free Trade Area as a counterproposal to the policy of hemispheric integration during the discussion of the FTAA timetable.

Finally, the greatest challenge is to develop strong institutional mechanisms to support hemispheric regionalism. In particular, these would involve the acceptance of more impartial dispute settlement mechanisms, which would imply relinquishing some degree of national sovereignty, and the creation of collective mechanisms to facilitate the integration of emerging countries into the globalization processes, as has been done in Europe. To this end, Chile is working to strengthen regional collaboration aimed at establishing an economic dialogue within the WTO. The recent Summit of the Rio Group confirmed the favorable disposition of Latin American countries toward this type of initiative.

In MERCOSUR, the lack of appropriate institutional mechanisms has been reflected in the informality of dispute settlement mechanisms, leading to the settlement of controversies through two extreme avenues: the good will of the heads of state or rapprochement between disputing parties. In the case of the United States, the lack of commitment to the development of adequate institutions is reflected in its resistance to place on the FTAA negotiation table, or in bilateral negotiations such as the one with Chile, more reasonable antidumping rules, to avoid perverse incentives that damage long-term trade expansion.

The lack of clear will with respect to these issues raises doubts in many quarters as to the depth of commitment to free trade. Motives are questioned because of the inability to prevent or mitigate protectionist attitudes in markets that are highly sensitive for exporters from emerging economies. Undoubtedly, this may lead to a light regionalism of scant legitimacy in the eyes of civil society, an issue that finally weakens the momentum toward liberalization throughout the continent.

Note

1. This decision by signatories to the General Agreement on Tariffs and Trade in 1979 allows derogations to the most-favored nation (non-discrimination) treatment in favor of developing countries. In particular, its paragraph 2(c) permits preferential arrangements among developing countries in goods trade. It has continued to apply as part of GATT 1994 under the WTO. Please see: http://www.wto.org/english/docs_e/legal_e/enabling1979_e.htm

9

Mexico's Trade Policy: Improvisation and Vision

Antonio Ortiz Mena L.N.

Mexico is, by far, the major trading power in Latin America. In 2000, its trade easily surpassed that of Argentina, Brazil, and Chile combined. It has been a member of the General Agreement on Tariffs and Trade (GATT) since 1986, was a founder of the World Trade Organization (WTO), and has free trade agreements (FTAs) with countries across the Americas, Europe, and the Middle East. In this chapter I argue that the transformation of Mexico from a closed economy to a major trader was the result of improvisation and crisis-led policy changes as well as vision and long-term planning. I also argue that, notwithstanding the image of Mexico as a major trade power pushing for trade liberalization across many fronts, the political economy of trade policy indicates that Mexico could become a stumbling bloc for multilateral trade liberalization.

The chapter proceeds as follows: after an overview of Mexico's current trade agreements and trade flows, I explain the transformation from a closed economy to a trading power, and then touch on the international push toward greater openness and the domestic challenges encouraging Mexico to return to closure. The interaction of these international and domestic forces will determine the trade policy options Mexico will follow in the near future, as well as whether Mexico's web of trade agreements will support or hinder hemispheric and multilateral trade liberalization.

Mexico's Trade at the Outset of the New Millennium

Mexico's position in world trade stands out because of the number of trade agreements it has subscribed to and the impressive growth in trade flows it

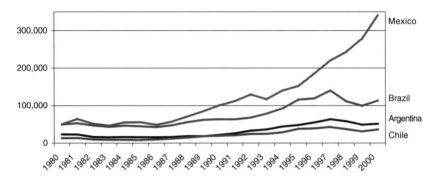

Figure 9.1 Total trade: Argentina, Brazil, Chile, and Mexico, 1980–2000 (US$ millions).
Source: World Bank (2001a, 2001b).

experienced throughout the 1990s. Mexico and Chile are the only Latin American countries that have FTAs with the two major world markets: the United States and the European Union. Apart from its numerous FTAs with Latin American countries (Bolivia, Colombia, Costa Rica, Chile, El Salvador, Guatemala, Honduras, Nicaragua, and Venezuela, and ongoing negotiations with Ecuador and Panama), it also has FTAs with the European Free Trade Association (EFTA) and Israel. At the time of this writing, Mexico had FTAs with thirty-two countries. The regional approach, coupled with unilateral liberalization and entry into GATT in 1980s, turned Mexico into one of the world's leading trade powers. As seen in Figure 9.1, during the 1990s its trade volume surpassed that of Argentina, Brazil, and Chile combined.

Another major change is how the significance of trade in the country's economy has changed over time (see Figure 9.2). At the time of the oil boom in the late 1970s and early 1980s, trade accounted for only about 25 percent of GDP, while it currently accounts for over 60 percent of GDP.

In terms of markets, the advent of the North American Free Trade Agreement (NAFTA) translated into a greater concentration of bilateral flows with the United States, which came largely at the expense of diminishing trade with the European Union, as shown in Table 9.1.

Despite the great number of trade agreements subscribed to by Mexico, not all are of equal importance. Currently 91 percent of Mexico's trade is carried out with countries with which it has FTAs, but 80 percent of this is accounted for by bilateral flows with the United States alone. In short, Mex-

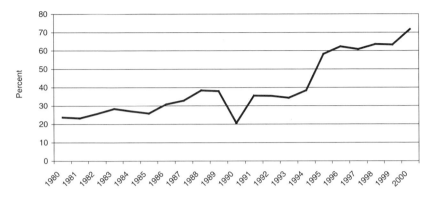

Figure 9.2 Mexican exports plus imports as percentage of GDP, 1980–2000.
Source: International Monetary Fund (2001).

ico is a leading trader with a very open economy that has become heavily dependent on trade relations with its northern neighbor.

The significant increase in Mexico's trade volumes, in contrast with the lackluster performance of other Latin American countries, can be attributed to both the entry into force of NAFTA in 1994 and to the high rate of growth of the U.S. economy during that time. Mexico's economy was closely tied to that of the United States throughout the twentieth century, whereas South American countries had more diversified trade relations. NAFTA granted Mexico privileged access to the U.S. market and fostered U.S. investment in Mexico. In addition, the United States experienced its longest economic expansion since World War II in the 1990s, and Mexico, with its open economy and close trade relations with the United States, was a direct beneficiary of that expansion. Finally, there was ample room for export growth due to

Table 9.1 Mexican Trade Profile: Principal Markets, 1990 and 2000

	1990 (%)	2000 (%)
United States	67	80
Latin America	14	11
European Union	14	6
Other	5	3

Sources: INEGI (1996); Secretaría de Economía (2001).

low levels of Mexican exports to the United States in 1982, but since then it has become ever more difficult to increase exports.

The downside of the forces behind the export boom is that the Mexican economy is greatly affected by developments in the U.S. economy, and negative developments in the North are quickly transmitted to the Mexican economy.

Mexican Trade Liberalization, 1980–2000

The 1980s: Unilateralism and Entry into GATT

By the late 1970s and early 1980s Mexico was one of the world's major oil exporters, at a time when oil prices were on the rise. In 1980 it was exporting in excess of US$10 billion worth of oil, and oil made up made up more than three-fourths of total exports (Ortiz Mena 1993: 62). Then-Mexican President José López Portillo (1976–1982) famously announced to all Mexicans that they should prepare to administer the newly acquired oil wealth. The oil-based export strategy within a closed economy was short-lived and ended in a severe economic crisis. During the 1980s, instead of administering wealth, Mexico had to deal with a macroeconomic crisis of major proportions.

It was precisely the economic crisis—and the need to both control inflation and secure foreign exchange to service the public foreign debt that had ballooned along with oil exports—that led to a drastic change in trade policy. Import tariffs were slashed and many import permits were eliminated to facilitate imports in an attempt to control inflation; the diversification of exports (in composition if not markets) was sought as a way to generate foreign exchange and find a new engine for growth given the depressed domestic market.

The details of this story have been covered elsewhere (e.g., Lustig 1992; Flores 1998; Ortiz Mena L.N. 2003a). Suffice it to say that the radical shift in Mexico's trade policy was crisis determined and not the result of a grand strategy. The first changes involved a unilateral opening of the economy. With renewed growth not forthcoming and inflation on the rise, the Mexican government finally decided to join GATT in 1986, during the early days of the GATT's Uruguay Round (1986–1994). Mexico had been close to joining GATT in 1979, but had balked at the last moment. The GATT negotiations represented a logical step after gradual (albeit very limited) trade liberalization started under López Portillo. President Luis Echeverría (1970–

1976) had likewise promised to start liberalizing the economy and foster exports, but ended up increasing the degree of protection.[1]

López Portillo reduced the proportion of imports subject to permits from 91 percent at the end of the Echeverría administration to 60 percent by 1979. In fact, an accession protocol very closely in line with what the Mexican government had pressed for was drafted and accepted by GATT (Malpica 1988). Instead of being assessed on its own merits and on the specific commitments undertaken by Mexico under the accession protocol, GATT accession became a lightning rod for discussion in Mexican political and business circles about economic development strategies.[2]

Despite the ample leeway that the government would have retained after GATT accession under the conditions obtained by Mexican negotiators, López Portillo chose to announce his decision against joining GATT during an emotionally charged ceremony commemorating the March 18, 1938 nationalization of the oil industry. On March 18, 1979, López Portillo declared that, although Mexico had secured an excellent accession protocol, there was no need to join GATT at a moment when the world was divided between those countries that had oil and those that did not. Mexico had oil and a unique window of opportunity to escape from poverty and underdevelopment. The state would be the leader in this process and was not about to let its hands be tied with multilateral rules on trade precisely when it needed to be very active in the design and implementation of the new oil-based development strategy.

Three years of irresponsible economic policymaking followed, ending with Mexico's inability to service its foreign debt, bank nationalization, and the imposition of exchange controls (Ortiz Mena L.N. 1987). The timid trade liberalization was also reversed after the decision against GATT entry and, by 1982, 100 percent of imports required a permit.

President Miguel de la Madrid (1982–1988) inherited an economy in full-blown crisis. Soon after taking office he implemented the Programa Inmediato de Reordenación Económica (PIRE), which consisted of shock treatment (a large devaluation and significant reductions in government spending coupled with a cap on wage increases) to attain macroeconomic stability. The program was not successful insofar as inflation remained high and renewed economic growth was not forthcoming. Some authors have argued that the failure lay in part because the program focused on stabilization and neglected much needed structural reforms, chief among them trade liberalization and privatization (Cohen 1989, cited in Lustig 1992). Significant trade reforms were not implemented until 1985, in the midst of a balance of payments crisis. The original trade reform program contemplated liberalizing (i.e., eliminating import licensing requirements) 35 percent to 45 percent of total imports by the end of 1985, but under the prevailing adverse circumstances the government decided to liberalize 64.1 percent of total imports by that date (Lustig 1992: 39).

The situation deteriorated from 1985 to 1986, especially given the drastic reduction in oil prices, which went from US$25.5 a barrel in 1985 to US$10 a barrel in 1986, greatly affecting the ability of the Mexican government to service its foreign debt, given that in 1985 oil accounted for approximately 60 percent of total exports. The government used exchange rate policy to help boost non-oil exports by decreasing the real controlled exchange rate of the peso against the dollar by 46 percent in 1986.

The combination of very low oil prices and peso depreciation contributed to a radical shift in Mexico's export structure in 1986; by year-end, oil exports accounted for only 32 percent of total exports, instead of 60 percent just a year earlier. Table 9.2 summarizes the export structure at the beginning of the De la Madrid administration, the crucial shift between 1985 and 1986, and the current situation. More that 80 percent of nonoil exports in 1988 were comprised of manufactures, and the export structure has remained similar ever since.

The rapid pace of unilateral liberalization in 1985 led the government to renew actions geared at GATT accession. The argument made by proponents of accession was that since Mexico was already liberalizing on a unilateral basis, it might as well receive some concessions in return through GATT accession, and that accession costs would accordingly be very low (Bravo Aguilera 2002). Despite this argument, it would seem unwise to liberalize unilaterally right before the country is about to undertake trade negotiations.

When Mexico finally joined GATT in August 1986, the accession terms it managed to negotiate still allowed ample room for discretionary policymaking. For instance, the strategy outlined in the De la Madrid administration's national development plan, which required a great deal of state intervention, was covered under the protocol and a high bound tariff rate of 50 percent was established (Flores 1998: 330).

Given the rapid pace of trade liberalization prior to GATT entry, membership did not have immediately felt effects—either positive or negative. In fact, as the economic situation deteriorated, Mexico proceeded unilaterally with further trade liberalization that went beyond its GATT commitments.

The peso was significantly undervalued throughout 1986 and 1987,

Table 9.2 Mexican Oil and Nonoil Exports, 1982, 1985, and 1999

	Oil Exports (%)	Nonoil Exports (%)
1982	70	30
1985	60	40
1999	7	93

Source: World Bank (2001a).

helping to offset a balance of payments crisis. However, as Lustig (1992) notes, the cost of this strategy was to generate macroeconomic instability in the form of higher inflation. In 1987, inflation threatened to surpass an annual rate of 150 percent, and the government attempted to curb it by using imports as a ceiling on domestic prices. These stopgap measures did not work and, in October 1987, the Mexican stock market crashed.

The economic crisis exacerbated political tensions. In June 1987, Cuauhtémoc Cárdenas and a significant group of politicians from the ruling Institutional Revolutionary Party (PRI) left the party. With time running out to stabilize the economy and set the basis for renewed growth before the July 1988 presidential election, time was running out for the De la Madrid administration.

The response was a stabilization program called the Economic Solidarity Pact that was implemented in December 1987 and combined orthodox and heterodox components. Structural reforms, and within it further trade policy reforms, were now an essential component (Kaufman et al. 1994). The Pact was also designed to improve government–business relations, which had deteriorated as a result of the trade liberalization measures that the government had implemented in 1985 without any consultations with business representatives (Flores 1998: 330). Under the Pact, the tariff ceiling was set as 20 percent (as opposed to 40 percent that was prevalent at the time, and below the 50-percent tariff binding set under GATT commitments), the mean tariff was reduced from 19 percent to just over 10 percent, and import permits were eliminated for virtually all products except certain agricultural items, automobiles, and pharmaceuticals (Lustig 1992: 53, 119).

The Pact finally signaled the beginning of macroeconomic stability, with monthly inflation decreasing to an average of 1.2 percent during the second semester of 1988, as opposed to the 9 percent monthly inflation observed during the first semester of 1987. Growth, however, was not forthcoming, and it was the task of the new Salinas administration to seek a new strategy for economic growth.

The 1990s: The Advent of Regionalism

By the time Carlos Salinas de Gortari became president in December 1988, the economy was relatively open and the country no longer relied as heavily on oil exports. However, even after opening up its economy, Mexico still faced two major problems: the burden of foreign debt service, which was unduly onerous in terms of export earnings, and its stagnant economy, whose average GDP growth from 1982 to 1988 had been close to zero.

Salinas instructed his finance minister, Pedro Aspe, to renegotiate foreign debt payments. This proved to be relatively successful and he then turned to the other major concern: a search for renewed economic growth (Aspe 1993).

During his campaign, Salinas mentioned the need for renewed growth but did not envisage a free trade agreement with the United States. Instead, he turned to Europe in looking for fresh resources. Growth could no longer be based on public and private foreign borrowing, so significant amounts of foreign investment had to be secured. The turn to Europe was not too surprising, as it fit with a long-held desire by the Foreign Ministry to diversify economic relations. In practice, diversification meant a turn away from the United States and an increase in economic interactions with Europe.

Developments in Europe, however, foreclosed this option. In 1989, the Berlin wall had fallen and West European countries were interested in the political and economic transformation of Eastern Europe. Their attention and, more importantly, their resources were concentrated on that region. When Salinas and his trade minister, Jaime Serra, attended the World Economic Forum at Davos in 1989, they were practically ignored by the Europeans. It was then that Salinas decided to test the waters and propose a free trade agreement to the United States. Serra approached then U.S. Trade Representative Carla Hills with the idea during the Forum (Salinas 2000). Hills was not enthusiastic about the proposal, preferring instead to concentrate all energies on the Uruguay Round of multilateral trade negotiations, but Salinas was able to effectively lobby President Bush and negotiations soon got under way (Cameron and Tomlin 2000).

Thus, Mexico decided to negotiate a free trade agreement with the United States only after the entry into GATT had not generated a significant increase in foreign investment and renewed economic growth, and after its overtures toward Europe had been rebuffed. It was not a product of either U.S. pressures or competition between Mexico and Canada for the U.S. market, as some authors have suggested (Gruber 2000).

During the De la Madrid administration, Mexico subscribed to a framework agreement to deal with bilateral trade issues. The Reagan administration had insisted on including a paragraph in the agreement, indicating that in the near future the two countries would seek to negotiate an FTA. De la Madrid argued that the proposal was unacceptable, given that Mexico had only recently begun to open up its economy and there was a need to assimilate the costs and benefits of significant trade policy changes. The agreement was subscribed to and the reference to a future FTA was struck (Bravo Aguilera 2002).

Likewise, the Canada–U.S. FTA had been in force since January 1989 and Mexico's trade relations with the United States had not been adversely affected by it. Rather, it was Canada that feared trade diversion and requested the opportunity to participate in the Mexico–U.S. free trade negotiations that had started on a bilateral basis in 1991 (Cameron and Tomlin 2000).

NAFTA represented a significant shift in Mexico's trade policy, and it was to have long-lasting effects in all areas of the economy. Amidst episodes of stop-go unilateral liberalization and an awkward entry into GATT, measures that can best be described as improvisation in the face of adverse economic circumstances, the decision to make the most of Mexico's proximity to the world's largest economy is perhaps the single decision approximating a vision and long-term strategic thinking regarding Mexico's trade policy options since the 1970s.[3]

First, NAFTA signaled a recognition that, at least in the short and medium term, Mexico's best option was to concentrate on the United States as its main export market, and import, investment, and technology source. Instead of attempting to distance Mexico from the United States in economic and political terms, as had been the norm throughout the preceding decades, Salinas decided to take advantage of Mexico's geographic location by ensuring privileged access to the U.S. market and implementing a series of domestic economic reforms aimed at supporting economic integration with that country (López Ayllon 1997). Given the increasing importance of foreign trade as a source of economic growth (see Figure 9.2), this meant that trade with the United States in particular acquired greater relevance for the well-being of the economy as a whole. From a Mexican perspective, NAFTA was an instrument designed to maximize the benefits and minimize the costs of an extremely close economic relationship among vastly unequal partners.

Second, Mexico had to go beyond most Uruguay Round liberalization commitments under NAFTA, so the adjustment costs for multilateral liberalization were relatively low (Ortiz Mena L.N. 2002).

Third, the ever-closer links with the United States—in both legal terms and in trade and investment flows—meant that Mexico's pride of place was secondary to its unparalleled access to the U.S. market. Any erosion of this advantage was to be seen with great suspicion. Mexico would look askance at multilateral (WTO) and regional (Free Trade Area of the Americas, FTAA) trade liberalization efforts if they adversely affected its privileged position, albeit publicly government officials were always careful to express Mexico's support for the FTAA and WTO negotiations.

Fourth, the two trade agreements with European countries (with the EU and EFTA) were negotiated at Mexico's behest and complement NAFTA. They are very significant, given their potential to diversify Mexico's economic relations regarding trade, investment and technology, and should be construed as being of a different nature than the Latin American agreements whose economic significance is limited.

Finally, NAFTA paradoxically made Mexico put Latin America within the purview of its trade policy. This was not so much the result of a strategy as a response by Mexico to political pressures from several Latin American Integration Association (LAIA) members. During NAFTA negotiations, Brazil and, with less insistence, Argentina, argued that under LAIA Articles 5, 44, and 48, Mexico had to award them most-favored-nation treatment; in other words, the same concessions it had awarded to Canada and the United States under NAFTA (Anaya 2002). Mexico was of course loathe to do that, and instead opted to follow a divide-and-rule policy by negotiating FTAs with individual Latin American countries (see Table 9.3).

In 1992, an economic complementation agreement with Chile had entered into force. It was largely a political gesture supporting the return to democracy after the long Pinochet dictatorship. During the Pinochet regime, Mexico received many Chilean exiles, and consequently relations between the two countries had been a bit strained.

After the entry into force of NAFTA, Mexico negotiated and subscribed to a significant number of FTAs with countries in Latin America. The Mexican government's official position was that the Latin American agreements were negotiated as part of its strategy to diversify economic relations (Anaya 2002). This position was either disingenuous or seriously flawed. As shown in Table 9.1, Mexico's trade with Latin America pales in comparison with Mexico–U.S. trade. In addition, given that economic diversification entails

Table 9.3 Key Developments in Mexican Trade Policy, 1979–2001

1979	Aborted entry into GATT
1982	Increase in trade barriers
1985	Unilateral trade liberalization
1986	GATT entry
1987	Economic Solidarity Pact
1992	Chile ECA
1993	Asia-Pacific Economic Cooperation forum entry
1994	North American Free Trade Agreement, Organisation for Economic Cooperation and Development entry
1995	Costa Rica FTA, Bolivia FTA, G-3 FTA
1998	Nicaragua FTA
1999	Chile FTA
2000	European Union FTA, Israel FTA
2001	European Free Trade Association FTA, Uruguay ECA, Guatemala, Honduras, and El Salvador FTA

Note: Years indicate when respective agreements became effective.

ECA, economic cooperation agreement; FTA, free trade agreement; G-3, Colombia, Mexico, and Venezuela; GATT, General Agreement on Tariffs and Trade.

not only new export markets but also investment and technology sources, the limited potential of these agreements is readily apparent.

Rather than agreements with an overriding economic rationale aimed at diversifying economic relations, these FTAs can be seen as an attempt to placate relations with Latin America and at the same time maintain political influence in that area. The G-3 FTA (with Colombia and Venezuela) was an offshoot of the three countries' close collaboration in seeking to foster a peaceful settlement of the civil wars in Central America throughout the 1980s.

The agreements with Central America can contribute to their economic development and, it is hoped, greater political stability. Trade agreements with small economies have very limited effects on the larger Mexican economy, but if benefits are not significant, neither are the potential displacement and adjustment costs. Conversely, these FTAs may indeed have an important impact on the smaller economies, thus contributing to Mexico's political leverage.

The FTAs with Bolivia and Chile, both associate members of MERCOSUR, and the 2001 economic complementation agreement with Uruguay are ostensibly aimed at limiting Brazil's ability to forge a united coalition in South America, thus giving Mexico more leverage in its economic and political relations with Latin American countries (Anaya 2002). However, whether establishing trade agreements with two associate members and an advanced economic complementation agreement with a MERCOSUR member state whose population is less than 2 percent of Brazil's is the best way to pressure Brazil is open to question, and seems more of an ex-post justification than the product of a detailed plan.[4]

The Political Economy of Mexican Trade Policy

From the time of López Portillo (1976–1982) up until the end of the Zedillo administration (1994–2000), trade policy was conducted by the chief executive with very little effective opposition, either from the Congress or civil society groups and organizations.

Just as López Portillo had personally decided against the entry into GATT, so did De la Madrid favor entry, under dire economic circumstances. Salinas managed to negotiate NAFTA despite numerous protests from diverse groups within Mexico. The Foreign Ministry had been against it, but all authority was granted to the Trade Ministry, which closely followed presidential instructions.[5] The agreement was approved by the Mexican Senate without much ado (Schiavon and Ortiz Mena L.N. 2001). Large business groups were well represented during all FTA negotiations through COECE (the Foreign Trade Business Organizations Coordination Council), and real opposition was effectively controlled (Ortiz Mena L.N. 2003a).

Thus, the political system and dominance of the PRI during the 1980s and 1990s were key ingredients in allowing the radical shifts in trade policy observed during that period. The ample discretion retained by the chief executive in trade policy meant that economic policy change could be effected with relative ease, at least regarding domestic constraints. The limits on economic policy options were posed more by the external economic environment and the macroeconomic situation of the Mexican economy than by domestic political opposition.[6]

The downside of executive discretion is that policy swings are common, given that economic policy reforms can be overturned or modified with relative ease (Cowhey 1993). It also makes establishing a strategic vision and adhering to it extremely difficult. For instance, De la Madrid first sought to pursue a gradual liberalization of the economy and then was forced by circumstances to speed up liberalization and abandon his initial gradualist approach. He thought that Salinas would follow a moderate course in that regard, but in fact liberalization deepened and an FTA with the United States was subscribed to, when just a few years earlier De la Madrid had considered that embarking on such radical policy change was ill-advised (Bravo Aguilera 2002). NAFTA itself can be seen as an instrument designed to ensure policy lock-in in this domestic political setting, and thus as a means to attract foreign direct investment that would not easily commit to entering a country in which policy swings were the norm.

Economic policymaking has become more pluralistic in recent years. In 2000, Vicente Fox, the candidate from the right-of-center National Action Party (PAN), won the presidential election after more than seventy years of PRI dominance. Representation in both chambers of the federal legislature has become more pluralistic and their members more assertive in foreign policy matters. In addition, intraexecutive divisions over foreign policy have become more explicit.[7]

This means that unless intraexecutive divisions are mended and the legislature accords the executive ample discretion for the conduct of foreign policy (including foreign economic policy), consensus will be difficult to attain and particularistic interests will permeate foreign economic policy design and implementation. In other words, under the current political setting it will be difficult to agree on a grand vision regarding foreign economic relations and putting it into practice.

Mexico's Trade Policy in the Next Decade

While all agreements pale in comparison with NAFTA in terms of trade volume, by 2000 Mexico nevertheless found itself as the hub in a hub-and-spoke FTA system and as the world's fifteenth largest trader. The key elements of the system were NAFTA and the FTAs with the European Union and EFTA, which gave Mexico privileged access to the two major world markets: the United States and Europe. The Latin American agreements constitute spokes of relatively minor significance.

This position was a product of tactical moves rather than a strategy sustained over a long period of time, but no matter the reasons behind the trade policies, there are incentives to keep the system in place.[8] The government's trade policy preferences are to maintain Mexico's privileged status with its network of trade agreements and, if possible, to cap it off with an FTA with Japan (negotiations were launched in 2002) and a deepening of NAFTA commitments.[9] It thus largely favors the status quo and has a negative agenda regarding hemispheric free trade negotiations (FTAA) and the multilateral

Doha Development Agenda launched in November 2001. Preferences of the major exporters coincide with those of the government (Ortiz Mena L.N. 2003a).

Import-competing sectors and especially some nongovernmental organizations (NGOs), such as the Mexican Trade Action Network, favor greater protection for local industries and granting pride of place to labor and environmental issues over trade and investment concerns (Ortiz Mena L.N. 2003a). The left-of-center Party of the Democratic Revolution (PRD), and more recently the PRI as well, have heavily criticized so-called neoliberal policies for allegedly generating poverty and greater income inequality, and regard NAFTA as part of the neoliberal policy package. They do not propose a coherent alternative trade policy, and intermittently make calls for protectionism.

How Mexican trade policy will evolve in the near future will partly depend on which interest group manages to get the upper hand in trade policy formulation, and this is affected by how the Mexican political system evolves. First, there is the issue of shifting authority between the Foreign Ministry and the Economics Ministry regarding foreign economic policy; the Foreign Ministry has traditionally been more cautious in assuming liberalization and international economic commitments, while the Economics Ministry has been the harbinger of free trade, including GATT accession and NAFTA (Schiavon and Ortiz Mena L.N. 2001). If a planned transfer of trade negotiating authority from the Economics Ministry to the Foreign Ministry takes place, it will be more difficult for free traders to maintain the upper hand in trade policy.

Second, Congress has become more active in international affairs. If international economic issues are deemed salient by members of Congress, this will make for smaller "win sets" regarding international trade negotiations and will favor the status quo (Putnam 1988). Lastly, the evolution of trade policy will also hinge on how FTAA and WTO negotiations develop, and on the Mexican government's reaction to pressures for greater liberalization. Four scenarios can be envisioned:

Greater closure. This scenario is likely if the PAN fails to attain control of the Chamber of Deputies in the 2003 mid-term congressional elections and especially if the PRD or the PRI win the presidency in 2006. It is also likely if similar results are obtained with a PRI triumph in either of those elections or an understanding between the PRD and the new PRI leadership is attained regarding a more protectionist trade policy.[10] This scenario would also be possible if high rates of economic growth do not occur by the second half of the Fox administration and opponents of neoliberalism manage to frame stagnation as the natural and inevitable product of neoliberalism rather than mismanagement of the economy and especially fiscal irresponsibility.

Stalled FTAA and/or WTO negotiations lead to status quo. Under this scenario, stalled hemispheric negotiations would lead to the status quo. Even if the Mexican government cannot opt out of a hemispheric trade deal, it may be wise for it to let the United States and Brazil slug it out without offering any constructive mediation. This would be the preferred scenario for the government and many export industries, both of which have a basically negative agenda for both FTAA and WTO negotiations (Ortiz Mena L.N. 2003a). Another alternative would be for very limited gains under either of those negotiation efforts, which would also lead to a virtual status quo for Mexico, with its privileged access to the United States and Europe.

Liberalization through coercive cooperation.[11] This scenario would take place if significant liberalization commitments were agreed to in either the FTAA process or the WTO. Despite strong domestic opposition for further negotiated or unilateral liberalization by import-competing sectors, some NGOs, and perhaps most exporters (concerned about an erosion of Mexico's privileged access to key markets), the government would attempt to comply in the face of strong domestic political opposition. This may result in foot dragging regarding its international commitments.

This scenario would also obtain if the Mexican government decides, despite domestic opposition, to deepen security cooperation with the United States. Strengthened security mechanisms derived from the 2001 terrorist attacks on the United States have made its borders less permeable, despite NAFTA provisions. If Mexico is to maintain its privileged access, it must deal head-on with U.S. security concerns (Hufbauer and Vega-Cánovas 2003).

Liberalization through voluntary cooperation. This is an alternative scenario under successful hemispheric and/or multilateral trade negotiations. The government would take a proactive stance seeking to maintain an edge over potential competitors in its access to the European and especially the U.S. market, and would be able to bolster domestic political support for greater liberalization.

Greater hemispheric liberalization might erode Mexico's privileges, and that could be forestalled by deepening NAFTA. If multilateral liberalization affects the gains Mexico made through its FTAs with European countries, it would have incentives to push for greater access to those markets by accepting an acceleration of the previously agreed upon tariff liberalization schedules and demanding a like response from European countries.

Another external threat derives not from multilateral trade negotiations per se, but as a result of China's entry into the WTO. While Mexico is protected by the waiver regarding the application of the WTO antidumping code and will be able to use its domestic legislation against unfair trade practices practically at its discretion during a transition period, exports from Mexico will face increased competition from the Chinese in third markets. This will start to make productivity based on low wages unsustainable in the medium and long term. Domestic reforms will be needed to maintain adequate productivity levels and to garner more support for greater liberalization.

The domestic challenges to free trade are in part a result of the pressures generated by years of trade openness that have not translated into significant poverty reduction, more equitable income distribution, or more balanced regional development. There are also pressures to include more small- and medium-sized enterprises (SMEs) in foreign trade activities (Ortiz Mena L.N. 2003a).

In order to address these concerns, the government will have to take a more proactive stance regarding poverty reduction and regional development. It will also have to make the case that trade liberalization is just part of a development strategy and is neither the cause of all economic and social ills nor the only means toward their solution.

For instance, it will have to create conditions for the prompt resumption of financing at competitive rates, especially for SMEs.[12] Significant progress in deregulation is also a must. Despite years of effort aimed at fostering deregulation, the results are still wanting; excessive regulation constitutes a real obstacle for the creation of new businesses.

The government will also have to work diligently to ensure that an effective social safety net is established, especially for the rural poor, many of whom regard NAFTA's agricultural liberalization provisions as their death knell. Only by ensuring that the potential benefits that trade openness and the web of FTAs represent are shared equally, and that in those instances where dislocations occur, a safety net and the possibility of jobs in a new activity are present, will it be possible to increase domestic political support for a very open economy (Rodrik 1999).

At a time of greater political pluralism, it is not politics as usual in Mexico. The government faces the challenge of securing a broad social agreement to maintain an open economy. If a social safety net is not guaranteed and complementary policies aimed at ensuring a more equitable distribution of the gains from trade are not implemented, pressures for closure will grow. This may produce an inchoate trade policy that will benefit no one.

Notes

1. The proportion of imports subject to permits increased from 68 percent in 1970 to 91 percent in 1976 (Lustig 1992: 115). See also Flores (1998), especially chapter 5.

2. For an overview of Mexico's accession to GATT, see Ortiz Mena L.N. (2003b).

3. Mexico's long-standing desire to diversify its trade relations was centered on Europe. However, NAFTA was at least partially responsible for allowing Mexico to realize that vision. As shown in Table 9.1, increased trade with the United States came largely at the expense of reduced trade with Europe, and this generated interest in Europe to capture lost ground, and to ensure favorable conditions for investment in the North American region.

4. In 1999, Brazil's population was 168 million, and Uruguay's was 3 million (World Bank 2001b).

5. In December 2000, the Ministry of Trade and Industrial Development was renamed the Ministry of the Economy.

6. This view is challenged by Flores (1998), who argues that domestic interest groups had a significant influence on trade policy in the 1980s and 1990s. Other authors (Kaufman et al. 1994; Pastor and Wise 1994) emphasize the high degree of independence of political elites in the formulation of foreign economic policy. I would argue that the concentration of power in the hands of the president and the corporatist mode of interest representation allowed ample room for political elites' discretion. The policy swings are a natural reflection of power concentration, given that dispersion of political power makes policy change much more difficult.

7. For instance, during the Zedillo administration the attorney general was in favor of Mexico's subscribing to establishment of the International Criminal Court, while the Foreign Ministry was against it. Likewise, during the Fox administration there have been frictions between the Foreign Ministry and the Economy Ministry over who has responsibility for the conduct of certain foreign economic policy issues, such as the participation of Mexico in the Asia-Pacific Economic Cooperation forum (APEC).

8. Several authors have dealt with the political economy of preferential trade agreements and the reasons why countries in a position like Mexico's would tend to favor the status quo and try to block further liberalization, especially at the multilateral level. See, for example, Wonnacott (1991), Krueger (1995), Haggard (1998), and Milner (1998).

9. See Pastor (2001) for an overview of possible alternatives to NAFTA deepening.

10. In March 2002, Roberto Madrazo, a staunch critic of neoliberal policies and the political and economic management by "technocrats" (see Centeno 1997), was elected as leader of the PRI.

11. The title is borrowed from Martin (1992), although she uses it to explain forced cooperation regarding the imposition of economic sanctions.

12. The Mexican financial sector entered into a deep crisis following the December

1994 peso devaluation. See Hernández and Villagómez (2001) for an analysis of the evolution of the Mexican financial sector since 1994.

References

Anaya, César. 2002. Interview by author of Mexico's representative in Latin American Integration Association in 1990s. Mexico City, January 31.

Aspe, Pedro. 1993. *El Camino Mexicano de la Transformación Económica.* Mexico City: Fondo de Cultura Económica.

Bravo Aguilera, Luis. 2002. Interview by author of Mexican deputy trade minister, 1982–1988. Mexico City, February 11.

Cameron, Maxwell A., and Brian Tomlin. 2000. *The Making of NAFTA: How the Deal Was Done.* Ithaca, NY: Cornell University Press.

Centeno, Miguel Angel. 1997. *Democracy Within Reason: Technocratic Revolution in Mexico.* University Park: Pennsylvania State University Press.

Cohen, Aslan. 1989. "Effects of Trade Liberalization on Exports." Berkeley: Department of Economics, University of California–Berkeley.

Cowhey, Peter. 1993. "Elect Locally—Order Globally: Domestic Politics and Multi-lateral Cooperation." In *Multilateralism Matters: The Theory and Praxis of an Institutional Form,* edited by John G. Ruggie, 157–200. New York: Columbia University Press.

Flores, Aldo R. 1998. *Proteccionismo versus Librecambismo: La Economía Política de la Protección Comercial en México, 1970–1994.* Mexico City: Fondo de Cultura Económica.

Gruber, Lloyd. 2000. *Ruling the World: Power Politics and the Rise of Supranational Institutions.* Princeton, NJ: Princeton University Press.

Haggard, Stephan. 1998. "The Political Economy of Regionalism in the Western Hemisphere." In *The Post-NAFTA Political Economy: Mexico and the Western Hemisphere,* edited by Carol Wise, 302–38. University Park: Pennsylvania State University Press.

Hernández Trillo, Fausto, and Alejandro Villagómez Amezcua. 2001. "El Sector Financiero Mexicano en el Tratado de Libre Comercio: Una Evaluación Preliminar." In *Para Evaluar al TLCAN,* edited by Arturo Borja Tamayo, 143–80. Mexico City: Miguel Ángel Porrúa.

Hufbauer, Gary Clyde, and Gustavo Vega-Cánovas. 2003. "Whither NAFTA: A Common Border?" In *The Rebordering of North America? Integration and Exclusion in a New Security Context,* edited by Peter Andreas and Thomas J. Biersteker, 128–52. New York: Routledge.

International Monetary Fund (IMF). 2001. *International Financial Statistics.* Washington, DC: IMF.

Instituto Nacional de Estadística Geografía e Informática (INEGI). 1996. *Banco de Información Económica: Datos del Comercio Exterior de México.* Mexico City: INEGI.

Kaufman, Robert, Carlos Bazdresch, and Blanca Heredia. 1994. "Mexico: Radical Reform in a Dominant Party System." In *Voting for Reform: Democracy, Political Liberalization, and Economic Adjustment,* edited by Stephan Haggard and Steven R. Webb, 360–410. New York: Oxford University Press.

Krueger, Anne. 1995. *Free Trade Agreements versus Customs Unions.* Working Paper No. 5084. Cambridge, MA: National Bureau of Economic Research.

López Ayllon, Sergio. 1997. *Las Transformaciones del Sistema Jurídico y los Significados Sociales del Derecho en México.* Mexico City: Universidad Nacional Autonoma de México.

Lustig, Nora. 1992. *Mexico: The Remaking of an Economy.* Washington, DC: Brookings Institution.

Malpica de Lamadrid, Luis. 1988. *¿Qué Es el GATT? Las Consecuencias Prácticas del Ingreso de México al Acuerdo General.* Mexico City: Grijalbo.

Martin, Lisa.1992. *Coercive Cooperation: Explaining Multilateral Economic Sanctions.* Princeton, NJ: Princeton University Press.

Milner, Helen. 1997. "Industries, Governments and the Creation of Regional Trade Blocs." In *The Political Economy of Regionalism,* edited by Edward D. Mansfield and Helen V. Milner, 77–106. New York: Columbia University Press.

Ortiz Mena L.N., Antonio. 1987. "An Inquiry into the Causes of the 1982 Economic Crisis in Mexico." Master's thesis. University of London, Institute of Latin American Studies.

———. 2003a. "Mexico and the WTO: A Regional Player in Multilateral Trade Negotiations." In *Trade Policy Reform in Latin America,* edited by Miguel Lengyel and Vivianne Ventura Dias. Basingstoke, UK: Palgrave.

———. 2003b. "Mexico in the Multilateral Trading System." In *The Kluwer Companion to the World Trade Organization,* edited by A. Appleton, P. Macrory, and M. Plummer. Dordrecht: Kluwer.

Ortiz Mena L.N., Tania. 1993. "Políticas Petroleras en México." B.A. thesis. Mexico City: Universidad Iberoamericana.

Pastor, Manuel, and Carol Wise. 1994. "The Origins and Sustainability of Mexico's Trade Policy." *International Organization* 48 (fall): 459–490.

Pastor, Robert A. 2001. *Toward a North American Community: Lessons from the Old World for the New.* Washington, DC: Institute for International Economics.

Putnam, Robert D. 1988. "Diplomacy and Domestic Politics: The Logic of Two-Level Games." *International Organization* 42 (summer): 427–460.

Riding, Alan A. 1984. *Distant Neighbors: A Portrait of the Mexicans.* New York: Alfred A. Knopf.

Rodrik, Dani. 1999. *The New Global Economy and Developing Countries: Making Openness Work.* Washington, DC: Overseas Development Council.

Salinas de Gortari, Carlos. 2000. *México: Un Paso Difícil a la Modernidad.* Barcelona: Plaza & Janés.

Schiavon, Jorge, and Antonio Ortiz Mena L.N. 2001. "Apertura Comercial y Reforma Institucional en México (1988–2000): Un Análisis Comparado del TLCAN y el TLCUE." *Foro Internacional* 41 (October–December): 731–760.

Secretaría de Economía. 2001. *Estadísticas Comerciales de México.* Mexico City: Subsecretaría de Negociaciones Comerciales Internacionales.

Wonnacott, Ronald J. 1991. *The Economics of Overlapping Free Trade Areas and the Mexican Challenge.* Toronto: Howe Institute; Washington, DC: The National Planning Association.

World Bank. 2001a. *World Development Indicators.* Washington, DC: World Bank.

———. 2001b. *World Development Report 2000/2001: Attacking Poverty.* New York: Oxford University Press.

10

Trade Strategies in the
Context of Economic Regionalism:
The Case of MERCOSUR

Alcides Costa Vaz

In the early 1990s, the Southern Common Market (MERCOSUR) emerged as a promising and challenging initiative of economic integration among four very asymmetrical developing countries: Argentina, Brazil, Uruguay, and Paraguay. MERCOSUR was part of the resurgence of regionalism, a structural trend in the world economy since the mid-1980s. It evolved from a bilateral integration process between Argentina and Brazil begun in 1986 as a response to common domestic political and economic challenges and to the external financial constraints both countries then faced.

However, the new bloc turned out to be more than the heir of the bilateral initiative of the 1980s, which was more effective in political than economic terms. Indeed, MERCOSUR played an essential role in support of the economic reforms both countries implemented in the early 1990s. The effectiveness of the bloc in performing this role helped to restore the credibility and economic functionality of regionalism in Latin America after three decades of frustrated experiences of economic integration. MERCOSUR also introduced a new approach and new mechanisms that helped to stimulate impressive growth of trade flows among the four countries and, to a lesser extent, of trade with other countries. In addition, it played a secondary but meaningful role in stimulating unprecedented levels of inflows of foreign direct investment to the region (Motta Veiga 2000: 266).

However, from the mid-1990s on, the euphoria of the trade bloc's first years receded as successive trade conflicts rose and external financial constraints dramatically changed the political and economic environment in which MERCOSUR had come into existence. Economic policymakers of the Southern Cone were forced to adapt their policies to a more restrictive and unstable external context while preserving macroeconomic stability domestically. Macroeconomic stability was maintained, but at the expense of the liberalization drive of the preceding years and, therefore, of regional integration. Low and even negative economic growth rates, competition for foreign investment and markets, and acute financial and sectoral imbalances began to impose growing constraints on MERCOSUR, often seriously straining its political and economic underpinnings.

MERCOSUR also faced challenges derived from its external agenda, where key issues included both the negotiation of trade agreements with its main neighbors and economic partners, and issues related to the enforcement of the Uruguay Round agreements. The simultaneous management of these challenging and complex internal and external agendas required increasing political and diplomatic resources and technical expertise. The strong political commitment of the four countries to the integration process was essential for the harmonization of conflicting interests, the creation of a minimally coordinated strategy of internal development, and external initiatives regarding the relations of MERCOSUR with nonmember countries and other economic blocs.

The purpose of this chapter is to assess the responses of MERCOSUR to the challenges that have arisen within its own development and to those related to the diverse international commercial negotiations in which it is engaged. How has MERCOSUR responded to distinct and often contradictory challenges regarding its development and external relations at different stages of its evolution? What policy models, principles, and objectives have oriented the dynamics of MERCOSUR and shaped its trade profile during its evolution? How have these been adapted to changing circumstances? What have been the main features, successes, and pitfalls of MERCOSUR's external relations?

The assumption underlying the present analysis is that the features of trade strategies pursued by MERCOSUR have been defined at each stage of its development in the interplay of (1) interests, objectives and possibilities as interpreted by governmental authorities responsible for their promotion through the bloc; (2) the micro- and macro-economic contexts in which integration occurs; (3) the governmental perceptions of the framework of incentives and interests at stake internally and externally; and (4) external injunctions which raise opportunities and constraints that, in turn, influence the bloc's domestic and external agendas.

In the following I present an outline of three stages that comprise the trajectory of MERCOSUR since its creation, and identify the elements and features of the bloc's commercial strategy as it shifted over time. The first section discusses the context and the strategy pursued in the so-called "transition period," which ranges from the signing of the Treaty of Asunción on March 26, 1991, to December 31, 1994. This period witnessed the inception of the free trade regime and the emergence of the basic instruments of a customs union. The second section analyzes the shift from the domestic to the external realm as the main locus of activity in MERCOSUR in the 1995–1998 period. This change was brought about by the negative externalities of successive international financial crises that severely restricted the chances for MERCOSUR countries to pursue more advanced objectives internally. Under such unfavorable economic conditions, external relations provided a valuable opportunity to reassert the bloc's cohesion and identity, to project itself internationally, and to address some strategic issues related to market access and the enforcement of multilateral trade disciplines. The third section is dedicated to the developments and shifts observed from 1999 to the present, a period in which MERCOSUR has undergone an unprecedented crisis. This section highlights some important features of the trade strategy currently pursued by MERCOSUR: efforts to achieve a better balance between the basic requirements for its internal consolidation and its external possibilities, a more flexible approach to the application of norms and instruments, and a more assertive position in international economic negotiations.

MERCOSUR's Trade Strategy in the Transition Period (1991–1994): Forging the Free Trade Regime and Customs Union

A predominantly integrative agenda and an inward orientation marked the dynamics of MERCOSUR and the trade strategy it pursued in the transition period. Like the preceding bilateral initiatives of Argentina and Brazil, MERCOSUR was a political project carried out in the economic and commercial realms. It is worth mentioning, however, that the economic content of this regional political project has not always been self-evident. The bilateral integration initiated by Argentina and Brazil in the mid-eighties was deeply rooted in political interests and objectives, such as the consolidation of democracy, the promotion of regional stability, and the overcoming of xenophobic positions internally, particularly among the military. This bilateral political project was expected to take the form of a *common economic space* to be built incrementally accomplishing three basic goals: (1) to stimulate a managed and balanced expansion of bilateral trade on the grounds of economic complementarity and political symmetry; (2) to foster productive and technological changes in key economic sectors through the expansion of bilateral investment flows; and (3) to promote cooperation in areas of critical importance for joint economic development such as energy, transportation, and technology. Sectoral agreements were the main instruments utilized to accomplish these objectives and to promote higher levels of economic interdependence between both countries (Seixas Correa 2000: 374).[1]

In other words, it was a strategy framed around the internal complementation and integration of productive sectors across the border with emphasis on those sectors capable of providing stronger positive externalities to economic growth and technological change. Capital goods were identified as a key sector, and represented a strategic nucleus for integration. Advancement in this sector was promoted through policy instruments designed to secure financial equilibrium, foster investments, and stimulate the creation of binational corporations. In this strategy, trade was expected to play an essential role, but it was approached carefully and selectively, since the main objective was to stimulate a balanced and managed growth of trade flows. Trade liberalization was expected to proceed smoothly, as long as it was compatible with this approach, and other trade and industrial policy objectives that were at the core of the development strategies that both countries pursued, as well as the integration process.

The development strategies of Argentina and Brazil underwent a dramatic change after 1990. The import substitution model of the 1960s and 1970s and the selective, gradual, and managed economic opening both countries tried to pursue in the late 1980s became irreparably flawed, and were gradually replaced in both countries by a liberal approach. The political agenda and objectives of the bilateral integration process were not entirely dismissed, but trade liberalization became its main driving force and, subsequently, became the central impetus of MERCOSUR itself. The broader notion of a *common economic space* or the daring objective of a common market, although preserved in MERCOSUR, gave way to some operational definitions of a free trade arrangement and a customs union in the short term.

It was the political decision to promote liberal economic reforms unilaterally and to coordinate their response to the Enterprise of the Americas Initiative announced by the Bush administration in June 1990 that paved the way for Argentina and Brazil to pursue a new strategy of economic integration. In other words, a regional strategy was based on convergent, unilateral economic reforms. In this sense, and contrary to the previous bilateral integration initiatives, the strategy envisaged to settle a new regional economic arrangement was not the outcome of a deliberate and jointly defined approach to common political and economic challenges. Rather, it evolved from the convergence of liberal economic policies pursued unilaterally by both countries. Its immediate appeal was the establishment of a trade liberalization program that could eventually serve as a leveling platform in other international trade negotiations.

The sectoral approach of the preceding years was therefore replaced by a new one centered on a broad trade liberalization program carried out through automatic, regular, and linear tariff reductions. Instead of limited lists of specific goods to which trade preferences would be granted—a feature that characterized previous initiatives of economic integration in the region—trade liberalization within MERCOSUR should encompass the entire universe of tradable goods, allowing each country to keep a small number of products under a temporary exceptional regime with clear rules and deadlines for their full incorporation to the free trade regime. Starting in June 1991, tariffs were scheduled to be reduced by 7 percent every six months, starting from a 47-percent margin of preference, so that a 100-percent reduction should be reached by December 1994.

This program was originally proposed by Argentina, and was formally agreed to bilaterally in 1990 in the Buenos Aires Act signed by Presidents Carlos Menem and Fernando Collor de Mello. In December of the same year, the program was incorporated into the Economic Complement Agreement No. 14, subscribed to by both countries under the Latin American Integration Association (LAIA). Finally, it was transposed to the Asunción Treaty (signed on March 26, 1991) with a few changes designed to accommodate new signatories Paraguay and Uruguay. These agreements formally marked the departure from the regulated and selective approach of the 1980s, and introduced strict commitments to tariff reductions and the establishment of a free trade regime within five years.

Paraguay and Uruguay were encouraged by these commitments from both major countries to attain, within five years, the objectives envisaged in the bilateral treaty of 1988. There was a significant political logic to joining as well, and for Brazil and Argentina to welcome these new members. The possibility of creating a trade bloc to negotiate collectively with the United States within the framework of the Enterprise for the Americas Initiative was extremely attractive. Such a bloc would represent an affirmative response to the proliferation of regionalism; moreover, it would grant credibility to the efforts of domestic economic reform and would prompt economic opportunities and favorable conditions for market access on a preferential basis.

Despite the ambitious aim of the Treaty of Asunción to establish a common market, and the short time span projected for its accomplishment (before December 1994), it regulated and provided the instruments for the settlement of commercial arrangements only. The centrality of commercial issues was reflected in the bloc's internal agenda through its first four years: the implementation of the trade liberalization program, the settlement of trade disciplines in nontariff areas, and the establishment of a common external tariff.[2]

The Asunción Treaty also referred to sectoral agreements and the coordination of macroeconomic policies as instruments for the establishment of the common market. The former did not materialize, however, as governments feared they could become channels for managed trade practices.[3] The coordination of macroeconomic policies also could not be carried out for several reasons. Great disparities in terms of exchange, monetary, and fiscal policies among the member countries, rising economic instability and inflation in Brazil from 1991 to early 1994, and opposite economic growth cycles between Brazil and Argentina created a highly unfavorable political and economic environment for policy coordination. In addition, economic authorities argued that the commercial objectives then pursued did not require high levels of economic coordination, and therefore there was neither immediate incentive nor appropriate conditions for this type of coordination. Policy coordination was simply put off, but this did not prevent commercial integration from advancing.

The attainment of objectives in the commercial realm, as well as the positive performance of intra-MERCOSUR trade observed in its first four years (which grew from US$4.2 billion in 1990 to US$12 billion by the end of 1994) were closely associated with: (1) the strong political commitment by national governments to market-oriented economic reforms, with MERCOSUR as a forefront initiative to support and promote them; (2) a favorable external economic environment, which stimulated the emergence of outward-driven trade strategies notably in Argentina and Brazil; and (3) the successful methodology and instruments envisaged to promote the phasing out of tariffs and settlement of the basic instruments of a customs union.

However, divergent political preferences between Brazil and Argentina as to the form and level of coordination of trade policies to be achieved, as well as significant differences in degrees of macroeconomic stability, led to mounting disagreement between the two most important partners in MERCOSUR. Structurally, these divergences between Brazil and Argentina in the transition period reflected acute differences in their respective productive scale and cost levels, levels of industrial competitiveness, and prevailing macroeconomic conditions. Growing microeconomic imbalances stemming from differences in trade and industrial policies reinforced structural diversity. The trade strategy pursued by MERCOSUR during this transition period was largely influenced by these structural economic differences and the manner in which they were translated into distinct microeconomic policy orientations in each country. Attempts to reach minimum agreement on those issues were directly related to the settlement of a free trade area and a customs union.

It is important to take into account the different trade policy preferences that emerged within the bloc. As the transition period unfolded, the perspectives of Brazil and Argentina in relation to trade policy within MERCOSUR grew increasingly contradictory. At the onset of intra-MERCOSUR trade negotiations, Brazil, the region's largest, most diversified and industrialized economy, had begun to shift its trade policy away from a managed trade strategy, which for decades had focused on the development of its large domestic market through import substitution. This managed strategy was reflected, among other aspects, in the antiexport bias Brazilian trade policy exhibited for decades (Guimarães 1997: 8). In this regard, the challenge that the country faced in the early nineties was to pursue trade liberalization—and indeed MERCOSUR represented an attractive, supporting environment—while at the same time preserving some important industrial sectors and exploiting market opportunities for those sectors within MERCOSUR and in the whole region in a sort of mercantilist approach (Bouzas 2001: 43). The way Brazil carried this out reinforced the perception by its MERCOSUR partners, especially Argentina, that in spite of the reforms initiated in March 1990, protectionism still persisted in Brazil's trade policy, even if restricted only to specific sectors deemed of strategic importance for its industrial development.

Argentina, on the other hand, aimed to redefine its economic outlook and the basic parameters of its insertion in world politics and the global economy. To accomplish these ambitious goals simultaneously, it engaged in foreign policy activism with the intent to develop a privileged relationship with both its main economic partners on one hand, and on the other with the remaining superpower. Its trade policy included a strong commitment to liberalization as a means of reinvigorating its productive infrastructure and obtaining concessions in terms of market access from its main trade partners, including Brazil.

That initial framework, under which Brazil maintained a limited but persistent protectionist bias while Argentina tried to exhibit deep commitment to the liberal agenda, changed significantly when considered from the perspective of intra-MERCOSUR negotiations in the first half of the 1990s. In Argentina, rising commercial deficits with Brazil reflected microeconomic imbalances. Pressure increased from domestic economic sectors that bore the costs of unilateral measures of economic adjustment and liberalization, as well as those derived from integration within MERCOSUR. Argentina's trade policy within MERCOSUR gradually incorporated some elements of managed trade. Brazil, in turn, sought to promote, consolidate, and lock in its economic reforms through MERCOSUR. In order to safeguard its interests in MERCOSUR as a privileged space for preparation for wider economic opening, Brazil needed to reject several proposals and unilateral measures proposed by Argentina with the purpose of regulating the process of trade liberalization within MERCOSUR.

Therefore, Brazil emerged at the end of the transition period as a more open economy in relation to 1991, while Argentina, even if it were not the original intention of the government, emerged as an economy in which several limits to trade liberalization had been introduced. For several economic sectors in Argentina, those limits meant a setback to the implementation of a liberal trade agenda. The regime of convergence toward a common external tariff (which was the core aim of the transition phase), the lowering of Brazilian tariffs, and the upward trend of Argentine tariffs reflected a turnabout in the trade policy orientations of both countries within MERCOSUR.

In brief, the trade patterns of MERCOSUR and its disciplines were defined within the narrow space left between attempts to harmonize differing national trade orientations at the subregional level, and the intent to achieve and consolidate jointly defined political and economic goals through economic integration. The trade strategy set forth in MERCOSUR during its first four years for the attainment of the objectives established in the Treaty of Asunción was based on three main principles: the non-negotiability of the phasing out of tariffs in intra-MERCOSUR trade, reciprocity, and a regular, incremental approach to trade policy goals.

The trade strategy aimed at generating preferential market access for

goods among the four member countries by phasing out tariffs and establishing common trade disciplines in relation to nonmember countries. An
important feature of that strategy was to grant priority to the negotiation of
less controversial issues and to build on successes achieved there to deal
with more controversial and complex ones. Therefore, efforts concentrated
on the phasing out of tariffs, while nontariff issues and the disciplines required to build a free trade regime or a customs union remained unfinished.
Progress in negotiations in these areas demanded the accommodation of
divergent interests and priorities through political and technical trade-offs
and side payments.

Trade-offs were vital to overcoming specific stalemates and to achieving
the basic objectives of the negotiations within the defined timeframe. The
fundamental and most important trade-off involved in MERCOSUR's commercial profile was of a political nature. Brazil conceded preferential access
to its large domestic market in exchange for the establishment of common
trade disciplines in the context of a customs union. Several other trade-offs
at the technical level were equally important because they allowed the definition of the structure and levels of the common external tariff, as well as
the regime for the exemption of sensitive sectors, in time for the free trade
regime and the customs union to be enforced from January 1, 1995, onward.

Summing up, MERCOSUR's trade strategy in its first years was marked
by the (1) emphasis on regular, automatic and horizontal tariff reductions;
(2) management of more complex nontariff issues through tentative mechanisms for harmonizing sectoral policies; and (3) resort to principles, trade-
offs, and side payments as the ultimate means of leveling asymmetries
among the four countries. This strategy was relatively successful in promoting trade liberalization and growth, as demonstrated by the performance
of intra-MERCOSUR trade in those years, although it should be taken into
account that several important dimensions of the free trade regime and the
customs union remained unfinished at the end of the transition period, or in
some cases even untouched.[4]

MERCOSUR's limitations were compensated for by the political commitment of national governments to economic reform and the favorable
external economic environment. Both these elements, however, would be
severely affected in 1995 by the rising instability of international financial
markets, which brought about the need to adjust the bloc's trade strategy to
confront an increasingly unstable external environment and by dramatic
changes in both countries' domestic situations. In Argentina, those changes
were associated with the gradual erosion of the underpinnings of the eco-

nomic stabilization program initiated in April 1991. In Brazil, however, the most important change was associated with successful enforcement of the monetary reform and stabilization program initiated in 1994. In both cases, although for different reasons, a conjunction of external and domestic factors led governments and corporations to divert their attention from MERCOSUR's internal agenda. A shift in the trade strategy of the transition period became inevitable.

1995 to 1998: Responding to Economic Constraints by Assessing International Opportunities

The completion of the trade liberalization program and adoption of the common external tariff coincided with the launching of the Free Trade Area of the Americas (FTAA) initiative in December 1994 and the outbreak of the international financial crisis following Mexico's currency devaluation. After 1994, MERCOSUR negotiated associative agreements with Chile and Bolivia, which were signed in June and December 1996. A framework agreement with the European Union was signed in December 1995.

This set of initiatives represented a landmark in the evolution of MERCOSUR and a turning point for its trade strategy. Having satisfactorily established a free trade area that encompassed over 80 percent of the tradable goods of its four members and set forth the basic instruments of a customs union, MERCOSUR's trade strategy shifted from internal trade liberalization to the external attainment of market access through the negotiation of trade agreements with neighboring countries. The Chilean and Bolivian markets were at the forefront, followed by the bloc's main trading partners in the developed world, notably the European Union and the United States. Negotiations with the Andean Community and Mexico soon followed as part of the renegotiation of preferences granted under the LAIA.

Regarding the internal agenda, attention shifted to completing the free trade regime and consolidating the customs union. As mentioned above, several aspects of the free trade regime had been left unfinished. In spite of the effort to identify and compare nontariff barriers with the aim of eliminating or harmonizing them, the issue became a source of intense disagreement among the four member countries. By the end of the transition period, there was slow progress in dismantling and harmonizing nontariff measures, along with assurances that the benefits of tariff elimination were not reversed by the application of nontariff restrictions. However, as microeconomic imbalances increased, governments became unwilling to deal effectively with that issue. The option of resorting to nontariff measures offered some space for policy discretion in facing economic imbalances and the negative commercial consequences of instability in international financial markets.

Aside from the issue of nontariff barriers, the achievements of the transition period in trade liberalization referred strictly to goods. As of yet, negotiations on services had not advanced to the point of allowing any sort of agreement. As domestic regulations in this area were also undergoing important changes associated with privatization programs, governments decided not to support any formal commitment to service liberalization until those reforms and their respective processes of privatization had been consolidated. The issue remained a focal point for the completion of the free trade regime in the post-transition period. Finally, a framework agreement on services was reached in December 1997 with the compromise of full liberalization ten years after ratification by each member country.

Regarding consolidation of the customs union, negotiations centered around the issues directly related to definition of the common external tariff, including its structure, levels, exceptions, and enforcement procedures. Definitions pertaining to other issues that make up complementary disciplines of the customs union (safeguards, antidumping, countervailing duties, policies that distort competition, etc.) were postponed to the following period. Considering that important sectors—sugar, automotives, informatics and telecommunication products, and capital goods—had been granted exceptional treatment,[5] and that several issues related to complementary disciplines were not fully agreed upon, the customs union that came into force on January 1, 1995 was far from perfect. From then on, its consolidation became the most important issue in the internal agenda of MERCOSUR, thus keeping trade issues at the top of the internal agenda.

In principle, the macroeconomic convergence between Brazil and Argentina and the positive impact on the bilateral trade balance brought about by the success of the economic adjustment program (Plan Real) in Brazil should have favored further progress in MERCOSUR's internal agenda. However, in reality, circumstances moved in the opposite direction. In fact, opportunities presented during the period of macroeconomic convergence for the consolidation and deepening of MERCOSUR's trade disciplines and progress toward a common market went underexploited. Despite macroeconomic convergence, microeconomic imbalances persisted, leading to several recurrent trade conflicts between these two countries. Despite being handled politically, outside of mechanisms for dispute resolution, these disputes regularly strained trade relations and revealed the bloc's institutional weakness. At the same time, external constraints increased due to the instability of international financial markets in the aftermath of Mexico's crisis in early 1995. In this context, preserving some margin of policy discretion to deal with domestic and external constraints became a preferable strategy for governments rather than strict submission to imperfect collective trade disciplines in the framework of economic integration.

From the perspective of MERCOSUR's internal agenda and evolution, it was clear that integration was no longer a driving force or priority in the economic agenda of the four countries, most notably Argentina and Brazil. Circumstances had complicated the likelihood of progress in the internal dimension, and therefore external agenda issues grew in importance for MERCOSUR (Vaz 2001: 48).

The following factors reinforced this focus on external relations at the expense of internal consolidation: (1) MERCOSUR countries wished to renegotiate bilateral trade preferences granted in the LAIA framework, given that they were the natural counterparts of negotiations with Andean Community members; (2) the effective start of the FTAA negotiation process with the Denver ministerial meeting of June 1995 posed the immediate need for MERCOSUR to strive for self-preservation as a trade bloc and as a recognized partner of the United States; and (3) negotiations with the European Union within the framework inter-regional agreement of 1995 for the establishment of a free trade area between the two blocs. These negotiations provided the underpinnings of the trade strategy that MERCOSUR started to pursue in 1995. The external arena had become MERCOSUR's dimension for activism. This strategy was largely determined by the value members placed on external negotiations as a means to reassert the bloc's credibility and cohesion, in order to face their own vulnerability to external financial crisis and to meet the opportunities of accessing the markets of their main trading partners in the developed world on a preferential basis.

Thus, the push toward external negotiations and MERCOSUR's related strategy can be seen as a byproduct of a mix of operational, defensive, and assertive concerns with the clear prevalence of a particular aspect in each context. Negotiations with the Andean Community were launched as a response to the necessity of redefining and adapting the trade preferences granted by each MERCOSUR member to other LAIA countries, and were justified by what can be termed an operational concern. As for the FTAA, the possibility of preferential access to the U.S. market was a powerful incentive. However, the huge economic asymmetries and the threat they posed to the very existence of MERCOSUR as a free trade arrangement, and the protectionist bias of the Unites States in relevant sectors for MERCOSUR exports made defensive concerns prevail. In the case of the trade talks with the European Union, MERCOSUR has adopted a more assertive stance toward market access for its agriculture exports. However, the possibility of a free trade agreement with the European Union has not provoked the same kind of concerns that arise with the FTAA. U.S. hegemony adds a political hindrance to the economic benefits of an eventual FTAA, thus dividing the relevant political preferences of Brazil and Argentina. Besides that, the European Union, in spite of its Common Agriculture Policy, is perceived as a reliable economic partner, less prone to unilateralism than the United States and more politically motivated in forging a multilateral world economic order.

The overall strategy with which MERCOSUR approached its external relations was not then, nor is it now, carefully designed or homogeneous. Rather, it is a complex and often ambiguous exercise of evaluating and balancing different perspectives on the incentives and risks of simultaneous trade negotiations in a context of rising financial instability and economic uncertainty. The heterogeneous, multifaceted profile of such strategy does not imply, however, that its main features cannot be identified. On the contrary, there are some common aspects of MERCOSUR motivations and behavior that help shed light on the rationale of its interests and on the way it has acted to promote and/or safeguard them in international negotiations.

One feature of the strategy that MERCOSUR started to pursue in 1995 was dealing with external negotiations independently of internal dynamics and agenda. In other words, MERCOSUR's external relations were to a certain extent disassociated from its internal dynamics in the sense that the latter did not formally constrain the former. On the contrary, having been given an international juridical profile by the Ouro Preto Protocol in 1994, MERCOSUR was willing and able to act as a negotiating partner to foster its own development. At the same time, internal issues and divergences should not pose restrictions for exploiting external opportunities. The intent was to have MERCOSUR's countries speak with a single voice internationally. The external agenda should then be dealt with as if it had no immediate, direct or necessary links to its internal agenda and domestic constraints. Having both agendas evolve in parallel fashion would represent the best option to maximize external opportunities and to project MERCOSUR internationally, while preserving higher levels of discretion to manage its internal affairs. Therefore, MERCOSUR engaged in external negotiations, using the achievements of the transition period to (1) reaffirm the bloc's identity and cohesion as a negotiating entity; (2) strengthen its credibility internally and with its external partners; (3) increase its attractiveness by emphasizing the economic potential of the bloc as a source of opportunities for trade and investment; and (4) strengthen its negotiating power vis-à-vis its trading partners.

Starting in the mid-1990s, this separation of its internal and external agendas has been a central feature of MERCOSUR's strategy to handle external negotiations. Although hardly sustainable over the long term, this strategy has brought about some immediate benefits. First, it has granted governments a certain degree of maneuverability and discretion in both spheres. Likewise, it has provided a wider range of tactical options in each negotiating stance in the face of demands and proposals of its counterparts. Third, it has blocked attempts by MERCOSUR's counterparts in trade negotiations to push for the acceptance of unfavorable or undesirable terms on issues related to MERCOSUR's imperfect trade disciplines.

A second feature of MERCOSUR's trade strategy was to treat each negotiation in its own terms, but to preserve some basic guidelines for all of them. This was, in part, a pragmatic recognition of a particular state of affairs, as each negotiation was subject to specific agendas, criteria, principles, procedures, instruments, and institutional frameworks. However, this should not necessarily preclude the possibility of either seeking a more integrated approach to some common issues or taking advantage of what was conceded, accepted, or defined in one negotiation process to bargain and obtain desired outcomes in another. Although attractive in principle, this has proved to be more of a potential rather than a frequently exercised component of MERCOSUR's strategy, as the political framework, the agendas, the pace of negotiations, and the expected benefits vis-à-vis its potential costs did not allow much room for the exercise of this bargaining strategy. To some extent, this sort of linkage has been observed in cases of MERCOSUR negotiations in the context of the FTAA and those with the European Union. This has become possible because strengthening commercial and economic ties with Latin America is regarded as an important dimension of broader international strategies for the United States and the European Union, major world economic powers and MERCOSUR's main economic partners.

Actually, the MERCOSUR–European Union 1995 framework agreement was widely interpreted as a reaction by the European Union to the FTAA initiative aiming at countervailing U.S. trade activism through a preferential arrangement in Latin America. Therefore, the linkage between both processes is not due to MERCOSUR strategy, but to the European Union's strategy. When pursued by MERCOSUR, the smaller partner in this economic triangle, this strategy tends to assume a predominantly defensive connotation in the sense that it represents a means of bridging asymmetries rather than an assertive way of promoting interests or reaching desired outcomes.

Third, based on the success of the strategy internally pursued in the transition period, MERCOSUR strove for broad-scope agreements without permanent exceptions and with clear criteria and rules for the full incorporation of sectors and products temporarily granted exceptional treatment. At the same time, the bloc rejected special treatment for less developed countries, thus sustaining the same principles of symmetry and reciprocity.

These principles were actively discussed in negotiations with Chile and Bolivia, and subsequently in the MERCOSUR–Andean Community negotiations. They have not yet been dismissed in the FTAA and the negotiations between MERCOSUR and the European Union, although in both cases the eventual agreements will necessarily have to abide by the rules of the World Trade Organization (WTO). Strengthening the rules of the world multilateral trade system and advocating reciprocity in regional arrangements were perceived as the first best options to safeguard MERCOSUR's commercial interests vis-à-vis its main trading partners. MERCOSUR has endorsed reciprocity, given that its members have opened their economies unilaterally, regionally, and multilaterally. What the bloc strives for, particularly in the context of the FTAA, is an adequate timeframe for the eventual agreements to come into force, to allow domestic sectors favorable conditions to prepare for direct and open competition with U.S. exports, and to deepen and consolidate its trade rules and practices to avoid being overwhelmed by competition in the short term.

This leads to another distinctive trait and objective of MERCOSUR strategy since the mid-1990s: to approach external negotiations as a means of seeking the full enforcement of Uruguay Round agreements and strengthening multilateral norms, while refusing to negotiate beyond WTO disciplines. This element of MERCOSUR's trade strategy is of great relevance because it involves two areas to which MERCOSUR is extremely sensitive: the ability for partner countries to resort to antidumping and antisubsidy measures to restrict exports, and restrictions on agriculture trade. This same principle of adherence to WTO rules lies behind MERCOSUR's position regarding environmental and social clauses in the FTAA advocated by the United States.

In contrast to the first four years, when the bloc benefited greatly from the trade strategy it pursued internally, the 1995–1998 period saw little internal progress. External trade relations also slowed considerably in that period. With the exception of the agreements with Chile and Bolivia, other initiatives did not bring effective results either politically or economically. Negotiations with the Andean Community did not advance. Those with the European Union evolved slowly, but without clear compromises on trade liberalization. The FTAA was still centered on the definition of methodology and timeframe of the negotiations.

However, the gap between expectations and external achievements must be attributed to factors beyond the nature of the agreements and to the dynamics of each negotiation. Among these are the constraints imposed by the adverse external economic environment, the priority granted to the management of domestic economic affairs and preservation of macroeconomic stability, the unwillingness of some MERCOSUR partners to effectively engage in negotiations (as in the cases of the European Unity and the Andean Community), and the low profile of domestic agents in relation to external negotiations in the aftermath of unilateral, regional, and multilateral economic liberalization.

Results of these external negotiations were various. Negotiations with the Andean Community were suspended in 1998, due to the impossibility of harmonizing diverse views and demands of both sides regarding rules of origin, special customs regimes, sensitive sectors, and the more fundamental issue (for the smaller Andean countries) of special treatment for less developed countries.

In FTAA negotiations, MERCOSUR was relatively successful at safeguarding its fundamental interests, namely gradualism and equilibrium of results, the broad scope of the agenda, the principle of "single undertaking," compatibility with WTO disciplines, and preservation of subregional and regional integration initiatives. The reaffirmation of 2005 as the timeline to start implementation of the FTAA, decided at the 1998 Santiago Summit, corresponded to a MERCOSUR proposal. However, it is entirely uncertain whether it will succeed at getting the United States to abide by strict norms concerning the application of antidumping and antisubsidy measures and countervailing duties in the context of the FTAA, or to give up environmental and social welfare clauses.

In relation to the European Union, negotiations under the 1995 framework agreement initially focused on deeper economic cooperation and a tentative agenda for gradual progress toward trade liberalization between the two economic blocs. MERCOSUR has made it clear that a trade agreement of that sort is only feasible if agricultural protections are effectively resolved. As previously mentioned, developments in these negotiations have also been very sensitive to the dynamics of the FTAA process. The prospects for a MERCOSUR–EU accord depend not only on the ability of MERCOSUR to promote its views and interests, but also on the results obtained in the FTAA negotiations as a source of incentives and/or constraints for the European Union to respond affirmatively to the demands of the Southern Cone.

Summing up, from 1995 to the end of 1998, MERCOSUR's trade strategy shifted its focus from the internal agenda to its external relations as the main arena for activism in terms of seeking opportunities for greater market access. This shift did not represent a rupture with the achievements of the transition period; rather MERCOSUR built on those achievements to define principles and guidelines for the negotiations that it engaged in with several trading partners. With the unprecedented macroeconomic convergence between Brazil and Argentina in the second half of the 1990s, it was the instability of international financial markets that acted as the main constraint on the revision of MERCOSUR's strategy.

This instability did not prevent the bloc from pursuing a coherent trade strategy, but it curtailed the development of a strategy in which internal accomplishments could be fully incorporated. Policymakers were forced to concentrate on the immediate impacts of international instability on national economies and on preserving macroeconomic stability. This severely reduced their ability to enhance the integration process with improved coordination of internal and external policies, a necessary step for the creation of an encompassing trade strategy. Moreover, the dispersion of effort caused by simultaneous negotiations made it difficult for MERCOSUR to develop a single and homogeneous trade strategy in that period.

Late 1990s: Striving to Harmonize Interests in Times of Crisis

The intensification of macro- and micro-economic imbalances between Brazil and Argentina in the aftermath of the Asian and Russian financial crises, Brazil's currency devaluation in January 1999, the progressive deterioration of Argentina's financial condition, economic stagnation in Uruguay and Paraguay, and decreasing rates of economic growth in the United States, Europe, and Japan have exposed the internal fragility of MERCOSUR and the limits of its external strategy. The unprecedented crisis that the bloc has experienced recently is expressed not only in the re-duction of trade flows among the four member countries, but also in the up-surge of unilateralism inside the bloc, the weakness of the mechanisms and institutions to counter it, and an overall loss of credibility.

In such a context, external restraints have accentuated internal vulnera-bilities, making it impossible to keep on managing external relations and the internal agenda independently. On the contrary, the acute crisis has made it imperative for policymakers to focus on pending internal issues and on addressing macroeconomic coordination and problems in the external agenda as necessary steps for reinvigorating MERCOSUR. Moreover, it has also become imperative to balance the bloc's internal and external agendas and to adjust its present trade profile to its external interests, possibilities, and challenges. As the agendas of both negotiations with the FTAA and the Eu-ropean Union evolve, it becomes clear that issues long neglected in the internal agenda of the bloc will have to be dealt with in the context of those negotiations and/or also in the context of the WTO negotiation round launched in the Doha ministerial meeting in November 2001.

As a consequence, issues such as dispute settlement, decision-making procedures, and the transposition of norms have risen in the bloc's agenda, along with those directly related to trade disciplines and consolidation of the customs union. It has become necessary to reinvigorate MERCOSUR from inside to avoid its gradual self-dismantlement and to preserve it as a viable and effective channel for negotiating with other countries and eco-nomic blocs regionally, transregionally, or multilaterally. These perceived needs led to the highly touted "relaunching" of MERCOSUR in 1999. That agenda was negotiated and formally agreed on under Argentina's *pro tem-pore* presidency in the second semester of 1999. It included previously pend-ing issues related to the implementation of MERCOSUR's trade disciplines, such as market access (especially nontariff restrictions), the transposition of harmonized norms to national legislation, dispute settlement, the appli-cation of the common external tariff, commercial defense, protection of competition, and incentives for investment, production, and exports. In ad-dition to these trade issues, others related to macroeconomic coordination (e.g., the harmonization of economic indices and statistics, and the settle-ment of common goals for fiscal matters, debt, and inflation) were introduced to move the integration process beyond trade liberalization (INTAL 2000: 90). Finally, the agenda included commitments to negotiate trade prefer-ences as a bloc and to resume negotiations with the Andean Community.

The expression "relaunching" was obviously flawed. In actuality, this revised agenda was an effort to update and adjust MERCOSUR to respond to internal challenges and to those posed by external negotiations in the short and medium terms. The operational approach of the relaunching agenda was similar to that applied in the Las Leñas Program in the transition period; that is, the voluntary execution of specific tasks through negotiations at technical and executive levels, according to strict deadlines. This approach was relatively successful at leading MERCOSUR to a free trade area and an imperfect customs union during the transition period, but it has not been equally successful in leading MERCOSUR out of the current crisis. Recent efforts have been countervailed, to a large extent, by the political and economic problems brought about by Argentina's acute financial crisis, as well as by economic imbalances in other member countries, including Brazil, and, finally, by important differences in policy areas and issues such as exchange regimes, dispute settlement mechanisms, the nature of MERCOSUR's institutions, and the FTAA.

In this context, it was almost inevitable that the debate should reopen over what is the most desirable and feasible form of integration among the four MERCOSUR members, although this contributed to widespread uncertainty regarding the possibility of preserving and attaining its original objective of a common market. At one extreme, many have argued that the bloc is doomed to failure and disappearance. Others suggest that even if it does not disappear, it will likely become increasingly irrelevant.

However, in spite of its fragility and inconsistency, MERCOSUR still represents an important political and economic asset that can play an effective role in providing economic opportunities and dynamism for its member countries, as well as in the definition of prospects for regionalism and multilateralism. MERCOSUR as an institution is neither easily disposed of, nor is it a self-sustaining strategic asset. Its importance and usefulness for member countries varies according to its effectiveness in addressing development needs and problems, political challenges, and external risks and opportunities from the viewpoints of each individual member. In other words, the strategic relevance of MERCOSUR rests on the perceptions and evaluation of each member country's policymakers and prominent economic actors as to the bloc's functionality in providing viable alternatives to address international economic constraints and domestic problems.

It is important to note that despite the initial skepticism of actors in most economic sectors about the prospects of integration, as time passed MERCOSUR came to receive wide political support and to play an important role in advancing liberal trade practices in member countries. The acute economic crisis that seized Argentina and spread to Uruguay, Paraguay, and Brazil fueled criticism of the economic policies to which MERCOSUR had been associated. Although only in relatively few instances has overt opposition to economic integration been expressed, in each member country an anti–free trade mood has arisen, along with a perception that the bloc does not play a meaningful role in addressing most immediate economic concerns.

This ambivalence has not prevented member countries to reshape their strategies for MERCOSUR in an effort to adapt to new and more restrictive circumstances. Some features of its present strategy, although not yet fully developed, can be identified. They derive from the assessment of MERCOSUR's current course and from previous formulations, and reflect a predominantly principled, normative, and voluntaristic view of the necessary conditions to reinvigorate the bloc.

One feature of this revamped strategy is emphasis on internal cohesion as a fundamental condition for restoring the bloc's self-confidence and credibility. In this regard, the prospect of a new multilateral round of trade negotiations under the aegis of the WTO and the acceleration of FTAA negotiations after the Quebec Summit, as well as the negotiations with the European Union, have played a positive role in terms of stimulating internal cohesion, in spite of the evident differences between Brazil and Argentina as to some important issues, especially in the FTAA process. These positive steps have not, however, been fully met in the quality and strength of MERCOSUR norms and institutions and in a sound commitment by its members to free trade policies and deeper integration levels. Even so, the bloc has so far managed to preserve itself internally and as an international negotiating entity, in spite of the ongoing loosening of its political and economic threads.

A second feature is the reassertion of the political commitment to perfecting the customs union and its disciplines and institutions. Rather than a mere rhetorical manifest, this commitment has practical consequences as it defines a clear agenda with specific issues to be addressed, thus stimulating the mobilization and convergence of efforts toward attainable goals. Nevertheless, this commitment has not found sound and equitable support among the member countries. Argentina has repeatedly insisted on downgrading MERCOSUR to a free trade area, with the support of some economic and political sectors in Uruguay and Paraguay. Such propositions have not progressed due to Brazil's strong stance on preserving and consolidating the customs union as an essential element of the bloc's (and the country's own) regional strategy.

A third feature reflects the effort to update the internal agenda of the bloc to cope with the challenges posed by external negotiations at the regional, hemispheric, transregional, and multilateral levels. This implies the establishment of some functional links between the internal and external agendas for the sake of reinvigorating the bloc, which would be an important change vis-à-vis the 1995–1997 period. A fourth feature of MERCOSUR's late trade strategy is the search of a more active profile in relations with its main trade partners, namely the United States and the European Union, and in trade talks within the WTO. In spite of its internal crisis, MERCOSUR maintains its assertiveness externally, notably in issues related to market access and in refusing to negotiate the so-called "gray-area issues" as a way of strengthening the multilateral world trade system and resisting the protectionism of its main trade partners.

Nevertheless, some of the basic requirements for the success of this strategy have not been met. Efforts to advance the agenda of relaunching have been bogged down because of the divergent perspectives of Brazil and Argentina, and by an ever-growing protectionist trend that has contaminated trade policies in both countries, as well as perceptions of the bloc's economic health. In addition, governments have failed to establish functional ties between the bloc's domestic and international agendas. Dealing with the immediate and short-term consequences of economic imbalances and their negative political, economic, and social externalities became a key issue in 2000 and 2001 not only in Argentina, where it led to a crisis of unprecedented proportions, but also in neighboring countries.

In such a context, policy coordination remains a desired objective rather than an actual accomplishment. Although important incentives for policy coordination exist, several obstacles remain. Domestic economic issues have systematically prevailed over those of the integration agenda. Restoring and preserving macroeconomic stability in the face of domestic and external constraints continues to be an essential economic goal of MERCOSUR countries. Besides that, measures adopted at the microeconomic level reveal important differences in policy preferences within each national government as to what MERCOSUR should be and the priority to be granted to it in face of other domestic demands. These differences make policy coordination even harder to achieve. As previously mentioned, although the four MERCOSUR countries have established some common macroeconomic goals, their achievement depends much more on domestic matters and corresponding economic policies than on incentives for cooperation associated with the regional project.

Conclusion

The analysis of the strategies by which MERCOSUR has dealt with trade issues internally and externally indicates that those strategies were not derived from any single, encompassing, long-term operational approach. Rather, they are the outcomes of several adaptive responses to changing contexts, possibilities, and constraints posed at each stage by internal and external political and economic environments. This conclusion meets the assumption that trade strategies and preferences are largely determined by the interplay of strategic political and economic objectives and international and domestic constraints.

Over the course of its first decade, as the bloc faced new challenges and contexts, it developed adaptive strategies to counter them. During its first four years, MERCOSUR took advantage of a favorable external economic environment to implement its internal commercial agenda through a voluntaristic approach in which automatic procedures for the phasing out of tariffs, and the harmonization of interests through trade-offs and side payments were key elements. In the following phase, the focus shifted to the external agenda as a means of exploiting political and economic opportunities to consolidate a political profile within a context of more restrictive economic conditions. In more recent times, the bloc has labored hard to harmonize and balance increasing different national interests, to create opportunities to reinvigorate itself, and to overcome the severe crises it faces. However, it has become more vulnerable than in previous phases to domestic and external injunctions, and is confronted with the prospect of stagnation or even retrocession. Avoiding these prospects requires the reassertion of its cohesion and its identity as a negotiating entity, the strengthening of its trade disciplines, and a more assertive profile in its relations with its main economic partners. So far, progress in each of these tasks has been uneven, while domestic and external economic circumstances remain unfavorable for the advancement of integration.

In the external realm, three developments are relevant to the shaping of MERCOSUR's destiny: the reassertion of U.S. political, economic, and strategic leadership as an immediate reaction to the terrorist attacks of September 11, 2001; the willingness by the European Union to advance steadily in the negotiations with MERCOSUR; and the fate of the Doha Round multilateral trade negotiations. The reassertion of U.S. leadership internationally has produced a two-pronged strategic effort. It has propelled political and military activism, even unilateral if necessary, in areas in which the United States feels that it has been threatened directly. The military campaign in Afghanistan and the war waged against Iraq in the first half of 2003 are evidence of such activism. At the same time, the U.S. government seems to have no alternative but to reinvigorate multilateral initiatives at global and regional levels to counter the rising feeling of insecurity and to restore confidence in international institutions and regimes. The willingness not to allow the 2001 WTO Doha ministerial conference to fail in launching a new round of trade negotiations was one striking piece of evidence of this element of the U.S. agenda. At the regional level, U.S. assertiveness implies a stronger commitment to the establishment of a comprehensive security regime in the Americas and to the successful completion of the FTAA negotiations.

MERCOSUR is not equipped politically or institutionally to act collectively in matters of security or defense, and there is no indication thus far that governments are willing to assign it any meaningful role in this area. At the same time, the renewed commitment of the United States to the establishment of an FTAA poses a direct challenge to the ability of MERCOSUR to negotiate with a more assertive United States. The lack of internal cohesion of the bloc and its economic vulnerabilities contribute to the current fragility of its position.

In addition to the weaknesses of Argentina, Uruguay, and Paraguay derived from a deepening economic crisis, Brazil also faced economic problems in the final months of Fernando Henrique Cardoso's second presidential term. These problems were associated with political uncertainties brought about by the prospects of victory of leftist candidate Luis Inacio Lula da Silva in the October 2002 presidential election and by the country's external economic imbalances and vulnerability. In the second semester of 2002, Brazil's real devalued strongly, inflation and unemployment rose, and investment halted, resulting in an extremely unfavorable economic environment in which economic and social inequalities generated or reinforced by the liberal economic policies pursued in the 1990s were exacerbated. The election of Lula da Silva and his Workers' Party with massive popular support was the political corollary of disastrous domestic economic conditions.

However, most domestic and foreign concerns about the new government's policies dissipated as the commitment to fiscal discipline, sound monetary policy, and macroeconomic stability was implemented. In foreign affairs, the new Brazilian government has indicated willingness to exercise an assertive role in regional and global affairs. As to the regional dimension, the exercise of political leadership to strengthen MERCOSUR, promote

South American integration, and reassert the country's key interest in the FTAA negotiations is to become the cornerstone of Brazilian foreign policy in coming years. Regarding world affairs, the general guidelines are to influence the global agenda in favor of balanced economic and social development and to strengthen multilateralism.

As for trade policy, fighting any form of protectionism that affects Brazilian exports, opening markets, exploiting trade opportunities in emerging markets, and promoting import substitution by stimulating production efficiency and competitiveness are the announced priorities of the new government. Reciprocity will be an important Brazilian demand in trade negotiations in which market access and further liberalization of important sectors of the Brazilian market are at stake. After the simultaneous unilateral, regional, and multilateral opening of its markets carried out in the 1990s, Brazil is certainly not willing to give up entirely the benefits of free trade, but it is also much less prone to accept further liberalization if clear and more immediate concessions by its main trading partners in key commercial areas are not seen as forthcoming.

These priorities taken collectively do not indicate any kind of departure from the trade profile the country has exhibited so far. Its trade preferences and strategies continue to be centered around the building of minilateralism at the regional level with MERCOSUR as its key component, transregionalism, and multilateralism. At the same time, bilateralism has not been dismissed. On the contrary, regardless of its commitment to reinvigorate MERCOSUR, Brazil is strongly willing to develop new trade partnerships, especially with emerging trade powers like China, and with other important countries like Russia, India, South Africa, and Mexico. This implies that MERCOSUR will be assigned an important role, as in the early 1990s, but perhaps a more limited one in the context of Brazilian foreign trade.

The paths chosen by Argentina to overcome economic crisis and the role played by Brazil in this regard are also key elements for the definition of the political and economic profile of MERCOSUR in the short and mid-term. The Argentine nightmare has affected MERCOSUR directly and in different ways. Most immediately, it led to a significant decrease of trade and investment flows. Politically, the crisis has raised uncertainties about the form and degree of integration that MERCOSUR might eventually assume. In its early stages, the crisis contributed to the gradual rise of managed trade practices that eroded the free trade regime. It forced Brazil and Argentina to give up efforts aimed at restoring and consolidating the common external tariff and the customs union, one of the main objectives of the agenda to relaunch MERCOSUR agreed upon at the beginning of Argentine President Fernando de la Rua's term in 1999. Negotiations on this crucial issue were resumed in early 2003 as part of the initiative launched by the new Brazilian government aimed at reinvigorating MERCOSUR.

However, it can be argued that the prospects for MERCOSUR's trade policies and strategies will become more clear only when the Argentine government is able to move away from the immediate and short-term requirements that have absorbed its policy energies in recent times. The end of the peso–dollar parity model brings with it the possibility of greater convergence with Brazil in terms of their respective exchange regimes. This certainly clears the way for a positive agenda as it removes a source of commercial conflicts between the two main partners and clears the way for future coordination of macroeconomic policies. However, a high level of uncertainty persists as to Argentina's future trade strategies and preferences and the role to be played by MERCOSUR. There is no doubt that at present, Argentina is closer to MERCOSUR than it was in the late 1990s. But Buenos Aires might be tempted again to seek a bilateral free trade agreement with the United States, as Uruguay also attempted, as a hedging strategy in case FTAA negotiations are deadlocked. This would create a de facto condition in which the trade disciplines of MERCOSUR and its trade strategy toward third parties would become severely, and possibly irreversibly, strained.

In such a context, the fate of the global multilateral trade system becomes a critical variable for MERCOSUR. The start of a new round of trade negotiations within the WTO will require a more vigorous and consolidated commercial discipline, improved institutions, and enhanced political willingness of its member countries for collective negotiations. The scope and complexity of the negotiation agenda as presently envisaged and the highly politicized debates it has already created make it necessary to strengthen the instruments that may contribute to aggregate positions and negotiating capabilities. Regional blocs like MERCOSUR serve this purpose. So far, MERCOSUR does not act as a single negotiating unit in the context of the WTO. However, there is no indication that its member countries are willing to give up the political and economic utility that the bloc may yet provide in the context of large multilateral negotiations.

Even if negotiations do not advance as expected or eventually fail, there will be strong incentives for countries to resort to economic regionalism as a second-best approach to trade liberalization. In such a scenario, regional initiatives might represent an important arena of political dynamism, providing a positive environment for the establishment of norms, rules, and practices that may eventually go beyond the regulations of the WTO. MERCOSUR has not endorsed this sort of "WTO-plus" proposition. However, these issues have been occasionally raised in the context of the FTAA in relation to environmental and social provisions. Whether WTO negotiations are successful or not, regionalism will remain an important underpinning of the world trade regime and MERCOSUR will certainly at some point have to face these issues.

At stake are the links between regionalism and multilateralism. In the late 1980s and the first half of the 1990s, there was fierce debate over the nature of regionalism and its consequences for the multilateral trade regime. Regional initiatives were then portrayed either as obstacles or as stepping-stones to global trade liberalization. At present, those expressions seem to be inaccurate in capturing the relationship between regional agreements and the multilateral trade system. These relations cannot be defined any longer simply in terms of either/or propositions. It is important to notice that, even in the case of an eventual failure of the WTO's new round of negotiations, the multilateral trade system will not be immediately or inevitably replaced by regional arrangements, no matter how strong and encompassing they are. What may develop then is a very complex system regulated by the WTO but with a wide array of areas subject to regional agreements. Regionalism would become a form of restricted multilateralism in which new commercial disciplines would be introduced, implemented, and legitimized under the form of a WTO-plus arrangement.

On the other hand, the advancement and success of multilateral negotiations will not mean the end of incentives for countries to seek and join regional agreements and integration mechanisms. What seems to be at stake then is the functionality of such agreements and arrangements regarding the accomplishment of interests and objectives of both national governments, on the one hand, and corporations, on the other, in an ever-changing political and economic international landscape. The ability of regional blocs like MERCOSUR to adapt and shift strategies in response to dynamic internal and external challenges simultaneously is a key criterion of their future performance.

Notes

1. Treaty of Integration, Cooperation and Development Between Brazil and Argentina (1988), Art. 2.

2. The Treaty of Asunción, Article 5.

3. Only one of such sectoral agreement was actually convened and registered with the Latin American Integration Association.

4. The harmonization of nontariff measures, trade liberalization of services, disciplines against unfair trade practices of third states, safeguards, and customs valuation were some of the important issues upon which no agreement was reached by the end of the transition period.

5. It was agreed that the common external tariff to be applied to capital goods should converge to the 14% level until January 2001; for informatics and telecommunications goods, a 16% level would be reached in 2006.

References

Bouzas, Roberto. 2001. "Aspectos Estratégicos de las Negociaciones del MERCOSUR." In *Las Américas sin Barreras: Negociaciones de Acceso a Mercados,* edited by Antoni Estevadoreordal and Carolyn Robert, 37–68. Washington, DC: Inter-American Development Bank.

Guimarães, Eduardo A. 1997. *Abertura Econômica, Política de Estabilização e Política Industrial.* Working Paper. Brasília: Instituto de Pesquisa Econômica Aplicada.

Institute for the Integration of Latin America and the Caribbean (INTAL). *MERCOSUR Report 1999–2000.* Report 6. Buenos Aires: INTAL.

Motta Veiga, Pedro da. 2000. "O Brasil no Mercosul: Política e Economia em um Projeto de Integração." In *Mercosul: Entre a Realidade e a Utopia,* edited by Jorge Campbell, 237–94. Rio de Janeiro: Relume Dumará.

Seixas Correa, Luis Felipe de. 1996. "A Política Externa de José Sarney." In *Sessenta Anos de Política Externa Brasileira, 1930–1990,* Vol. 2, edited by José A. G. Albuquerque, 260–84. São Paulo: Cultura Editores Associados.

Vaz, Alcides C. 2001. "Mercosul aos Dez Anos: Crise de Identidade ou de Crescimento?" *Revista Brasileira de Política Internacional* 44, no. 1: 43–54.

Part IV

Conclusion and Prospects

11

Conclusion

Vinod K. Aggarwal, Ralph Espach,
and Joseph S. Tulchin

This volume has explored the motivations behind the trade strategies of Argentina, Brazil, Chile, and Mexico from the reform period in the early 1980s to the present. A comparison of these strategies, which consist of combinations of initiatives at the unilateral, bilateral, regional, and multilateral levels, shows dramatic divergence. The differences in these paths reflect a variety of choices among economic, political, and security objectives, as well as the relatively fixed constraints and opportunities specific to each country that derive from its resources, geography, and history of economic development. The theoretical framework developed in Chapter 1 presents a categorization of trade accords and explores the reasoning and calculations underlying each country's strategic trade profile. As a first-cut analysis, Aggarwal and Espach set aside issues of domestic politics and capacity that influence trade policy formulation to provide a baseline assessment focused on the strategic options presented in each case.

The initial assessment states that Chile has actively undertaken unilateral liberalization, complemented by bilateral and multilateral trade approaches, as a strategy to enhance its economic competitiveness and minimize risks, in contrast to seeking political leverage through membership in a regional bloc. In the case of Mexico, the deepening of ties to the United States through the North American Free Trade Agreement (NAFTA) has enhanced the country's long-term political and economic prospects, but at the cost of increased dependence on a single market and a more limited set of strategic options. The political and strategic advantages that accrue to Brazil from regionalism, and its ability to use the regional bloc it dominates as a tactical advantage in negotiations with the European Union and the United States and in other concerns, entail a trade-off between economic efficiency and negotiating leverage. Finally, Argentina's commitment to regionalism has gained it limited political and strategic advantage, and the protections that the Southern Common Market (MERCOSUR) provides to several large regional industries (many dominated by Brazilian companies) have cost Argentina in terms of economic competitiveness. While MERCOSUR has benefited its members in many ways, in terms of promoting the emergence of globally competitive industries, its record thus far has been disappointing, especially when compared to Chile's go-it-alone, multilateral approach to trade.

The framework in Chapter 1 is intended as a parsimonious analytical basis for a comparative exploration of these countries' trade policies. To explain more fully the origin and development of these trade patterns, these hypothetical strategic trade-offs require further elaboration. The other chapters in the volume explore and provide useful challenges to the initial analysis by focusing on specific elements of trade policy or individual country cases. Aggarwal and Espach's framework and predictions provide us with a relatively static picture of opportunities and costs. However, as countries engage in strategic action in a dynamic environment, the cost of trade-offs may be mitigated, difficulties may become opportunities, and fortunes may be reversed. This will depend in part on the effectiveness of government responses to the challenges and opportunities offered them today and in the future. In Chapter 2, Tulchin expands on the analytical framework to emphasize the position of a nation's trade policy within a broader context of international relations and power. In an increasingly dense and multi-layered international system, trade agreements—aside from their economic logic—are one of several instruments for the enhancement of a country's legitimacy as a partner in the making of international rules. And, in a reciprocal fashion, elements of that legitimacy can strengthen a nation's hand in trade negotiations. This investment in "soft power" should not be over-looked as an asset of national strategic action within a dynamic, unpredictable environment. This type of resource may prove critical as these nations with fewer elements of traditional hard power seek to be heard in negotiations over complex and far-reaching international institutions including the World Trade Organization (WTO) and the Free Trade Area of the Americas (FTAA).

This conclusion reviews the findings from our contributors' analysis, and assesses how well the abstract analysis from the introduction holds up when considered alongside the many factors and considerations introduced by the case studies. Before turning to this task, however, we first explore the vexing problem of attempting to assess systematically these distinct national trade strategies. To wit, how can we assess "strategies" from the outcomes we observe in terms of bilateral, regional, or multilateral agreements?

The Nature of Strategy

The question as we see it is whether states are actively pursuing coherent sets of policies that can be considered a "strategy," or does the variation simply reflect an artificial and ad hoc potpourri that results from some combination of the vagaries of domestic politics, a changing ideological landscape, and simple opportunistic liberalization choices? The framework in Chapter 1 conceptualizes trade policymaking as the pursuit of trade policy profiles by rational, unitary actors following their specific national interests. The drawbacks of rationalist conceptual models are broadly recognized, and we do not intend to summarize or comment upon a half-century of debate. By employing a rationalist model of state interest formulation and activity, Aggarwal and Espach postulate that despite the messiness of actual trade policy formulation, there is enough divergence among these cases over a sufficiently lengthy period to indicate fundamental differences of intent and strategic orientation. The outcomes we observe, in terms of regional trade patterns and participation in various efforts at liberalization, are useful indicators of this divergence—even if they are affected by factors other than the realization of strategic trade policy.

The principal alternative to this view is that each of these countries has a rather similar trade policy orientation, but the divergence observed in implementation is the result of differences in their capacities to implement long-term plans. Information provided in the case studies about institutional weakness, the power of special interest groups, especially industry associations, and the demands on the executive to engage in domestic coalition building lends support to this type of interpretation. The fact that each of our case study countries has sought to implement a free-market, export-promotion economic model in the 1990s also suggests that their differences may not be strategic, but incidental. We find this view, which is common in the mainstream media, to be lacking.

Certainly, trade policies can be affected as much by special interest lobbying or short-term executive prerogative, or some other form of response to domestic concerns, than by strategic planning. Long-term national economic and strategic plans may well get hijacked by short-term interests or political instability or may reflect the dominance of special interests over long periods of time. Indeed, consistency in trade policy is rare even in the most stable and institutionalized democracies. Aggarwal and Espach's analysis assumes that there is strategic thinking and planning at the national level, although perhaps this is conducted more effectively in some governments than others. Moreover, this strategic planning lies behind each of the

observed trade profiles. From this perspective, the consistency of the pattern of trade policy divergence over the past fifteen years is solid enough to
discard the notion that it is the result of each country's failing in its own way
to implement liberalization unilaterally and multilaterally—the preferred
avenue of neoliberals. To some extent, these governments are indeed failing to realize their ideal strategic trade policies; most, if not all, countries
are. But there is more going on than this. The divergence among these national trade profiles reflects fundamentally different strategic visions and
objectives. The interpretation that differences in trade policies are the result
primarily of weak state capacity instead of differing strategic agendas also
neglects the dramatic differences among these countries. These differences
include the sizes of their domestic markets, their natural endowments, degree and form of industrialization, the institutional nature of their policy formulation process, and—partly a result of these other factors—their political
self-identification. To many outside observers, the differences among the profiles of Argentina, Brazil, Chile, and Mexico simply reflect various degrees
of failure or success, driven by corrupt or feckless political systems, at implementing the policies widely accepted as "best" for their development.

We do not entirely disagree. State capacity is an extremely important
issue, as the case study chapters make eminently clear. However, the role
played by capacity as a determinant variable is different in each case. State
capacity is demonstrated both in a government's ability to formulate strategies and its capacity to carry them out effectively over time. The case studies of Argentina and Chile suggest two opposite conditions. In Argentina,
as Ablin and Bouzas suggest, weak capacity for the formulation of trade
policies calls the concept of strategy into question. One of Chile's advantages, on the other hand, is its centralized institutional capacity. Rosales's
description of Chile's multifaceted strategy is handily supported by the
country's success at establishing a variety of trade agreements since 1990.

The analyses of the Brazilian and Mexican cases are more ambiguous.
With Brazil, the element of state capacity has a dual and neutralizing effect,
at least in regard to the impressive capacity of Itamaraty, Brazil's foreign
ministry. Due to the professionalism of its diplomatic corps, Brazil is a formidable negotiator. However, the institutional capacity of Itamaraty also has
negative value, in that the ministry has traditionally worked to prevent the
inclusion of outside social and governmental groups in the policy formulation process. Similarly, observers of the Mexican state rarely argue that the
central government suffers from an inability to formulate and carry out its
policies, once its priorities are established. In this regard, NAFTA has had

a bolstering effect, by increasing the pressure on various Mexican government agencies—including the foreign ministry and the office of drug control policies—to improve their performance relative to their partners in Canada and the United States. In sum, we argue that while state capacity is an important element of the conditions these governments face, it is not the principal determining factor behind the divergence in their trade strategies.

In our analysis we seek to emphasize that in addition to their economic concerns, these countries frequently use trade policy as an element of the pursuit of political interests within the international arena. For example, Chile, heavily dependent on the exportation of copper and niche market agro-industrial goods, faces a different menu of strategic alternatives than massive Brazil—one of the world's largest economies and with century-old aspirations of becoming a global power. Mexico's geographic location and unique relationship with the United States presents extraordinary constraints and possibilities. What may be more exceptional than the divergence we observe among these countries' trade profiles is the fact that they share any common economic and foreign policy orientation at all.

This may seem a simple point, but it is often overlooked. Through the 1990s to the present, trade and economic relations involve far more than the creation or diversion of jobs and investment. They also involve strategic alignment and positioning. In the post–Cold War era, when the regional hegemon is also the global hegemon, and shows a propensity for the muscular pursuit of its interests abroad, these political and strategic calculations are likely to play an increasing role in the foreign policies of Latin American nations. As Tulchin argues in the second chapter, trade strategy is one of several means by which governments seek to expand their influence in the international community, and expanded influence and the economic benefits of expanded trade can be mutually reinforcing.

We have argued that national trade policy profiles reflect particular sets of economic, political, and strategic rationales that involve trade-offs among different objectives. The chapters in this volume that focus on specific areas or implications of trade policy, or on national or regional case studies, support this claim. Moreover, each of our authors identifies other factors as well at the social or institutional levels that may influence either the preferences of trade policymakers or their abilities to effectively formulate and implement a consistent foreign economic policy. Table 11.1 summarizes the key elements from those chapters.

In each country case, a wide range of factors, from geographical attributes and population size to the characteristics of state–business institutions

Table 11.1 *Summary of Principal Factors Affecting Trade Profiles of Mexico, Argentina, Brazil, and Chile in the 1990s*

	Geography	Market Size	Domestic Politics and Institutions	Business and Sectoral Dynamics	Security
Mexico	Proximity to the United States, history of bilateral trade, and complementary factor endowments encouraged regionalist policy	Limited internal market and access to United States, made trade vital for economies of scale and encouraged regionalist strategy	Membership in trade groups an instrument for committing country to liberalization Currently, democratization is placing new pluralist pressures on policymakers	PRI dominance limited influence of business and labor opposition to trade liberalization Increased influence of export sectors; decline in political strength of import-competing sectors	Trade accords complemented cooperative regional security efforts Multilateral trade agreements envisioned as platform for expanded presence in other issue areas
Argentina	Proximity to Brazilian market encourages regionalist policy History of balanced trade with United States and Europe reduces potential for dependence on Brazil	Potential gains from access to Brazilian market encouraged regionalist strategy Proximity to Brazilian market in the formation of regional trade initiatives	Early stages of trade liberalization bolstered democratization, part of shift from military dominance Membership in trade groups an instrument for committing country to liberalization Lack of bureaucratic autonomy limited capacity for strategic trade policy	Weakness of business associations reduced political capacity of export sectors to push agenda	Early stages of trade liberalization reduced long-standing regional tensions

Brazil	Enormous size and number of neighboring countries encouraged regionalist policy	Limited importance of trade as share of GDP reduced political salience of trade policy. Enormous market yields increased bargaining power	Early stages of trade liberalization bolstered democratization. State capacity for strategic trade policy constrained by clientilism, resulting in patches of protectionism. Dominant influence of foreign ministry on trade agenda supported paradigm shaped by competition with United States	Strong resistance from beneficiary groups under import substitution industrialization yielded gradualist liberalization. Brazilian business poorly organized, while some industry groups enjoy particularistic ties. Weakened political capacity of exporters to support free trade policy	Early stages of trade liberalization reduced long-standing regional tensions. Trade relations envisioned as a platform for expanded presence in other issue areas
Chile	Relative isolation reduced incentives for regionalism, increased interest in multilateralism. History of balanced trade with United States and Europe encouraged further multilateralism and outreach to East Asia	Exports required for developing industrial economies of scale	Early trade liberalization implemented under authoritarian government that stifled opposition, facilitated economic liberalization	Political preference given to export interests. Successful coordination between state and business associations increased support for and gains from free trade	Early stages of trade liberalization reduced long-standing regional tensions. Strategy of linkage between trade agenda and support for human rights and democratic institutions

or state ideology, influenced the trade policy outcome. Most of our four cases share critical features, such as the importance of past regional ties and security concerns, or the role of trade policy as a concrete commitment to the models of democratic governance and economic liberalization. There are important differences as well. Looking forward, what do these factors that lie behind the observed trade profiles indicate regarding future trade relations in the Americas? We offer the following reflections.

Looking Forward: Case Study Trade-offs and Their Implications for the Future of National Trade Policies

Mexico: Hub Market

In the introductory section we argue that Mexico has pursued a hub market strategy centered on NAFTA. This approach entails a fundamental trade-off of improved economic stability for reduced political autonomy. On the upside, the advantages of such a strategy are clear. From an economic standpoint, following the devaluation in 1994, Mexico's economy rebounded well and enjoyed healthy growth and increased foreign investment throughout the 1990s. Although these gains were unevenly distributed within Mexico, and massive shifts within the domestic economy have caused severe hardship for many Mexicans, especially rural workers, Mexico's growth rate was among the highest in Latin America. How much of this was due to NAFTA itself is unclear. Regardless of the trade accord, Mexico's economic growth has for decades been linked to the health or weakness of the U.S. economy, Mexico's critical export market. But NAFTA clearly deepened this trend. The more important effect of NAFTA is that it also deepened regional interdependence, which has made Mexico an indispensable partner of the United States.

To the extent that economic interdependence leads to increased collaboration on several fronts, including management of the border, anti–drug trafficking and crime prevention, and environmental cleanup, NAFTA will generate numerous long-term benefits. Close cooperation with the United States and deepening economic integration may encourage the modernization of Mexican state institutions, and improve its economic competitiveness as well as its state capacity much faster than likely would have occurred without NAFTA.

On the downside, Mexican openness to U.S. and Canadian influence through many channels both public and private will cause tension within a political system and society already undergoing tremendous change. As Ortiz and Wise suggest in their chapters, the principal question is: How will the Mexican government manage these political tensions without succumbing to instability?

As a foreign relations policy, NAFTA's potential payoff is also very high, but it faces significant challenges. The shift since the early 1990s toward close, warm relations with the United States was a watershed in Mexican international relations. Expectations in Mexico—and particularly within the Fox administration as it took office in 2000—were high that collaboration would increase on several fronts, in particular the legalization of temporary migration. Before September 11, 2001, this appeared to be the case. President Bush, reluctant to involve himself with complicated, distant foreign affairs, had personally highlighted improved relations with Mexico as a key element of his agenda.

After the attack on the World Trade Center, however, U.S. relations with Mexico floundered as the Bush administration turned its attention almost wholeheartedly to a global campaign against terrorism, and then against Saddam Hussein's regime in Iraq. President Fox's progressive initiative toward the United States was ignored, sullying his administration's image at home. His foreign minister, Jorge Castañeda, who made improved cooperation with the United States on several fronts a top priority, resigned in frustration in January 2003. Nevertheless, cross-border cooperation on several issues continues, in particular at the interagency and local levels, and with greatest effect in the border region of both countries. In many respects, this is NAFTA's best legacy. On the other hand, as predicted by the analytical framework in the introduction, Mexico's throwing its lot in with the United States has its advantages in the form of an insurance policy against disaster, but its effects will likely vary depending on the level of attention given to it by the U.S. federal government.

There is another advantage to Mexico's early commitment to regionalism. Contrary to expectations, the Bush administration has proved willing to continue government protection for U.S. steel and agriculture. Despite the optimistic rhetoric of the president and Trade Representative Robert Zoellick, this trend does not bode well for the future of the FTAA, which is entering its most difficult period. As Ortiz explains, Mexico's regionalist hub-market strategy and its increasing transregional economic ties reduce the importance of the FTAA, which for Mexico was never very great to begin with. To some degree, Chile's recent free trade agreement with the United States lessens Mexico's advantage as being the only developing country bridge to the U.S. market (thus a "hub market"). On the other hand, with foreign direct investment flows to Latin America on the decline, and with the United States seeking bilateral agreements with Central American countries as well as others, these advantages are unlikely to ever again be as beneficial as they were in the second half of the 1990s. In the lexicon of corporate strategy, through its early membership in NAFTA Mexico successfully garnered the one-off costs of being a first mover.

In terms of economic relations, Mexico has sought to address its overwhelming dependence on the U.S. market by establishing several transregional free trade agreements, including with the European Union and MERCOSUR, and is currently in negotiations with Japan and Singapore. Mexico has joined Chile as one of the world's foremost bilateral free traders. However, as Ortiz suggests, the extent to which these agreements will reduce dependence on the U.S. market is far from certain. Clearly, NAFTA and U.S.–Mexican bilateral relations will continue to have preeminent importance, but these broader partnerships are valuable for Mexico nonetheless. Furthermore, the success of NAFTA has greatly increased Mexico's role in the United Nations and in hemispheric affairs.

Argentina: Regional Partner

In several respects, our assessment of the Argentine case is the most pessimistic of the four. Our introductory analysis suggests that MERCOSUR's lack of institutional consolidation, the unevenness of its long-term benefits, and its failure to improve the competitiveness of Argentine goods and industries in external markets have limited the benefits of the country's regionalist strategy. Membership in MERCOSUR did little to help Argentina avoid financial breakdown. Fluctuations in the value of the peso against the Brazilian real even contributed, in small measure, to bringing it on. In contrast to Mexico, there was little political payoff from Argentina's deepening ties to the regional giant. Brazil's economy and financial resources provide no safety net against catastrophe, as in the case of the United States and Mexico. In addition, the free trade talks between MERCOSUR and the European Union, have also broken down as MERCOSUR slogs through difficult political times. Menem sought to balance trade dependence on Brazil with a strategic partnership with the United States. But the benefits of such a partnership never were clear to Argentines and appear to have disappeared entirely in the aftermath of default, as the United States demonstrated little sympathy for Argentina's plight vis-à-vis the International Monetary Fund (IMF).

In Chapter 6, Ablin and Bouzas suggest that Argentine trade policy reflects little in the form of strategic intention or calculation, but instead was arrived at largely through decisions made under short-term pressures. As of this writing, with its national politics and financial system still shaky, significant trade talks are on hold. The nation's strategic trade options—whether to continue its commitment to regionalism, or to reduce Brazil's influence and pursue agreements bilaterally—are sharply constrained in the short term by the caution of potential partners. In addition, the new economic policies that will emerge as Argentina recovers will dramatically affect the future form of MERCOSUR and long-term prospects for regional integration. For example, the brutal devaluation of December 2001 has turned Argentina fiercely competitive in the export of its traditional commodities, a trend with uncertain implications for its trade policy henceforth. However, despite the current weaknesses of MERCOSUR and Argentina's doldrums, the regionalist strategy should not be seen as a total failure. The non–zero sum nature of international trade expansion, which is the underlying rationale for unilateral and multilateral liberalization, may manifest itself during times of economic expansion, but what strategies are best for addressing a more difficult, zero-sum competitive environment? As we consider in the case of Chile, future developments such as the continued growth of Chinese export industries, the possibility of a prolonged Brazilian or U.S. recession, or a period of armed conflict involving the United States, could alter the climate for international investment and trade. In such a case, regional accords that have political and security elements linked to economic issues may prove useful and sustainable whereas shallow transregional free trade pacts, with little political rationale, may yield relatively few benefits. MERCOSUR may seem to have generated for Argentina only limited gains in terms of economic expansion and competitiveness, but a political partnership with Brazil—if further developed—may yet prove useful.

Brazil: Regional Leader

Brazil's trade profile emphasizes the nation's predilection to consider trade policy as part of a larger strategic or political agenda, rather than an element of broad, laissez-faire liberalization. In addition to its numerous benefits in terms of improving regional relations and supporting democracy, MERCOSUR has developed for Brazil into an instrument for greater control over a moderately paced program of liberalization. The decline of the trade bloc's legitimacy—due to the economic weakness of the region as a whole,

and the breaching of tariff commitments by several members in late 2001—
has affected Brazil, but not to the same extent that it has Argentina. With its
massive internal market and advanced level of industrialization, Brazil is
well positioned in international trade negotiations, even with a weakened
MERCOSUR.

The generosity of the IMF toward Brazil, even as its prominent trade
partner Argentina collapsed, indicates that as with Mexico, Brazil may
now be perceived by the United States as an economy deserving of extra-
supportive treatment. The fact that Brazil and the United States will share
leadership of the FTAA negotiations over the next two years during its most
difficult phase will also elevate Brazil's position regardless of its caution
toward free trade and limited extra-regional ties (especially when compared
to Chile or Mexico). Indeed, as critical attitudes across South America toward the neoliberal economic model continue to build, FTAA terms and
conditions advocated by the left-leaning President Lula are likely to enjoy
popular support. The recent free trade agreement between Brazil and Mexico, which covers key sensitive sectors including autos and auto parts, is an
important signal that the MERCOSUR club may no longer be so restrictive.
Similar to Argentina, as the Lula government settles in within the context
of a less prosperous and generous international environment, as well as a
more unilaterally minded United States, it will surely reassess the gains and
limitations of a regionally focused trade policy. It may be that MERCOSUR
is reinvigorated, perhaps even expanded, by a Lula government keen on
countering U.S. influence. If so, we agree with the analysis by Costa Vaz
that this will require a deeper commitment from Brazil to the institutionalization of MERCOSUR—for instance, through effective mechanisms for
trade dispute resolution and macroeconomic coordination.

Is Brazil likely to shift from its tendency to treat trade policy as part of
a larger strategic, political agenda? Is it likely to move beyond the ambivalent, "hedging" attitude that Motta Veiga describes? We think not. Brazil's
inclination in its foreign policy toward longer-term, global aspirations is
rooted in its self-identity as a continental country and the insular nature
of its foreign ministry—neither of which will change in the foreseeable
future. President Lula is likely to bring a less cooperative spirit to Brazil's
economic relations with the United States and Europe, as these powers continue to protect or to subsidize segments of their markets critical to Brazilian
exports. Lula's new foreign minister, Celso Amorim, is one of Itamaraty's
most experienced negotiators, and will be an important asset in the difficult upcoming negotiations with the United States. In the future Brazil may

choose to engage more in bilateral trade agreements, but more likely out of strategic, rather than purely economic, rationale. Either way, the prospects for Brazil's further strengthening of its position as an important economic player on the world stage, and for MERCOSUR, will be deeply affected by how well and quickly Argentina can recover, and if Brazil is itself able to avoid financial collapse.

Chile: Multilevel Trader

If Brazil's strategic trade policy is largely an instrument for the enhancement of political power at the expense of rapid liberalization and economic competitiveness, Chile's is the reverse. The introductory chapters as well as Rosales's contribution in Chapter 8 highlight the economic—and for Tulchin, political—successes of Chile's deeper liberalization combined with multiple transregional free trade agreements. Chile is one of the world's leaders in transregional bilateral free trade. The recently completed free trade agreement with the United States makes Chile virtually a de facto member of NAFTA, and the accord with South Korea was the first between countries of South America and East Asia. Chile is also in negotiations with Singapore and Japan. These numerous memberships are a compliment to the competitiveness of Chilean exports and the skill and energy of its diplomatic team. Due largely to this competitiveness, and to some degree to Chile's modest restrictions on short-term capital flows, the Chilean economy has managed to remain relatively stable during the region's recent turbulence. Chile remains a model case for the neoliberal economic doctrine of unilateral liberalization and multilateral free trade.

Chile has foregone the protectionist benefits that come from membership in a regional bloc. Instead it has welcomed the international market pressures that have driven its industries to modernize and increase their competitiveness in both the home market and abroad. How has Chile been affected by the political costs of acting independently, without the leverage or protection that come from bargaining collectively? Thus far, Chile has been successful. In fact, it may work to Chile's advantage when negotiating with much larger nations such as South Korea and the United States that the relatively small scale of its industries poses little threat to domestic special interest groups. There is little that is controversial in signing a free trade pact with Chile, from the U.S. perspective, compared to the expected costs of trading with Mexico or Brazil. Also, Chile benefits from the relative stability and effectiveness of its national state institutions, which improve the country's ability to corral domestic interests in order to meet commitments. Again, this is especially significant when compared against the complex, multilevel politics that prevail in federalist systems in Argentina, Brazil, and Mexico. The multiple agreements with their spreading network of rules and dispute resolutions have earned Chile significant nontrade benefits, as in flows of foreign direct investment.

On the other hand, as we suggest above regarding the Argentine case, in a more conflictive international environment Chile's independent path may leave it vulnerable if trade agreements take on a more political tone. This viewpoint rests on the assumption that there are deep divisions between the interests of industrialized and underindustrialized nations and that trade between them, despite its natural benefits to both, will at some point generate zero-sum situations that will require difficult political choices. The plight of Mexico's small- and mid-sized farmers is one such problem that the government will address either by angering and disappointing an enormous segment of its population or the United States, most likely the former. With the relatively high quality of its human capital, and the competitiveness of its producers—most of whom suffered through the shaking out process of liberalization in the 1980s—Chile expects such costs to be manageable. The most recent developments seem to support Chile's strategic bet, although some observers wonder whether the United States and South Korea may have won excessive concessions in their negotiations (see *The Economist,* January 4, 2003). MERCOSUR's weakness and the inability of its members to expand significantly their market share abroad speak to the wisdom of Chile's decision to reject full membership. However, if FTAA talks intensify and Brazil can maintain a coalition to push for favorable terms, these may prove discriminatory against Chilean producers. Outside of this possibility, however, the Chilean trade-off of political clout for economic flexibility and trade partner diversity seems to be paying off.

Indeed, by seeking its economic partnerships independently, Chile may have improved significantly its image abroad as a reliable partner. As a member of both the Asia-Pacific Economic Cooperation forum and the NAFTA grouping (through its bilateral agreements), and with a free trade agreement with the European Union, Chile has enhanced its presence as a global actor. Although the benefits of international reputation are notoriously hard to determine and fragile, Chile's image abroad as South America's most stable and prosperous country (with a nod to Uruguay) makes it an attractive economic or political partner, perhaps as a go-between with larger, more cantankerous Southern nations such as Brazil and India. Chile's trade policy of aggressive, independent multilateralism has been an important part in building that image.

Prospects for the Future

Argentina, Brazil, Chile, and Mexico—and Latin America in general—now face a considerably more challenging and uncertain international environment than that of the 1990s. Both of the main engines of Latin America's economy, the U.S. and Brazilian domestic markets, may face a prolonged period of recession or sluggish growth. The future progress of the WTO and the global free trade project will be sorely challenged by the refusal of the European Union, the United States, and Japan to allow fair competition in agricultural goods. The continuing growth and sophistication of Chinese exports threaten to reduce prices worldwide for many goods that Latin America sells. Within the region, political resistance to liberalization and free trade is growing, and there appears to be a trend toward electing leaders who will challenge the neoliberal model more directly. The FTAA process, the centerpiece of the enthusiasm for pan-American partnership in the 1990s, is now in the hands of the Lula and Bush administrations, neither of which has shown any stomach for the political sacrifices that free trade demands.

The analysis in this volume is based on the decisions and trends of the 1990s and the early 2000s. Our central argument is that longer-term political and strategic calculations must be considered along with economic theory to understand the divergence we observe among these countries' trade policy profiles. Considered together, these different trade strategies entail certain trade-offs and bets, mostly in one form or another between economic efficiency and political autonomy. As the international political and economic climate changes, we expect that the outcomes of these trade-offs and bets will also likely change.

Contributors

Ambassador Eduardo R. Ablin is director of the Argentine National Council on International Negotiations and Cooperation.

Vinod K. Aggarwal is a professor of political science and director, Berkeley APEC Study Center, at the University of California–Berkeley, and a fellow at the Woodrow Wilson International Center for Scholars in Washington, D.C.

Roberto Bouzas is professor of economics and international relations at the Universidad de San Andrés in Buenos Aires, and senior research fellow at the National Scientific and Technical Research Board (CONICET).

Alcides Costa Vaz is professor of international relations and executive coordinator, Center for MERCOSUR Studies, at the University of Brasília.

Ralph Espach is a doctoral student in the Political Science Department of the University of California–Berkeley.

Sylvia Maxfield is lecturer of government and social studies at Harvard University.

Antonio Ortiz Mena L.N. is professor and chair of the International Studies Division at the Center for Economic Research and Instruction in Mexico City.

Ambassador Osvaldo Rosales is an economist and the director general of international economic relations at the Chilean Ministry of Foreign Relations in Santiago.

José M. Salazar-Xirinachs is chief trade advisor and director of the trade unit at the Organization of American States in Washington, D.C.

Joseph S. Tulchin is director of the Latin American Program at the Woodrow Wilson International Center for Scholars in Washington, D.C.

Pedro da Motta Veiga is director general of the Foundation Center for the Study of Foreign Relations in Rio de Janeiro.

Carol Wise is associate professor at the School of International Relations of the University of Southern California.

Index

Note: Numbers followed by *t*, *f*, or *n* refer to tables, figures, or notes found on those pages.

domestic resistance (*continued*): Mexico, 226, 227, 228; multilateral trade liberalization, 15; neoliberal model, 275; outcomes related, 37

Dominican Republic: price effects of FTA with Central America, 141; US intervention (1965), 48

downward mobility: Argentina, 99; Brazil, 99–100

Duhalde, Eduardo, 50, 106

dumping, 42

dynamic time-path question, 145

EAI. *See* Enterprise for the Americas Initiative

East Asia: competition, 124, 199; developmental state model, 60; education, 99; small business, 98

East Asian financial crisis, 25

ECLAC. *See* Economic Commission for Latin America and the Caribbean

e-commerce, 205

economic benefits of liberalization, proposed, 19

Economic Commission for Latin America and the Caribbean (ECLAC), 123–24, 180

economic complementarity: Chile, 195, 197; Mexico with Chile, 222

Economic Complement No. 14, 236

economic crises: Argentina, 160; impact for RTA partners, 142

economic efficiency: unilateral liberalization, 13

economic explanations of trade preferences, 5–6

economic growth, 92t, 95–96; Chile, 60–61; intra-MERCOSUR trade, 237; market reforms, 94; Mexico, 96–97, 220, 268

economic reforms. *See* market reforms

Economic Solidarity Pact ("Pacto"), 67, 219–20

economies of scale: bilateral geographically concentrated trade, 20; regional level, 23

education: East Asia compared, 99; regressive distribution, 99; spending levels, 97; US wage penalty, 102

"education president," 103

efficiency gains, bilateralism, 20

EFTA. *See* European Free Trade Association

electronic commerce, FTAA groups, 93

employment: oligopolies, 98; small business, 98

Enterprise for the Americas Initiative (EAI), 88, 235–36, 236–37

entrepreneurs, Chilean, 189

environmental protection: Americas Fund, 199; Brazil, 39; Bush administration, 83; Clinton era, 89; FTAA, 111; FTAs in Latin America, 122; globalization agenda, 17; Latin American opposition, 90; NAFTA effects, 102

Europe, FTAA, 28; mercantilism, 41; Mexico, 220–21, 229n

European Economic Community: WTO, 151n

European Free Trade Association (EFTA), 214, 222

European Union: agricultural protection, 48; Argentina, 172; Brazilian view, 182, 185; exports to Argentina and Brazil, 129; MERCOSUR, 21, 27–28, 101, 241, 243, 244, 247–48, 252, 253, 254; MERCOSUR-European Union 1995 framework agreement, 245–46; MERCOSUR talks, 270; Mexico, 27, 214, 222; US compared, 244

exchange rate regimes: Argentina, 96, 161, 162–63, 164, 170, 172n–73n, 256; Brazil, 178; Chile, 207, 208; instability effects, 142; MERCOSUR, 170; Mexico, 97, 218

export industries, Chile, 14

export-led growth: Argentina, 159, 171; business-government relations, 63; Chile, 60–61, 90, 194, 205, 207–9; Mexico, 90, 215–16; strategic alternatives, 265

rules of origin (*continued*): RTA weakness, 147; tariff shift, 151*n*; value added, 151*n*

safeguards, 133
Salinas de Gortari, Carlos, 67, 224
sanctions approach, 148
"second-best policies," protectionism, 43
sectoral agreements, MERCOSUR, 235, 236, 237
sectoralism, 7, 8*t*; overview of free trade agreements, 10*t*
sectoral level, liberalization infrequent, 9
security objectives, 6
September 11 attacks: Mexican border, 227; Mexican foreign policy, 269; recession, 84; Summit of the Americas agenda, 126; United States as hegemonic power, 41; US leadership, 253–54; victories at Doha, 51
Serra, Jaime, 220
service sectors: Chile, 205; domestic regulation, 147–48; GATS, 132, 133, 148; MERCOSUR, 242
Silva, Inacio Lula da (Lula), 110, 254, 272, 275
Singapore, 201
single-undertaking principle, 147
skill differentials, 98
small business: East Asia, 98; employment, 98; Mexico, 69, 228
smaller nations: bilateralism, 20; FTAA process, 144; motivations compared, 125; RTAs, 150*n*
small industry, Brazil, 73
small- and medium-sized enterprises (SMEs), 228
SMEs. *See* small- and medium-sized enterprises
social capital, business-government relations, 62
social investment: Argentina, 99; Brazil, 99–100; Chile, 23; Mexico, 97, 104, 228–29; NAFTA, 104; US, 103
social stratification: Brazil, 97
Sociedad Rural Argentina (SRA), 76

soft power, 262; Argentina, 45; argument summarized, 38; Brazil, 49; Canada, 51; Chile, 17–18, 46, 50–51; Chile's special status, 46; post–Cold War era, 47; trade advantage, 46; trade preferences, 49; trade strategies, 39
Southern Cone, recession, 84
South Korea, Chile FTA, 201–2
Soviet Union in 1930s, 42
spaghetti bowls, 20, 135–36, 137, 138, 144
SRA. *See* Sociedad Rural Argentina
state capacity, 264–65
state-centered models, 39; Brazil, 109–10
state sovereignty: hemispheric regionalism, 211; Mexico, 33; North American private sector, 89
state-to-state bargaining, 39
strategy, concept of, 263. *See also* trade strategies
structural adjustment: Argentina, 160, 162; Mexico, 68, 217–18
subregional agreements: Chile, 191–92; limits, 86; macroeconomic stabilization of 1980s, 87; trade disputes, 138–40; Western hemisphere (listed), 112*n*
subregional integration, locking in macroeconomic stabilization plans, 88
Summit of the Americas: democratic provisions, 122; FTAA process, 126; listed, 150*n*; Miami, 199; Quebec City, 93, 211; Santiago, 92–93, 110, 200
symmetry and reciprocity, principles of, 246

tariffs: Andean Community, 132; Argentina, 61, 162, 169; Brazil, 178; Chile, 194; early US debates, 42; Latin vs. US burdens, 109; lists of exceptions, 132; MERCOSUR, 236, 240; Mexico, 216, 219
tariff shift model, 151*n*
taxes, on trade, 144
tax policy, Brazil, 186
technical assistance, trade-related, 135
technocratic leadership, Mexico, 34